CROSVILLE
THE FIRST FORTY YEARS

by

John Carroll

and

Duncan Roberts

Edited by T B Maund
and
Designed by Alan Townsin

Venture *publications*

CONTENTS

FOREWORD

This is the story of the first half century of a bus company whose first service was started, almost by accident, in financial desperation, but whose name became, with the goodwill of its passengers, a byword to millions in Cheshire, Merseyside, North and Mid Wales.

It is not the first history of the company, but it is by far the most extensive yet published, and being well researched, tells the story 'warts and all'.

Whilst the story of Crosville's fleet will be a source of fascination to many, the company could not have survived and subsequently prospered without the loyal service of many staff of all ranks. To them the book is dedicated.

I am sure this volume will bring much interest, pleasure and indeed reminiscence to many.

David Meredith FCIT, FIMgt
Director & General Manager July 1976-February 1986
Managing Director March 1986-February 1989

The 1929 PLSC Lions were rebodied by Eastern Counties in 1935. Number 383, by now B10, stands patiently at Oulton Broad, Lowestoft for Boughtons' photographer in this official ECOC view.

George Crosland Taylor was born near Huddersfield on 30th January 1857, the second of four children of millowner Henry Dyson Taylor and his wife, Sarah, nee Crosland. At 16 Crosland, as he was always known, entered the family business, learning all aspects of the woollen trade. He also became a keen student of chemistry. The family was obviously well-to-do and the young man was able to follow his inclinations. In his early 'twenties he visited Australia and, on his return, determined to become involved in all things electrical, a phenomenon in the process of being harnessed. On the death of Henry about 1880, Crosland was free to pursue his interest with vigour and, after visiting the Paris Exhibition in 1881, founded with his brother James in the following year, G C Taylor & Co which later became the Telegraph Manufacturing Co, at Neston, on the Wirral Peninsula. That proved not to be the best of locations and a new factory was opened at Helsby, the company eventually becoming the British Insulated and Helsby Cable Company which, in the 1940s amalgamated with

George Crosland Taylor

Callender's to form the British Insulated and Callender's Cable Co Ltd – BICC. James was also a director of the Birkenhead tramcar manufacturer, G. F. Milnes & Co Ltd, the first recorded family connection with public transport.

The Taylors were prepared to turn their hand to almost anything mechanical or electrical. In 1906 Crosland bought two sample cars and a chassis, together with the drawings and patterns, which had been built by the French company, Morane. In June 1906 he rented Crane House, Chester, and a warehouse from the Shropshire Union Railway and Canal Company with a view to assembling and selling cars of the French design. It was soon realised that much more capital was required and so the Crosville Motor Co Ltd, with an authorised capital of £5,000 (£3,750 issued), was incorporated on 27th October 1906 to take over the business of motor manufacturer and agent. Various associates and acquaintances were persuaded to invest in the company in which Crosland's son Edward took an active part. The name was derived from the first part of Crosland and the surname of Georges de Ville, his French associate.

Besides constructing cars, the company was engaged in motor vehicle and boat repairs and maintenance and it soon became apparent, after only two cars had been constructed entirely at Crane Wharf, that there was still insufficient space and much larger premises were needed. An additional 2,250 shares were issued and 2,500 of the original shares were surrendered as a gift to the company by Crosland. In 1908 car making ceased and the business was confined to agency work and repairs.

None of the cars was sold on the open market, three of the total of five being retained by the family with the other two going to a director, C W Catt, perhaps in lieu of dividends. Edward was appointed general manager on 23rd June 1909, at a salary of 35 shillings per week and he joined the Board in September 1910 when Catt's son, who had replaced his father the previous year, resigned.

In 1909 a Mr Lightfoot, of Kelsall, bought a 23-seat Lacre motor bus to replace the horse-drawn service between Kelsall and Chester. This innovation appealed to the then office manager, Jack Morris, who suggested to Crosland that Crosville should start a motor bus service between Chester and Ellesmere Port, as the rail journey was indirect and involved a change of trains at Hooton. Edward bought an old Herald charabanc in Swansea but then went on a visit to the United States where he met, and soon afterwards married, an American lady, emigrating permanently to the USA in January 1911.

In the meantime, on 13th December 1910, Crosville wrote to Chester City Council asking permission to start from the Market Square, 'preferably from opposite the Town Hall'. The application was granted, subject to satisfactory tests of the vehicles by the Electrical Engineer (sic)

Claude C Taylor

At the start the company conducted a business as a general carrier. A De Dion lorry, FM 43?, is seen circa 1912. The haulage business ceased around 1919, when the prospects in passenger carrying were seen to be brighter.

and the Chief Constable, who was to decide on the exact starting point. Crosland offered the management of the business to his second son, Claude, who gave up his job at the Cable Works. The Herald proved to be a financial and mechanical disaster, refusing to start whatever was done. Another abortive purchase was a Germaine wagonette, acquired for £50 at an auction in Chester. This vehicle went well down hills but refused to go up! The Ellesmere Port service finally started on 2nd February 1911 using a large Crosville car and a second-hand Albion charabanc. On 24th April 1911 Claude replaced Edward on the Board. He was content with the surname Taylor and usually signed himself 'Claude C Taylor' or 'C C Taylor'.

The dire situation of the company is illustrated by the following extracts from the Balance Sheet.

Year End 30 April	Book Debts	Cash in Bank	Cash in Hand	Revenue A/c Surplus/(deficit)
	£ s d	£ s d	£ s d	£ s d
1909	521.16.11	360. 8. 6	4.12. 5	31.17. 2
1910	863.13. 1	262. 5.10	4. 7	(1557.17. 3)
1911	1092.11. 5	NIL	14.15. 6	(1990. 1.11)
1912	704.13. 3	NIL	2.17. 3	(4084. 5. 5)
1913	470. 2. 7	97. 5.11	85. 7. 5	(4105. 8. 0)

The pioneering days were times of great contrast. In this view, The Grey Knight, a 1913 Lacre, is seen carrying a well-to-do party, albeit before registration as FM 535. Note the pneumatic tyres on the front wheels only; the solid-tyred rear wheels were chain-driven. The plate on the toolbox reads 'Hunter & Odd Ltd, Motor Body Builders, Sydney', and this is presumably the then village near Crewe and not its more famous cousin.

The other extreme, No. 11 (FM 964) a 1915 Daimler Y is seen nose down in Offa's Dyke, near Mold. According to the note on the back of the photograph, the driver lost control on the gravel which can been seen on the right side of the shot.

The following year, the adverse balance was wiped off the books by the surrender of a further 2,500 shares, and goodwill to the value of £1605. 8. 0.; a dividend of 5% less tax was paid for the first time on the Ordinary Shares.

After this period of financial uncertainty, the fortunes of the company steadily improved under the control of the two family directors. The First World War gave the company a tremendous boost supplying transport to a munitions factory at Queensferry. Although new Daimler buses ordered by the company were commandeered by the War Department, they managed to obtain some inferior Lacre chassis and built up a fleet of 20 to 30 buses to meet the needs of the factory.

Soon after the end of the war, the third Crosland Taylor son, Winthrop James, aged 24, joined Crosville, starting on 19th January 1919 as traffic superintendent at Nantwich, where he also drove buses from time to time. James had served in the Royal Marines during the War and had been awarded the Military Cross. He was appointed to the Board on 13th October 1919.

Crosland died in January 1923 and the Chair was taken by Claude. Two additional directors were appointed, Edwin Gardner, who had been Secretary since 1908, and John Davies. The Assistant Secretary, Henry Middleton, was appointed Secretary. The following year saw two more Taylors joined the Board, Mrs Mary Taylor, widow of Crosland, and Dr James George Taylor MD. Henry Middleton died in July 1925 and Arthur William Smith replaced him as Secretary.

In 1929, the Board was dissolved on the sale of the company to the London, Midland and Scottish Railway Company, with Claude and James being retained by the LMS as employees. Within a year ownership had changed again, this time to Tilling/BAT and Crosville Motor Services Ltd. was formed as a Tilling and BAT subsidiary, under BET management. These events are described in detail in Chapter 6. The new Chairman was William Simpson Wreathall (1879-1939) but Claude was appointed Managing Director, joining Messrs Ashton Davies, OBE MInstT, and O Glyn Roberts, OBE, as representatives of the LMS, plus George Cardwell (Tilling/BAT) and Charles D Stanley (BET). Cardwell was also a director of the North Western Road Car Co. Ltd.

Claude died at the age of 45 on 31st March 1935, following a short illness that resulted in peritonitis. This meant that for the first time since the formation of the original company in 1906, there was no Crosland Taylor on the Board of Directors. On Claude's death, James was appointed General Manager, a position which he held until he retired on 31st December 1959. On nationalisation in 1948, James was appointed a director in accordance with Tilling Group policy of general managers sitting on Boards. He died, aged 73, on 4th October 1967.

There is fleeting mention of another member of the family, Miss Alma Crosland Taylor, who was a shareholder in the Crosville Motor Company just before it was sold to the LMS. She may have been Crosland's older sister (his younger sister was Hannah) or perhaps his daughter. She almost certainly was the inspiration for naming Crosville's first new bus, Eaton saloon-bodied Dennis, FM 387, 'The Alma'.

INTRODUCTION

The Crosland Taylors, photographed in Chester in 1922. Edward, who had settled in the United States; Claude, who ran the company from 1923 until his untimely death in 1935, and James, General Manager from then until 1959. The boy was George, Edward's son.

It is quite remarkable that a firm the size of Crosville, which survived four changes of ownership in the 53 years from 1906 to 1959, retained a connection with the founding family over the whole of that period. It is perhaps even more remarkable that the name 'Crosville', with such a personal connection to the founder, should still appear on buses almost 90 years since it was first established. Such is the legacy of the Crosland Taylors.

Crosville is a company about which much has been written, in particular the two books by W J (James) Crosland-Taylor, *Crosville – The Sowing and The Harvest* and *State Owned Without Tears* have become much-lauded classics, supreme for their readability and the revelations they made into the working of one of the country's largest bus companies.

James was the younger brother who made it to the top through the early death of his brother, Claude, who had guided the fortunes of the company since their father had passed on in 1923. At that time, he ranked as a Divisional Organiser but with some additional responsibilities which kept him closer to the seat of power than his peers. This arose purely as a carry over from the old days when the brothers owned much of the company. His appointment as successor to Claude was a surprise to many of his contemporaries but it was a time of centralised power and he undoubtedly had the greatest knowledge of company affairs.

He wrote his books from a position of great privilege and it is important to put his rather idealistic view of the company into proper perspective. He deals kindly with his late brother but there is evidence of some strain, or even jealousy, which is reflected in events which are left out of the book or skimmed over very rapidly. Respected researchers have been known to remark that the Crosville depicted in the first book was not the Crosville they knew in the company's formative years. It seems strange that, although relations with Chester Corporation receive some attention, it is not revealed that Claude was for some years a member of the city council and was Mayor in 1926-27, a vicarious honour for the company. By contrast, in later years, the attainments of employees who became mayors or council chairmen were publicly lauded.

Two men who started their careers with Crosville and achieved high positions in the National Bus Company, the late Cyril Buckley and the late D S Deacon, privately expressed reservations about the accuracy of the overall picture painted and the judgement of James who, for example, resented being left out of the negotiations with Birkenhead Corporation in favour of H H Merchant. But the latter, at least nominally equal in rank in the company's hierarchy, had an unequalled knowledge of the Wirral area. James asserts that Crosville would have got what they wanted under the Road Traffic Act 1930 without surrendering territory but it is unlikely that they would have got the express services which the Agreement facilitated. Buckley, who later controlled the Merseyside area and later still became general manager of Crosville, said it was the finest thing that ever happened to the company! No credit was given to Ashton Davies, Chief Commercial Manager of the LMS for the part he played in welding together the bus and railway interests and securing agreements with difficult councils like Liverpool and Birkenhead.

An article by James in *Bus and Coach* for August 1962 on Major H E Hickmott, managing director of Ribble until 1945, is full of errors and fantasies. He mentions a meeting with Hickmott to discuss what they should do about Liverpool Corporation; at the time, that body was considering what to do about them! The events mentioned are all well documented and several dates quoted are many years out. In 1924-25, Ribble's careful diplomacy gave them entry into the city centre while Crosville buses were still stuck out on the boundary at Garston. They subsequently rode on the back of Ribble's efforts, a fact which would not have been forgotten by Hickmott who, in 1929, wanted to prevent Crosville buses using the A57 between Prescot and Liverpool, which they were entitled to do under an inter-company agreement. Hickmott and James Crosland Taylor, men of totally different backgrounds and temperaments, must have been strange bedfellows. Charles Klapper in *The Golden Age of Buses* also comments on the discrepancies in Crosland Taylor's description in *The Sowing and the Harvest* of the events leading to the railway takeover and the facts as published at the time which are recorded in Chapter 6.

It follows that the picture of Crosville as wholly benevolent to both employees and the communities served should be treated with some reserve. All the pioneer bus companies were hard taskmasters and Crosville was no exception. While they did their best to provide adequate services, they were first and foremost profit-driven. It was the way things were done in those days and are now once more. In its wholly independent days up to 1929, the company consistently paid 10% dividends. After 1930, these were diluted by the over-capitalisation resulting from the allegedly injudicious purchases by the LMS in their year of sole ownership. Expensive adventures they undoubtedly were but no analysis has ever been made of the effect on the company if the purchases had not been made. The Brookes brothers, who owned White Rose of Rhyl, controlled a strategic section of the North Wales coast and also had a large depot at Denbigh; they had considerable political and commercial influence in the district. Before acquisition, Crosville hardly had a minimal presence in Prestatyn or Rhyl and the express services into the White Rose area were hedged round with restrictions prohibiting the carriage of passengers over certain sections of route.

Llandudno Royal Blue, a BET company, had penetrated as far as Llanberis and Caernarfon and into Anglesey and stood in the way of Crosville consolidation over a wide area of what is now Gwynedd. The integration of these two operators with Crosville opened up the whole of the North Wales coast and had an overall beneficial effect which was difficult to quantify.

James was fortunate in having the guidance, in the early years of his general managership, of W S Wreathall whose political and financial skills contributed enormously to the prosperity of the companies of which he was chairman in the consolidating years following the passing of the Road Traffic Act, 1930. His untimely death in 1939 was a great loss to the industry. Crosville also had a plethora of dedicated employees at all levels who spared no effort in the service of the company. James pays tribute to Wreathall and also mentions, in particular, the self-sufficiency of the Welsh employees who kept the services running as if they were their own and reduced costs in very thin territory.

But there were some strange practices which one would have expected good management to eliminate. Notable was the extraordinary system of displaying route information– the Widd plate, a sheet of paper sandwiched between two layers of celluloid with a border of some base metal. They were named after the firm which made them and were displayed in frames under the front canopy and at other points down the nearside.

They were kept in racks in the depots and soon became damaged and in need of renewal. They replaced the perfectly normal roller blind indicators which had been used in the mid-1920s.

The plates and the size of lettering varied, depending on the length of the contents but, at very best, they were visible for only a few feet and one wonders how many passengers were left behind over the years because they could not see the destination, particularly at night when illumination was poor. D S Deacon told how, on takeover of the Western Transport Co in 1933, he was assigned to drafting Widd plates for the acquired routes. The destination blinds were ripped out of the whole fleet and presumably destroyed, even though the buses continued to run the same routes for many years. The mind boggles at such pointless vandalism carried out in the name of economy, destination equipment being considered too expensive to maintain! There had been a payment by the company to Widd for the secrets of making them. Perhaps the payment had to be justified. The last plates lasted until the 1950s but the agreement was still in the strong room in 1986.

The company displayed the same eccentricity when Tilling-style destination equipment was introduced in 1946. The numbering of the routes, carried out reluctantly, one feels, hardly improved passenger information and the deficiencies were not rectified until the very end of the Crosland Taylor era.

But, in matters mechanical the company set high standards. The buses were generally well turned out and the ingenuity displayed in augmenting the fleet to meet the challenges of the 1939-45 War and the immediate aftermath was remarkable to say the least.

Crosland Taylor writes of working to gain tenths of a penny per mile; most other companies did this too and Crosville, with its very seasonal Welsh traffic, was really no worse off than Devon General, East Kent, Ribble or Western National. Merseyside was the solid financial base, the route between Birkenhead and Chester in all its permutations contributing 11% of the whole company's revenue in the immediate post-World War II years.

When changes in social habits eroded the traffic, this base started to crumble and there was nothing left to support the remote rural Welsh services. Political factors prevented contraction at a commercially desirable rate and the company, like other subsidiaries became, at times, indebted to its parent, the National Bus Company but never to the same extent as some of the others. Forced division into English and Welsh companies immediately prior to deregulation was a disruptive factor which, coupled with the intransigence of labour from which both companies suffered, ensured that their entries into the newly deregulated and privatised world were difficult in the extreme.

At the time of writing, Crosville Cymru is prominent in North Wales while, in England, there are still Crosville buses though their owner is declared as PMT Ltd, Woodhouse Street, Stoke-on-Trent and they are decorated with badgers – and there is a dormant Crosville company still in existence.

The Market Square in Chester, so long to be the best known of the three city terminals of the Company. This 1919 view shows six Daimlers including 11 (FM 964), 37 (FM 1384), 24 (DU 1560), 16 (FM 1103) and finally one Lacre.

A typical scene in 1927 shows a Chester City open-top tramcar passing under the City wall at the Eastgate whilst a new Crosville Leyland Lion poses for the camera. The Eastgate was to form the backcloth to many formal Crosville photographs – until modern traffic management – and the demise of the Company ended this historic link.

THE PIONEER YEARS
1911-18

Bearing fleet number 2, although not the second bus owned, 'The Alma' (FM 387) a 1911 Dennis with Eaton body, is seen with another respectable-looking party savouring the delights of the early motor bus. The open rear platform was a feature of many early Crosville buses, perhaps reflecting Parisian influences on the Crosland Taylors. The removable side windows had been taken off for this occasion.

In May 1911 the company applied to Chester City Council for permission to run the Ellesmere Port service on Sundays and to introduce a new service to Kelsall, using a second-hand Albion charabanc bought from Lawton's of Liverpool. It is believed that a Dennis bus, known as 'The Red Dennis', was acquired from Mr Lightfoot of Kelsall who, in 1909, had put a 23-seat Lacre in service on what had been a horse bus service. This Dennis was put to work on the Ellesmere Port service, together with a new Eaton-bodied 23-seat Dennis, named 'The Alma'. which featured a full-width open platform at the back in the Parisian style. This style of saloon body became commonplace in the Crosville fleet until about 1924, when the surviving Daimlers were rebodied with Leyland-style bodies. Some accounts state that Lightfoot's Chester-Kelsall service was acquired in 1911, along with his Lacre saloon but Claude Taylor, writing in the first issue of *The Crosville Social Review* in 1927, states that Lightfoot's Kelsall service continued to run but went from bad to worse and suggests, but does not record, Lightfoot's eventual demise.

In September 1911, the Chester Silver Motor Co applied to the City Council for licences for four motor buses to ply for hire from Chester to Ellesmere Port, Farndon, Kelsall and Tarporley. Before granting the licences the Town Clerk wrote to Crosville to ask their opinion of the proposed competition on the Ellesmere Port and Kelsall routes. Their reply is not recorded but can be imagined. Licences were granted, subject to the Council being satisfied that the company had the resources to provide a continuous service on the routes. This was an offshoot of an established company, North Wales Silver Motors but they had difficulty obtaining bus bodies and it was not until 10th October 1912 that the licences were confirmed. In December 1913, the company exchanged the two single-deck licences on the Kelsall and Farndon routes for two double-deckers. There is no evidence to show that the Ellesmere Port and Tarporley

Protection from the elements was getting a little more sophisticated by 1915 when No. 10 (FM 963) was completed. A Daimler Y with a body built by Hora of south east London, it remained in the fleet until about 1924. Unusually this vehicle has an enclosed rear.

An 1917 Lacre, No. 18 (FM 1087) with an unidentified 23-seat body, again when new. This vehicle had only a short life in the Crosville fleet and had gone by 1922.

routes were actually operated. In 1915, the company's vehicles were commandeered and the Kelsall and Farndon services were withdrawn, an arrangement being made with Crosville to take over the former but not the latter, until they could obtain further vehicles. There was no mention of Ellesmere Port or Tarporley. The Silver Motors service in Chester was never, in fact, reinstated, Crosville being left in sole possession.

In the meantime, Crosville's Ellesmere Port service was extended to New Ferry on 25th January 1913, operated in two parts, with a connecting service for Ellesmere Port meeting the New Ferry service at Backford. At this time there were about five vehicles available for service. The depot was at Crane Wharf. The fleet was doubled in 1913, when Daimlers were introduced, far superior to the mixed bunch of buses already owned, and more were ordered for delivery in 1914 but, following the outbreak of war, these chassis were commandeered by the War Department. The company's fortunes changed for the better, a profit of £21 being declared in April 1913, rising to £1,302 the following year.

Further competition in Chester was threatened in September 1913, when A A Hawkins, of the Wrexham and District Electric Tramways Ltd, was granted licences for eight motor buses to operate on three services radiating from Chester, to Wrexham, Flint and Mold. The services started operation soon afterwards. In May 1914 he applied for an additional 10 motor bus licences and permission to run to Hawarden and, possibly, to Seacombe via Saughall, Neston and West Kirby. In October, however, loss of buses to the military caused the withdrawal of the Flint route and abandonment of the other plans. But for the outbreak of war, the bus map might have been very different as the resources of the Wrexham company were substantial.

NANTWICH & CREWE

In 1913, the company decided to establish another operating base away from Chester. Northwich Urban District Council refused licences for a Chester service, preferring instead to support a local man, Thomas Wilkinson, who formed the Mid-Cheshire Motor Bus Company Ltd, registered on 9th

January 1914 and operating initially from a garage in Brockhurst Street, Northwich. Crosville had more success at Crewe where the Council had been considering applying for parliamentary powers to run 'trackless trams' within the town, later amending this to motor buses, within the borough and to Willaston, Nantwich, Haslington and Sandbach. However, on 1st December 1913, the Council granted Crosville licences for two motor buses, two drivers (W G Wright and H E Yeates) and one guard (sic) (Paul Newnes). Two buses were sent to the Victoria Cocoa House Yard, in Pillory Street, Nantwich, and two services were started between Nantwich and Crewe, via Willaston and Shavington and between Crewe and Middlewich, via Church Minshull, Over and Winsford. Two new Daimler saloons were licensed, one in March 1914 (FM 641) and the other in May (FM 703). The Nantwich service was soon extended beyond Crewe to Sandbach. The other local councils adjacent to Crewe had not adopted licensing powers under the Town Police Clauses Acts, 1847-89 so in these areas Crosville had no licensing problems.

In December 1913 Crewe Council also licensed two vehicles of the British Automobile Traction Co Ltd (M 5575/77) to operate from Macclesfield to Crewe, via Congleton and Sandbach. In February 1917, because of wartime petrol rationing, this service was curtailed at Sandbach, connecting with the Crosville service thence to Crewe. The full service was restored in 1919 but from Congleton, not Macclesfield.

On 22nd June 1915 the bus service of retired railway engine driver, John Gregory, of Furnival Street, Crewe, was acquired, along with four steam omnibuses and part of another for £450. There is no record of the steam buses being used by Crosville in Crewe. However, Gregory continued to license up to three motor buses and a charabanc until about 1916. Three of Gregory's motor vehicles were licensed by Crosville in September 1916, when Mr Gregory renewed his driver's licence, so he may have worked for the company after disposing of his business. There is an intriguing minute in the Chester City Council records when, on 15th July 1915, Crosville was granted licences for a new Daimler motor bus, for use principally on the Kelsall

Pioneering the Crewe services was this 32-seat Daimler Y type, again with Eaton body. The vehicle, new in 1913, was rebodied in 1924. It seems likely that the body orders were placed with Leyland but not all were necessarily executed by them. Other rebodied vehicles with Leyland-style bodies can be seen on page 85 and 86.

route, and for a steam charabanc in connection with their Chester services! The timing certainly fits in with the Gregory takeover and the company did operate Foden steam wagons, mainly on a contract for Frost's Flour Mills. There were also some Daimler lorries and tractors for agricultural contracts. When it was decided to stop operating the goods side of the business in 1919 the four Foden steam wagons were auctioned in Manchester, where they made an average of £1,750 each – about four times their true worth!

Under wartime conditions, the use of steam traction for buses was by no means far-fetched as there would be a demand for every serviceable vehicle and one which did not use rationed petrol would be especially valuable.

On 15th October 1915 Crosville bought the Crewe Town Services of Ward Bros., including one London General petrol and two Tilling-Stevens petrol electric omnibuses for £1,750. The Tilling-Stevens were retained, becoming Crosville's first double-deckers. They kept their red livery throughout Crosville ownership, contrasting with the grey of the rest of the fleet. Although motor buses had been run only from 1913, Ward Bros. was an old-established firm which had catered for horse-drawn passenger and goods traffic since the turn of the century. They continued in business operating motor taxis and horse-drawn wagonettes after selling the motor buses. The Crewe Town Services operated on a 20-minute headway.

The only other operator of a passenger service in Crewe at this time was Jim Gibson of Nantwich Road who had a 24-seat charabanc. He was no longer running by 1916, perhaps because his vehicle was commandeered, but he re-appeared after the war with a motor bus and a charabanc in June 1919.

Residents of Edleston Road, Crewe, complained about the noise and vibration from 'speeding omnibuses' and a speed limit of 8mph was imposed on all buses using the road. Crewe Council was also obsessed with the amount of spray and road dirt thrown up by motor buses and demanded that Crosville should improve the mudguards on its vehicles. After lengthy wrangles, during which the Council threatened

not to renew the bus licences, the company started putting canvas 'splashers' on the mudguard edges but these wore out at an alarming rate.

A garage was built in Station Road, Nantwich, in 1915. It had a capacity of nine buses and replaced the primitive facilities at the Cocoa House Yard.

MORE CHESTER SERVICES

There were many demands for new bus services which were thwarted by wartime conditions. The withdrawal of Mr Aldred's horse bus service between Upton and Chester around the end of 1914 prompted local residents to invite Crosville to provide a service. When the company rejected the route as not viable, the City Council was approached. Crosville offered to hire a bus to the Council at 9.5d per mile for a guaranteed minimum of 600 bus-miles a week (£23.75). The City Council also considered running a one-man electric bus but, after cost estimates had been prepared, both alternatives were rejected and the matter was deferred until after the war.

Another route first mooted in 1915, this time by Hoole Urban District Council, was between Chester, Hoole and Newton. Crosville asked for an annual guarantee of £250 but when the City Council declined to contribute half, this service, too, was deferred.

One route which Crosville was keen to start was between Chester and Queensferry and permission was given in Chester in January 1916 but Crosville was unable to obtain licences from Connah's Quay Urban District Council and yet another proposed service was put in abeyance. However, the opening of a government munitions factory at Queensferry in 1916 enabled the company to acquire more buses to operate an elaborate series of shift services, which were under the direct control of the Ministry of Munitions. The services were regulated by the Chief Supplies Officer and Traffic Manager at the factory. The public service application was resurrected in July 1918 and licences granted for a Lacre, FM 1092, and a Daimler, HF 147, to

An early view at Trelawny Square in Flint from the Company's own collection shows the exposed, almost Parisian air of Daimler 29 (FM 224) with London Improved body.

operate a route from Chester Market Square, via Parkgate Road, Mollington and Great Saughall, to Connah's Quay. The time and fare tables were approved on 10th October 1918 and the service was subject to a mileage payment to Chester City Council of 2d per bus mile under the Local Government (Emergency Provisions) Act of 1916.

Finally, an application to re-establish the service abandoned by Chester Silver Motors in June 1915 between Chester (Old Nag's Head Hotel, Foregate Street), Rowton, Saighton, Aldford and Farndon was approved by the Watch Committee on 28th November 1918.

All further plans for expansion were thwarted by the war. Unavoidable service reductions in 1916 caused by petrol rationing and a shortage of new buses brought complaints from local councils but the government would not allow any production of passenger chassis. In January 1917 Crosville applied a minimum fare of 1½d and increased all other fares by 50%, to bring them in line with railway fares increases.

In 1911 Crosville carried 80,000 assengers over 13,300 miles This figure grew steadily until the year ending 30th April 1916 when about 1,200,000 passengers were carried over 182,000 miles. This trend continued until the 1950s.

Originally No. 12 (FM 603), this Daimler was renumbered 25 and at the same time gained a Leyland style body by Vickers of Crayford.

16

Those familiar with the former Crane Wharf Head Office will recognise the scene for this view of No. 61 (FM 2093). This is the yard at the right hand end of the buildings which remained more or less unchanged until demolition in the late 'eighties. The building at the rear proclaiming itself to be an organ works continued thus until recently and still stands today in recognisable form. The vehicle is an all-Leyland 36GH7 with 32-seat bodywork which was to serve the Company from 1921 until 1928.

1. Chester

Until 1919, Chester depot was at Crane Bank with the repair shop but, the following year, the building was extended and the premises divided. As the fleet expanded, more space was needed and, in 1924, a separate depot on land leased from the City Council until 1995, was opened across the road at Tower Fields, New Crane Street, the Crane Bank premises being used solely as workshops. Continued expansion necessitated the provision of yet another site, the old roller skating rink in Liverpool Road, being opened as a bus depot (inevitably called 'The Rink') in April 1927, the 1924 site then becoming yet another extension to the workshops.

Crosville successfully applied for licences to operate the Chester-Hoole circular service commercially on 10th February 1919, a significant change of attitude from 1915. There was a mileage charge of 3d per bus mile in both the city and the county and the minimum fare was 3d, 5d being charged for a ride round the circular. The service was successful and the initial hourly service was soon increased to 20-30 minutes, needing three or four buses.

The New Ferry direct and Ellesmere Port services were separated, some competition being experienced on the latter from J M Hudson who was also pioneer of the infrequent route through the hamlets of Stoak and Stanney. After a period of 'chasing', Hudson was bought out and became Crosville's private hire manager, a position he held for very many years. An out-station was set up at the Great Eastern Hotel, New Ferry, facilitating early departures from New Ferry and, from October 1919, a lengthy service from New Ferry to West Kirby, Hoylake and Meols via Thornton Hough and Heswall was commenced.

In general, services along the main roads from Chester were developed by Crosville while many smaller operators pioneered services, often on certain days only, to and from the remoter villages. A service from Chester to Helsby, Frodsham, Runcorn and Warrington was authorised on 4th December 1919. This was worked in different ways for some time, with one bus running from Chester and connecting with another at Sutton Corner. June 1920 saw the authorisation of the Chester-Mold circular via Hawarden and Ewloe and via Buckley and Broughton, worked in both directions. Chester Corporation had a lengthy tram route to Saltney to which the company gave protection in the form of a 3d minimum fare. The Chester-Nantwich-Crewe service, linking two separated parts of the company's services (see below), started in 1920. This became an important trunk route being later linked with another service to provide a through route to Newcastle-under-Lyme, on the borders of the Potteries.

In July 1921, a local service to Eccleston which councillors had been asking for for seven years, was approved and another local route, to Upton, was started in the same year. About the same time, a direct link was established between Chester, Neston, Parkgate, Heswall, West Kirby and Meols, at first twice daily but later expanded; John Pye of Heswall had unsuccessfully applied to Chester Council to run on market days and Saturdays, having, he said, received permission from all the other licensing authorities. His application was refused, on the grounds that there were no stands available for further motor vehicles and the

Although service buses were offering passengers rather more cover from the elements, excursion vehicles still tended to be open or at least convertible affairs. This 1923 charabanc is again an all-Leyland 30C1 which just survived into LMS days in 1929. Number 90 (FM 2477) displays its leather benches for public approbation. Note that 12mph was the legal speed limit until 1928.

Committee were of the opinion that the district was already sufficiently served. Pye appealed to the full City Council in July, but the Committee's decision was upheld. Crosville services to Caergwrle via Dodleston, Kinnerton and Hope and to Tattenhall and Bickerton commenced running in 1922.

In September 1922, a licence was approved to Crosville for a temporary service with a flat fare of 3d over the Old Dee bridge between Lower Bridge Street and Queens Park, pending completion of the pedestrian suspension bridge. The service could have run only for a few days as, at the beginning of October, the owner of the private estate roads objected and threatened legal action if the service were not withdrawn.

Because of congestion, about October 1922 Crosville moved the terminus of the Connah's Quay, West Kirby and Parkgate services from the west side of the Market Square to Delamere Street. Buses still used the east side of the

Square on services to Ellesmere Port, New Ferry and Blacon and the south side for Hoole, Kelsall and Farndon. There were thus three separate terminal points as Lower Bridge Street was used for services to the south-east. This state of affairs was to continue for many years and was a severe handicap to arranging connections between services.

Several independent proprietors had their applications to start services into Chester refused in 1921-22 and one wonders if the Crosland Taylors had made friends with some councillors! The value of Claude's membership of the council is a matter for some speculation. In October 1921 R Jenkinson, an established operator of Berwyn Garage, Buckley was refused permission to run in from Buckley and, the following month, George Taylor, (no relation) of Nicholas Street Mews, Chester, was refused licences for a series of routes radiating from Chester to Buckley; Tarvin and Kelsall; Blacon, Saughall and Shotwick; Mollington, Saughall, Shotton and Connah's Quay; Eccleston and to

A typical vehicle of the 'twenties was No. 112 (FM 2617), an all Leyland 30A9 20-seater of 1923.

Ellesmere Port, all to start from his offices in the Market Square. He was refused on the grounds that 'a local operator already provided a very efficient service on the routes'. However, he received a charabanc licence to ply for hire 'for advertised tours, football matches, race meetings, etc.' Taylor became a well-established coach operator though plans for a network of long distance services for which the City Council granted licences in 1929, materialised only to a very limited extent.

Robert Roberts of Buckley was another hopeful whose application in January 1922 for a licence to operate between Buckley and Chester via Penymynydd was refused. Both he and Taylor had the support of the Chester and District Chamber of Commerce, who wrote to the City Council, pressing their case and suggesting that fares had recently been reduced on routes where there was competition (Chester-Ellesmere Port and Chester-Farndon) but not on those where there was none. Both Crosville and Wrexham and District Transport refuted the Chamber of Commerce claims and giving plausible reasons why fares on some routes were higher than on others. The Council stood their ground and Robert Roberts' subsequent appeal to the Ministry of Transport, was unsuccessful.

Among the successful applicants were William Manning, of 7 Lower Bridge Street, Chester, (Chester and Marford) and Gauterin Bros., of Farndon, (Farndon and Chester). Manning's fate is uncertain but the Gauterins, licensed in January 1922, sold their two-bus business to Crosville on 26th October 1925. Applications in 1922 by John Hendrick of Holt (Chester-Holt) and D R Goudie, of Higher Kelsall, were both turned down. The latter's proposal was for a 'coach service' and it was probably intended to be run with a charabanc. Another aspirant for a Kelsall service, this time via Hargrave and Huxley, was G West (Reliance) in 1924 and he met with no more success. However, he seems to have run unlicensed and was reported for running between Eaton, Cotebrook, Utkinton and Chester in 1929. He was licensed on Saturdays on 17th January 1931, three weeks before the cut-off date under the Road Traffic Act, 1930.

In 1923 Chester City Council became more sympathetic towards new applicants and Arthur Lloyd of Mancot Royal, applied to operate between Shotwick Aerodrome and Chester solely for air force personnel. Unfortunately, his vehicle was rejected as unsatisfactory so he was not licensed but he carried on running, picking up passengers in Bridge Street, St. Werburgh Street and Canal Street. He reapplied in January 1926 and was granted a licence, but, the following month, it was rescinded on appeal by Crosville, who submitted a time table for a route from Chester Market Square, via Northgate Street, Canal Street, Sealand Road, Blacon Point, Sealand Road Racecourse, Welsh Road corner and Shotwick Aerodrome to Garden City (Queensferry Hotel). Lloyd sold out to Crosville on 11th March 1926, and went to work as a fitter at Crane Wharf. After a full career with Crosville, he retired at the end of 1961 as Area Engineer, Wrexham, Crewe and South Cambrian Areas.

To return to 1923, J Shelbourne, of Swan Cottage, Kinnerton, was granted a licence to run between Kinnerton and Chester and Zacchaeus Woodfin, of Tarvin, was authorised to operate between Tarvin and the Queen's Head Yard, Seller Street, Chester. No more is known about Shelbourne but Woodfin extended his area of influence over the next few years, sometimes at the expense of Crosville whose competing applications were refused. By the time he sold out, on 2nd February 1931, one week before the licensing provisions of the Road Traffic Act, 1930 came into force, his routes extended to Tarporley, Burton, Huxley and Barrow, by tortuous routes serving many rural hamlets. Crosville succeeded in opening up new routes to Guilden Sutton and to Ince and Elton and, in 1924, to Garden City and Queensferry.

Another successful operator, T O Maddocks of Tattenhall, was granted a licence on 15th October 1925 to run between Tattenhall and Seller Street, Chester, the same terminus as used by Woodfin. His business expanded to embrace routes to Bunbury and Broxton and also between Tattenhall and Whitchurch; it was acquired by Crosville on 1st July 1934. However, the service of Joseph Rogers of Tilston, between Malpas, Tilston and Chester, granted in December 1925, did not last so long, being taken over by Crosville on 10th February 1927.

It is of interest to note that, on 12th June 1924, Green's Motors of Haverfordwest, were refused licences to operate between Chester and Wrexham. One is tempted to think

Pneumatic tyres were fitted by 1925 when No. 187 (FM 3325) was delivered. Crosville maintained a remarkable selection of chassis types suited to the various volumes of traffic on offer. Luggage accommodation was still on the roof although the means of access to it looks precarious.

that this was, in fact, intended to be part of a long service linking Chester with West Wales and, if so, it was remarkable for the period.

Chester Corporation showed no interest in establishing its own bus services until about 1925 but now there were signs of an awareness that they were likely to be left behind. Their antiquated Edwardian narrow gauge tram system linked the General railway station to Saltney with short branches to the Tarvin and Christleton Roads. On 12th February 1925 Crosville was granted a licence to operate between General railway station and Sealand Road and exactly a year later a route to Hoole via Lightfoot Street and Westminster Road was authorised. Meanwhile, in March 1925 the Tramways Committee had inspected a Shelvoke and Drury 'Freighter' bus and this spawned the idea that the Council should consider the viability of a Council-run motor bus service. Crosville offered to buy the tramways undertaking and convert it to motor buses in 1927 but this was rejected and two further years elapsed before a Bill was promoted in Parliament, seeking to give the City Council powers to run buses within a ten-mile radius. Crosville and Wrexham & District Transport, with some other local operators, objected and the radius authorised in the subsequent Chester Corporation Act, 1929, was 3½ miles from the Town Hall which still gave the Council plenty of scope to extend beyond the tram termini. The operators, for their part, agreed not to compete with the Corporation in this area.

There were still entrepreneurs who thought they could successfully compete with Crosville. One was C B Ellis, proprietor of the Cestrian Motor Omnibus Company who, in June 1926, proposed unsuccessfully to run between Chester and Ellesmere Port and between Chester and Connah's Quay, via Saltney or Saughall. However, a month later, Charley Burton, trading as the Tarporley Motor Co, was granted a licence to operate between Utkinton and Chester, via Cotebrook, Eaton, Tarporley and Tarvin, despite objections from Crosville and Woodfin. The Town Clerk met the three parties and approved an agreed time table. This service passed into Crosville hands on 31st July 1930, having been bought by the LMS Railway.

In July 1927 a schedule of all motor bus services operating into Chester was prepared for the Watch Committee and a condensed version is reproduced in the Appendices.

There was then little scope for new services and most applications were for improvements to existing services or operation on more days per week. Thus in 1927 the Higher Kinnerton service, hitherto Saturdays only became daily and was extended to Caergwrle via Pitchford House and Hope Village. The company was similarly authorised to run the Chester-Farndon route daily and extend two Saturday trips to Hanmer via Shocklach, Worthenbury, Threapwood and Sarn.

On 17th May 1928 Crosville and North Western jointly applied to replace their connecting service at Abbey Arms with through buses between Chester and Northwich; the joint licences were granted, Crosville losing two licences in favour of North Western, but the net service level was maintained. Crosville had been reported for running an unlicensed service on Saturdays, between Chester and Vicar's Cross. The company maintained that it was not

unauthorised but was a duplicate put on as a short-working of the Kelsall service to ease overcrowding. There was some debate as to whether the loadings did justify the extra bus but, to clear the air, the company applied for a variation to the Kelsall time table to incorporate this short-working which was granted.

Horace Phillips, of Caerphilly Road, Cardiff, applied to operate eight buses between Chester and Oswestry but he was refused, as he would have followed the Wrexham and District Llangollen route as far as Acrefair. W H Roberts and Co Ltd applied for a licence to run between Chester and Sandycroft but this, too, was refused. It was then reported that the firm had been operating without a licence between Saltney and Chester on 28th September, to which Mr Roberts replied that he had been carrying passengers on a contract and promised not to ply for hire. The Chief Constable was asked to 'keep an eye' on Mr Roberts! In February 1929, E F Millward, of Cobridge Motor and Engineering Works, Stoke-on-Trent, was unsuccessful in obtaining a licence for a service between Chester, Winsford, Middlewich, Sandbach, Kidsgrove and Hanley, despite support from the Town Clerk of Stoke-on-Trent. Millward was apparently taking up and setting down passengers outside the city boundary but Crosville was serving all the towns except Kidsgrove and Hanley and connections from Newcastle were good.

2. The Thrust into Wirral

The detailed development of the Wirral network is related in T B Maund's *Crosville on Merseyside* but the salient points are worth repeating, particularly as some new information has come to light since it was published. Woodside ferry, 15 miles from Chester Town Hall with a 10-minute service of boats to Liverpool, was an obvious prime objective for Crosville. At New Ferry, which had been reached in 1913, the buses were 2½ miles away but, in between, there was a Birkenhead Corporation tramway, worked by noisy, cramped cars of a unique design dictated by a low railway bridge. The tramways manager, Cyril Clarke, was a doughty individual with empire-building ambitions who started his first bus service in July 1919 and saw the whole of the Wirral as potential territory. Powers obtained in 1914 permitted municipal operation to Bromborough, two miles south of New Ferry with the consent of the local council, but, fortunately for Crosville, who soon started a local service over this part of the Chester route, the local authority was sympathetic towards the company and hostile to Birkenhead whom they regarded as Big Brother, anxious to swallow them up. They refused to allow Birkenhead's buses into their territory and convinced an arbitrator that they were right.

The company applied for licences to the Hoylake and West Kirby UDC on 11th April 1919; Claude Taylor appeared before the Committee on 9th July and licences for nine buses and 12 drivers were approved on 10th September on condition that, in the event of the council establishing its own bus service, there would be no competition. This was a serious ambition at the time but it was rejected by a Town's Meeting in 1920. The Council favoured an unknown Liverpool operator, British American Motor Co, granting them licences for unspecified services but they could not

The twelve Leyland Leviathans bought new by Crosville in 1926 were used in the Wirral area where the service was more urban in character. Number 222, in the grey livery, loads at New Ferry depot for Bromborough on the local service which was handed over to Birkenhead Corporation in 1930.

get licences elsewhere so never started.

The New Ferry-Meols service was started in October 1919 and in May 1920 the company was successful in getting licences to run from West Kirby to Wallasey Village, plans to reach Seacombe ferry and New Brighton being thwarted by Wallasey Corporation. David Randall, who had worked at Nantwich before joining the army in the 1914-18 war, went to West Kirby to open a small depot in Bridge Road, taking two Daimler CKs (probably 40-41). The West Kirby-Wallasey service started on 28th July 1920 and the traffic was good in the summer but sparse in the winter. Birkenhead remained an inviolable bastion, buses running from West Kirby via Frankby and Upton, being obliged to terminate at Boundary Road, by the waterworks, right on the top of Bidston Hill and half a mile from the trams, up a steep hill! This was an extreme case of local authority pride overriding public benefit.

Despite the handicap of the gap between New Ferry and Woodside, the traffic grew rapidly, eventually forcing the Corporation, under pressure of public opinion, to run the trams on Sunday mornings. The company's plans to run buses down to New Ferry pier, the approach to which was entirely in Lower Bebington, was thwarted by the suspension of the ferry service in January 1922 when the pier was demolished in an accident. Premises in New Ferry Road, near the Toll Bar were purchased in 1922 and rebuilt as a combined depot and bus station; they still exist, largely unchanged, as a market. Following the start of a New Ferry-Mold service in 1923, Birkenhead Corporation allowed one Sunday morning bus to start from Rock Ferry pier.

In 1922, as a result of an appeal to the Ministry of Transport, Crosville managed to get their buses down the hill from the waterworks to Claughton Village on a tram route to Woodside and the West Kirby services were rapidly expanded, a new depot for 27 buses being opened in Orrysdale Road in 1923. The same year, Birkenhead Corporation sought powers to run buses anywhere, with the permission of the Ministry of Transport, and Crosville entered a petition as a result of which the clause was deleted from the Bill. Late in 1922, Crosville had engaged Harry

England, managing director of Yorkshire (West Riding) Electric Tramways Ltd as a consultant to help them. In correspondence which has survived he criticised Claude Taylor for not doing more to get the buses right into Birkenhead, describing the Corporation's stance as a 'most selfish and untenable attitude'. In his reply, Taylor wrote '. . . we have not pushed it for the sake of peace and quietness'. This *laisser faire* approach throws grave doubts upon his judgement and management ability as a successful outcome would probably have trebled the income from the Wirral services. Crosville at last went on the offensive, proposing to extend the New Ferry routes to Woodside and the Claughton Village services to Park Station, Central Station and Woodside. Protection to the tramways was offered on the 'Birmingham conditions', a formula whereby the bus operator charged double the tram fare for local traffic and handed half over to the Corporation.

The Corporation took so long to reply that the company, interpreting the delay as a refusal, appealed to the Ministry. The Corporation requested a delay and then started negotiating with Crosville. They discovered that the Ministry was sympathetic to the extension of country services into town centres, with suitable protection for local facilities and, taking a census, calculated that Crosville's New Ferry services alone, were carrying over half a million passengers a year. In November 1923, following a report by Clarke, the Corporation seemed to have accepted the extension of Crosville routes to Woodside etc. as inevitable and the Chief Constable was busy working out suitable routes.

Crosville's only competitor of any importance in Wirral was John Pye of Heswall who had built up a network of services between Heswall and Singleton Avenue on Birkenhead's Prenton tram route and another between Parkgate, Neston and Prenton tram terminus. The success of his business was based on the roundabout railway route between Heswall and Birkenhead via Hooton. He originally had other ambitions such as the Chester service mentioned above and links with Moreton and Wallasey but the volume of his Birkenhead traffic absorbed all his resources. It became rather an embarrassment for the Corporation, too,

John Pye of Heswall sold his business to Crosville at New Year 1924. The vehicles taken over were numbered into yet another series, this time with a P suffix: Pye 8, Crosville 8P, was an Albion with unknown make of bodywork, perhaps constructed by one of the many small firms which built on Albion chassis in the Glasgow area at the time. The vehicle lasted less than a year with Crosville.

as the trams had difficulty in coping and had to be run on Sunday mornings. Consequently, there was not too much opposition when Pye started to run 'contractors' buses' through to and from Woodside at the peak hours. As all fares were prepaid, this did not amount to plying for hire.

Towards the end of 1923, Pye's backer, an uncle, was urging him to sell and negotiations started with Crosville. A deal was agreed, it is said on 7th November, but this has never been confirmed. The price was £25,000, including £7,500 in shares, the most expensive purchase for some years to come.

The next part of the story is one of Crosville's great enigmas. From an apparent position of great strength, the company capitulated to the Corporation, dropping its plans to extend its services to Woodside, accepting Park Station as a compromise for the West Kirby services and, beyond belief, voluntarily surrendering its right to appeal to the Ministry of Transport against the Corporation's future decisions. In return it got the transfer of the Pye licences and agreement to new services of no great importance from

Rock Ferry pier and between New Ferry and Moreton. The Pye services were taken over on 22nd January 1924 (backdated to 1st) and the first formal agreement between the Corporation and the company was signed on 26th February.

No explanation has been found for this extraordinary *volte face* which again casts considerable doubt on the judgement of the Crosland Taylors. Clarke said that he had seen a periodical which made the Ministry's view on town centre penetration clear whilst sitting in the waiting room at Crane Wharf yet the Crosland Taylors do not seem to have had time to read it! Maund speculates in *Crosville on Merseyside* that, having found £17,500 in cash for the Pye purchase, there was a cash flow problem but, unless it was very temporary, this is not borne out by the building, within a few months, of a lavish bus station at Heswall, one of the first in Britain, on the valuable town centre land acquired from Pye; it is now bounded on the east side by Pye Road. This is a mystery now unlikely to be solved.

Crosville's progress towards Liverpool was set back for

Another Wirral company who sold a Heswall service to Crosville was Hardings of Birkenhead. In this instance the vehicles did not pass to Crosville. Typical of the Harding fleet was this Leyland charabanc.

A Crosville Leyland Leviathan LG1 in the red livery leaves King's Gap, Hoylake for Liscard with a good load. These clumsy-looking vehicles were completely eclipsed by the lower built and vastly superior Titan when it was introduced only a couple of years later. The Leviathans only survived five years, up to 1931.

a few years though access to Park Station, on the Mersey underground railway, brought benefits. Seasonal services into North Wales, worked from West Kirby depot, were started from Park Station, Singleton Avenue and Wallasey Village, the latter being extended to Liscard in 1925. A Singleton Avenue-Neston-Chester service, which ran in the 1924-25 summers, was less successful. Even in their restricted form, the Wirral services thrived and generated much of the revenue for expansion elsewhere. A further attempt by Birkenhead to widen their operating radius in 1926 resulted in a further agreement with mutual concessions.

Double-deck Leyland Leviathan buses were placed on the Liscard and Park Station-West Kirby and New Ferry-Bromborough services in 1926; they were clumsy, solid-tyred vehicles with hard seats but they shifted the crowds and all these services had 10-20 minute summer frequencies by 1927-28. Industrial development at Bromborough Port and Stanlow generated significant workers' traffic and the urbanisation of the Wirral villages benefited all the company's routes. But there could be no meaningful progress within the framework of the iniquitous 1924 Agreement.

It was the sale of the company to the LMS Railway Co in 1929 that triggered a solution to problems of access to town centres on both sides of the Mersey.

3. Runcorn, Warrington and Widnes

The Chester-Runcorn-Weston Point service commenced in 1919 and, by 1923, there were two through return journeys on Tuesday and Thursday, three on Saturday and five on Sunday; on all other days the service ran only between Helsby Cable Works and Weston Point. In 1920 a service was started between Weston Point, Runcorn and Warrington, connecting at Sutton Corner with the Chester service. By May 1923 the service was frequent and there was an alternative route via Moore, and three on Sunday. A depot was established in West Road, Weston Point.

The Crosland Taylors saw both Warrington and Widnes as useful jumping-off points to gain access to Liverpool and obtained permission from Warrington Corporation to run a service to Rainhill and Prescot, along the A57 road, except for a diversion through Great Sankey village, which started in October 1921. The Corporation had a tram route as far as the borough boundary at Sankey Bridges and exacted a toll of 1½d of the 3d minimum fare which the company was obliged to charge. The Prescot route connected there with Liverpool's trams but its traffic scarcely increased during the 1920s, running about every three hours with an extra trip on Saturdays. It was worked initially by a bus from Weston Point.

Liverpool Corporation, with an extensive tramway system which was still being extended, vigorously opposed all attempts by private bus operators to run into the city. On 8th June 1922, they approved three Crosville routes from Widnes, one to Gateacre and two to Garston (via Hunts Cross and via Hale and Speke). At Garston they were not allowed to approach the trams too closely, the stand being fixed out of sight round the corner in Island Road South (now Horrocks Avenue), though this was later changed. At Gateacre, they did not even reach a tram terminus, a transfer being necessary to a Corporation bus which, in turn, connected with a tram at Calderstones Park.

On 16th October 1922, two Daimlers were sent to a new out-station at the Railway and Commercial Hotel, Victoria Road, Widnes, and following a day's route learning, three services commenced on 18th October. One bus operated between Widnes, Speke and Garston, making five return journeys on Monday to Friday, six on Saturday and four on Sunday. The other bus worked the two remaining services, to Penketh and Warrington and to Gateacre, with three return journeys on each on Monday to Friday and four on Saturday. From 16th May 1923, a second bus was allocated to the Garston route, doubling the frequency but the route via Hunts Cross was not started. The bus for the Prescot service was also garaged at Widnes. Widnes Corporation had its own bus system, using Tilling-Stevens petrol-electric vehicles, and its operating powers allowed it to run buses outside its boundaries. Within the borough there was a restriction on passengers using Crosville buses and a toll paid to the Council, as a result of a gentlemen's agreement, not formalised in any way.

A new service which commenced in 1923 between Prescot and Huyton had been started by the same David Randall who had worked at Nantwich and later opened West Kirby depot. His Ormskirk-based business had failed as did his Huyton-Prescot service and a later venture at Market Drayton. There were trips via Huyton Quarry and via Huyton Lane and some eventually ran through to Bowring Park tram terminus.

Towards the end of 1923, a new depot was opened in Chester New Road, Warrington, and the Widnes out-station was closed. About the same time, a frequent Runcorn local service was commenced serving Weston Point, Weston village, the Isolation Hospital, Highlands Road, Doctor's Bridge, Delph Bridge and Halton. A further local service started on 5th February 1925 between Helsby and the Transporter Bridge. By 1926 there were three buses allocated to the route operating a daily hourly service. The Runcorn locals were to some extent competitive with Trevor Garner whose business was bought on 10th February 1927.

From 1st October 1924 a Warrington local service served Walton every 20 minutes daily with a few trips extended to Hatton. The town terminus for all services was on the east side of Bridge Foot, in Mersey Street, which was also used by other out-of-town operators.

4. Entry Into Liverpool

In 1924-25, Ribble Motor Services Ltd of Preston conducted careful and diplomatic negotiations with Liverpool Corporation, resulting in their obtaining permission to extend their buses from the city boundary at Aintree into Canning Place, in the city centre. A set of ground rules which were applied to all country operators in due course forbade the carriage of local passengers within the city boundary and imposed a 6d minimum fare.

On 13th February 1925, two months before Ribble buses started running through from Preston to Liverpool, Claude Taylor wrote to the Town Clerk, Liverpool as follows:-

'We understand the Corporation are granting facilities for another omnibus company to run their buses right through the city to a stand in Canning Place. The Widnes-Garston service is not a great success due to the need to change to a tram.' He went on to quote the terms under which Widnes and Birmingham allowed company buses to run within their boundaries and asked 'On what terms would you allow us to extend our service to Canning Place?'

Liverpool imposed the same conditions as had been negotiated with Ribble and, typically, laid down some back street routes to be followed. Crosville had lost money on the Gateacre service which had been reduced to weekend operation by May 1923 and then suspended altogether but had applied to Liverpool to extend it to Wavertree where there were better tramway connections. Surprisingly, they did not ask for this service to run into the city and it was not reinstated through to Wavertree until July 1926. The city boundary was at Netherley Waterworks, then far out in the

country but the Corporation would not relax its restriction on local passengers even though there were no municipal services whatsoever. An authorised alternative route through Childwall was never taken up because it was pointless if local traffic could not be picked up and set down.

From 1st August 1925 the Widnes-Garston service was extended hourly to Canning Place North, Liverpool, with most journeys at the Widnes end extended through to Warrington. Crosville had, at last, broken through to the teeming millions of Liverpool.

From 8th July 1926, a daily seasonal service was started from Liverpool to Loggerheads, where the company had bought land with a view to establishing a resort to encourage traffic. It used the Transporter Bridge between Widnes and Runcorn, running thence via Chester and Mold; there was a connection at Loggerheads for Ruthin and Denbigh. From 1927 there was a seasonal route between Warrington and Loggerheads but a winter service through from Liverpool to Denbigh in 1927-28 was not successful and was not repeated.

A service between Warrington and Wavertree via Farnworth, Cronton and Huyton commenced in October 1927 but was suspended after less than a year, officially because of the condition of the roads but probably also because the traffic was poor. Liverpool depot at the corner of Church Road and Edge Lane, Old Swan, was opened in 1928, enabling the Liverpool services to be worked more economically. In October 1928, the company was permitted to extend the Warrington-Prescot service right into the city at Mount Pleasant. The Widnes-Wavertree services were extended to Edge Lane in 1929 and to Mount Pleasant a few months later.

On 3rd October 1928 a joint two-hourly (hourly Saturdays) service with North Western commenced between Runcorn and Northwich via Dutton and Barnton.

5. Nantwich and Crewe

When James Crosland Taylor arrived in Nantwich on 19th January 1919 he found four buses operating, two Lacre and two Daimler saloons, the Tilling-Stevens double-deckers having been sold in February 1918. Crewe Town services to and from the railway station required three buses – two for Lion and Swan, West Street, and one for Merrill's Bridge; another was needed for the Sandbach route. The Winsford and Middlewich route had been discontinued during the war, Middlewich and Winsford now being served only on Sunday by an extension of the Sandbach service. The Lacres started easily but would not keep going, while the Daimlers were difficult to start but, once hot, would keep running.

'To start a Daimler – first man heats some petrol in a tin (!) and pours same into the induction taps while second man swings the starting handle. (Third man arms the fire extinguisher?) This ensures that the engine starts but washes the oil off the sleeves, so first man immediately adds engine oil to the engine.'

The Crewe Town Council, with many railway employees as members, was especially demanding and apparently particularly hostile to Crosville. Throughout the 1920s, all manner of pointless bureaucratic obstacles obstructed the company in the provision of an efficient service. Besides

Number 82 (FM 2365), a 1922 Leyland G7, exhibits some of the features which Crewe Town Council wanted altered, poor mudguards and the comparatively high step which they wanted changed to a liftable arrangement, a forerunner of today's DiPTAC requirements.

the demand for anti-splash mudguards, previously mentioned, the Council asked the company to provide a lower step on its vehicles. Crosville replied that steps could not be altered 'because, when fully laden the steps were close to the floor, also they caught in the road when the bus hit a pothole'. Many steps had been lost that way. The Council then requested drop-steps, to which Crosville replied that 'Drop steps are not satisfactory – they wore out quickly and conductors were inclined to forget to raise them. They had been tried on the Chester-Ellesmere Port service but were not successful.' The only answer was to have stronger rear road springs. Two new buses were due for delivery in July and they would have the stronger springs and lower steps. The Council were not impressed and insisted that drop steps be fitted, which Crosville duly did, 'against their better judgment'. The complaints about buses splashing because of inadequate mudguards surfaced from time to time until 1924 when the Town Clerk wrote to the local MP, E G Hemmerde, urging him to support a clause in the forthcoming Road Traffic Bill 'to stop this irritating and unnecessary nuisance'.

Enter Jim Gibson

Jim Gibson of 24-28 Nantwich Road, resumed operations in Crewe in July 1919 with one motor bus and one charabanc. Another motor bus and a taxi licence were also granted to W H Gibson, of Edleston Road. In fact, Jim Gibson's motor bus was another charabanc. W H Gibson planned to operate a six-seat motor bus between Edleston Road and Queen's Park but there is no evidence that he ever did and various Gibsons ran charabancs on excursion and private hire work for some years. At the annual Hackney Carriage Inspection in September, Crosville presented five buses while Jim Gibson presented his two charabancs. British Automobile Traction Co Ltd (BAT) were granted licences for 23 vehicles, virtually their whole fleet, on the strength of a letter from the Chief Constable of Macclesfield. Preferential treatment for BAT and its successor, the North Western Road Car Co,

whose presence in the town was minimal, continued over the next few years. In October, Crosville was granted eight motor bus licences for CC 1096, FM 603, FM 703, FM 805, HF 147, DU 2007, FM 641 and FM 1092, the last three also being licensed in Chester. Only a week later the company applied for six licences for new motor buses FM 291-2, FM 1382-5, all due to enter service on 15th October 1919.

In December 1919, the company sought permission to start an hourly service between Crewe Station and Church Coppenhall (Cross Keys Hotel), via Cemetery Road. The new service was approved on 11th March 1920, subject to a mileage payment to the Council, the amount not being specified, and an agreement to give two weeks' notice on each side. The Council opposed an application by Crosville to increase all fares by 1d, with a 2d minimum and this resulted in a compromise of a ½d increase with a 1½d minimum. Crewe Council obviously wanted their pound of flesh twice, as the extra ½d requested was to meet the cost of the mileage charge.

A suggested summer service between Boots Corner and Queen's Park materialised as a circular, operated on Wednesday, Saturday and Sunday afternoons with alternate journeys via Wistaston Road and via Hightown, from 8th September until mid-October. This service was also subject to a mileage payment. Meanwhile Crosville had researched the history of these two routes and claimed that, in the case of the Church Coppenhall route, John Gregory had previously operated on Fridays and Saturdays. In the case of Queen's Park, Gregory had run his steam buses along this route on Sundays en route to Nantwich, and Crosville had themselves operated a circular via Wistaston Road, Queen's Park and West Street for exactly a year after taking over Ward's buses in October 1915. The company did not wish to disturb the agreement for the Church Coppenhall route but requested the Council not to insist on one for the Queen's Park circular and this was agreed.

In September 1920 Crosville submitted 12 vehicles for inspection, while Jim Gibson's fleet of charabancs had grown to four. BAT were granted licences, again by proxy, for 11 vehicles.

By the end of 1920, services were running between Nantwich, Wybunbury and Crewe (3-4 daily) and Crewe, Madeley and Newcastle (6-8 daily) and there were several market day services in the area south of the Crewe-Nantwich road. Chester depot provided the vehicles for the Chester-Beeston-Tarporley-Nantwich service. In November 1920, the Potteries Electric Traction Co (PET) applied for licences for its entire bus fleet of 29 but restricted its enterprise to a service between Hanley and Crewe.

New Competition

Crosville had enjoyed a monopoly on its Nantwich to Crewe and Crewe Town services but, from January 1922, Crewe Council began to grant motor bus licences to more applicants. In January 1922 Donald Taylor, 82 High Street, Haslington, was granted a licence for a 14-seater, while Jim Gibson began running on the town services. Crosville complained to the Town Council about granting licences to proprietors of small motor wagonettes and buses to ply for hire on their various motor bus routes, and asked 'that the Council make it a condition that they do not interfere with the regular omnibus service'. The Council replied that they considered every application on its merit and promptly proceeded to grant a licence for a 14-seater to H O Adams, 119 Wistaston Road. Four 20-seaters were also licensed to Crosville at the same time. PET were also granted licences for an additional three motor buses and three charabancs. A 14-seater was licensed to another operator, Albert Victor Peach, in August 1922 and Crosville again complained of the competition.

The Council, hoist by their own petard, found themselves with a traffic congestion problem caused by the bus traffic and the operators agreed to specific routes and stopping places in the town centre. They were urged to arrange their time tables so as to do away with the existing competition, 'which added to the congestion of the streets and was not in the interests of the community.' The opportunity was taken to call attention to overcrowding on Crosville buses and

certain anomalies in the fare structure. The desirability of buses being labelled (sic) was also urged. The competition continued, however, and in September Crosville introduced a 14-seater Crossley (FM 2184), a type of fast vehicle favoured by the company for 'chasing' competitors. It was licensed 'subject to the provision of permanent ventilation on both sides'. Gibson ran a fast Leyland on benzole fuel and Crosville replied by fitting a powerful fire-engine motor to one of its Leylands.

Crewe Council Gets Cross

The Council, having been assured of Ministry of Transport support in disciplining the operators, decided to issue licences for three months only instead of annually and Jim Gibson and the Crosland Taylors were summoned to appear before a sub-committee on 30th November 1922. Crosville's case was that the company undertook to run their buses only in accordance with their published time tables, provided they were not interfered with by their competitors, and they reserved the right to put on other buses as they thought fit, contending that they, not the Council, were in the best position to judge this. Claude Taylor admitted that his company had put on extra buses to compete with Gibson's buses, a copy of the time table having been lodged with the Council. The extra service was taken off after four days when Gibson withdrew his competing buses.

Jim Gibson then appeared and admitted he had not run his buses according to the approved time table, asserting that he was prepared to adhere to it in future, provided he had the protection of the Council. As requested, the two operators submitted copies of their proposed new time tables within ten days and, with a few exceptions, these were approved. Comprehensive new regulations were then drafted by the Council.

Despite the above regulations (or maybe because of them) there was no improvement and Messrs Gibson and Crosland Taylor were hauled before various Council committees time after time. In desperation, the Council made it a condition that licensed vehicles were not to be

The allegedly unlicensed vehicle which was used in Crewe was No. 6 (FM 641) The Busy Bee. A 1913 Daimler CD it is seen in Early Street, Crewe, behind another Daimler – of British Automobile Traction Co, Macclesfield branch, the forerunner of the North Western Road Car Company.

used for chasing or shadowing a competitor.

The Council adopted a policy of restricting licences believing that this would eliminate competitive tactics and, although BAT, who entered the town on only one route, had all their vehicles licensed, yet Crosville were only allowed barely enough licences to cover their published time tables in the Crewe area. The company was reported by the police for operating an unlicensed bus (FM 641) and warned accordingly. At this point Crosville appealed to the Ministry of Transport but the Council persuaded the Inspector of the validity of their actions and the appeal was disallowed.

Crosville were still interested in extending their area of influence in Cheshire to include Northwich and the Crosland Taylors met the directors of the Mid-Cheshire Bus Co in October 1923. A high proportion of the mileage was workmen's traffic and the directors wanted to sell. However, there was a big difference of opinion about the value of the business and Crosville declined to buy. The following year, George Cardwell of North Western purchased the business and Crosville's eastward expansion was effectively blocked for almost half a century. An agreement was reached as to areas of influence but, for a number years, through passengers between Chester and Northwich had to change buses at the Abbey Arms.

The absurdity of the outdated licensing system was highlighted in August 1923 when Crewe Borough, Nantwich Urban District and Nantwich Rural District Councils conferred together and agreed to co-ordinate the issue of

---

The Services So Far

At this point it is perhaps worthwhile summarising Crosville's Crewe and Nantwich area services as they were in May 1923. Besides the Crewe Town services and railway works specials, the following daily services were operated:

NANTWICH-MERRILL'S BRIDGE-CREWE: 8-9 weekdays and 6 Sundays
NANTWICH-SHAVINGTON-CREWE: frequent
NANTWICH-WILLASTON-CREWE: frequent
CREWE-SANDBACH-MIDDLEWICH-WINSFORD: 7-8 to Sandbach weekdays; 2 Middlewich, 3 Sandbach and 3 Winsford Sundays. Some through to/from Nantwich
CREWE-WESTON-BETLEY-MADELEY- NEWCASTLE: 4 weekdays, 3 Sundays.
NANTWICH-WYBUNBURY-HOUGH-CREWE: 3-4 weekdays and 3 Sundays.

All Sunday services commenced around midday.

Market day services.

NANTWICH-WHITCHURCH-HODNET: Fridays
NANTWICH-MARKET DRAYTON-HODNET: Wednesdays
NANTWICH-ACTON-FADDILEY: Thursdays & Saturdays
NANTWICH-WRENBURY: Thursdays & Saturdays
MARKET DRAYTON-NORTON IN HALES: Wednesdays
NANTWICH-CHURCH MINSHULL-CREWE: Thursdays, Fridays and Saturdays, some part route only.

CHESTER-TARPORLEY-NANTWICH, 2 Tuesdays & Thursdays, 3 Saturdays (worked from Chester depot).

In the early 'twenties Claude Taylor would dearly loved to have taken control of the Mid-Cheshire company's area. That had to wait until 1972 and the hand of the National Bus Company. This 1920 view of Leyland MA 4098, which passed to North Western, reflects on what might have been.

A half cab Leyland delivered in 1925 and seen here in a Leyland Motors view, No. 161 (FM 3218) was a 36SG9. The 36 denoted the horse power rating of the petrol engine. Dual-door bodywork for 40 seats was still specified although all new vehicles from 1925 onwards had pneumatic tyres from new, Crewe Watch Committee at least now being mollified by these new deliveries and conversions of earlier vehicles.

omnibus licences from 30th September. The Clerk to Nantwich RDC sought the assistance of the other councils in appealing to the Ministry of Transport against its decision not to allow any more local authorities to take on omnibus licensing powers. Just imagine the nightmare of continually seeking licences from three different local authorities for a simple route such as Nantwich to Crewe. Some councillors in Crewe were still in favour of a municipal bus service but several proposals failed to gain Council approval. A joint municipal undertaking with Nantwich, Sandbach and other local authorities was suggested but, despite a great deal of talk, nothing was done.

The Pneumatic Revolution

Crewe Council's tactics now turned towards ensuring that the newly available heavy duty pneumatic tyres were fitted to all its licensed motor buses as soon as possible. To that end the Town Clerk had written to Crosville on 12th October 1925 and received a reply to the effect that, at that time, it was not possible to put pneumatic tyres on their 40-seat SG buses but all buses up to 26 seats were being converted, so that all the Crewe Town buses would be fitted by the end of January 1926.

The Council now insisted that, in future, all vehicles must be submitted for examination before licences were issued. This alarmed both Crosville and NWRCC, the former because it was difficult to take buses off service so that they could be inspected, particularly those which had to be inspected by more than one licensing authority, and the latter because of its policy of undertaking maintenance and repair work in Stockport and sending 'float' vehicles to cover for those away from Macclesfield. The real purpose, apart from the desire of some members for the Council to operate their own municipal buses, was to force the conversion to pneumatic tyres. In September 1926, it was resolved that all Crosville buses running on solid tyres be licensed only until 1st January 1927, though, convinced of the practical problems, this date was extended to 31st March. Crosville explained that, because of the coal dispute, it was impossible to get the steel for the wheel conversion sets for the Leyland SG9 type, of which there were several allocated to Crewe though at least a dozen of another type,

not specified, but probably the Daimlers, had been converted. But the Council stuck to their guns and somehow the materials were obtained to convert the remaining six buses by the end of March.

A Licence Famine

Despite the virtual elimination of large scale competition in the town, the Council continued to devote considerable energy and resources to harassing the bus operators, in particular, Crosville. In a special exercise on a Thursday and Friday in January 1927, when the company held 39 licences and wanted three more, only 30 buses were recorded on the Thursday and 31 on the Friday. James Crosland Taylor explained that four vehicles were kept at Madeley and 33 buses were used on Saturdays, leaving only six to cover breakdowns. The company was obliged to supply full details of their vehicle rosters which showed that, on Saturdays, 33 buses were required for service, leaving six spare, of which two were used at Madeley and sometimes had to come to Crewe. Of the six additional licences applied for two would be required for the new Crewe-Chester service and four as spares. The complete schedule would be: Buses on service at some time or other – 35, Spares – 10, total 45. The ten spare licences were required as follows: Reserves in garages, Crewe, Nantwich or Madeley for overloads, wet nights and local breakdowns – four, paint shop – two, central repair shop – four. Spares of 25% were generally regarded as fair and reasonable at that time and the six extra licences were at last granted.

Competition had developed with Crosville, Peach and Taylor each claiming that the other was running ahead of the authorised times between Crewe and Haslington. In May, the Council's inspectors had a blitz on buses waiting on the Square longer than the permitted 15 minutes so it seems that, despite undertakings to keep to the timetables, some pirating was still going on. The matter was resolved from 10th November 1927 when Crosville took over the Peach and Taylor businesses. One of Taylor's drivers, Len Thornhill, eventually became garage foreman at Crewe and his son, Alan, became Area Engineer, Clwyd, in 1973 and, at the time of writing, is employed by Crosville at Ellesmere Port.

The Council's protests to both Crosville and North Western about their attitude towards trade unions were vigorously resisted and at a meeting on 14th June 1927, Claude Crosland Taylor for Crosville and George Cardwell for North Western told the councillors that wages and conditions of labour were an extraneous matter and not within the jurisdiction of the Council. Cardwell refused to listen or discuss the matter in any way. The members then turned their attention to standing passengers allowed, up to one third of the seating capacity being allowed; on workmen's services this was increased to one half.

In October 1927 a base was established at the Red Lion Yard, Middlewich and a new twice-daily service commenced in 1928 between Middlewich, Winsford and Chester, via Over and the Abbey Arms, while the Chester-Crewe route was extended to Newcastle-under-Lyme, running eight daily return journeys. In addition a frequent local service was operated between Newcastle and Madeley and there was a new branch off the daily Newcastle-Woore-Knighton service between Woore and Audlem, extended to Whitchurch on weekdays.

More Competition

A new threat to business was looming when, on 16th August 1929, Samuel Jackson and Sons, Engineers, of Wistaston, proposed to run a service of buses between Nantwich, Crewe and Sandbach, via Willaston and Shavington, and asked Crewe Council for licences to ply for hire in the borough. They proposed to use the most modern type of bus possible, could assure the public of an efficient and regular service at more reasonable fares and would be pleased to submit a time table and list of fares. The buses were to be Crossley 6-cylinder saloons and there would be 1d stages, whereas Crosville had a 2d minimum. New employment would be created for local men.

The original application was refused by 5:3 votes but Jackson would not let matters rest and on 28th September wrote again to the Council asking whether a spokesman might appear before the Committee, together with a legal representative. This was agreed and both Jackson and his solicitor, Mr J P Whittingham, attended the October Health Committee meeting following which they were invited to re-apply for licences. Meanwhile, Crosville suggested that if the Committee allowed applicants to attend to put their case, it would only be fair to permit existing proprietors to state any objections they might have simultaneously. As a result, the application was referred to a special meeting on 18th December, where all parties might appear before the Committee, severally but not collectively. In the meantime Jackson, under the name of Malbank Motor Services, had already started operating with the knowledge, and clearly the blessing, of the Council because, on 14th November 1929, a Crosville representative was interviewed about the practice of the company running buses immediately before and behind Jackson's unlicensed buses!

Jackson and Crosville, with their legal representatives, duly put their cases on 18th December and, after much discussion, Jackson got licences for two buses. He confirmed that he had no intention of operating an internal service within the borough and would consent to restrictive licensing conditions preventing this.

A Fares War

Competition between Crosville and Malbank was fierce. Both Jackson and Crosville had originally considered 7d return between Nantwich and Crewe, an overall distance via Willaston of ten miles, to be an economic figure. Crosville's fare had been higher than this but was reduced to 7d to compete with Jackson. Further reductions were

A delivery to LMS Crosville in 1929 was this Lion LT1, with Leyland 35-seat bus bodywork. It was withdrawn in 1937.

Crewe Watch Committee seemed to conduct itself in a manner reminiscent of the Metropolitan Police where vehicle specification was concerned. Number 108 (FM 2613) was a Leyland GH7 of a type which fell out of favour following the appearance of the first Lions in 1926. The vehicle exhibits its conversion to pneumatic tyres and the deep steps wanted locally. A suggestion that the rear door be used for boarding and the front for alighting was rejected by the Company though at the beginning of the 'seventies a fleet of Bristol RELL6G where the reverse was the case was introduced to the town! The grille in the nearside cab door is thought to have been added to improve ventilation in the full-width cab, apt to be marginal.

made, until the return fare came down as low as 4d and, during this period Crosville and Jackson lost some £7,000 between them. They then agreed to co-ordinate their services, resulting in a decision to recast their fares on the basis of 1d per mile, considering this to be an economic figure at which to run.

The whole matter was aired at the May Council meeting; the current 10d return fare between Crewe and Nantwich was based on this mileage scale. Jackson's figure of 7d return had been reached after only six weeks' experience of running buses. Both operators were working the Crewe-Nantwich service, whereas Jackson had taken over the Crewe-Sandbach route (7 miles) and the Nantwich-Wettenhall-Winsford route (12 miles), neither of which made money. Both Crosville and Jackson were criticised for increasing their fares between Nantwich and Crewe. Crosville stated that they had agreed not to increase their fares only if Jackson was not granted a licence. As he had been, they had been forced to raise the fares in order not to make a loss. Jackson wrote that he regretted any misunderstanding that may have arisen from his fare lists as discussed in December, but the lower return fares were only intended for workmen. The wool had been pulled firmly over the Council's eyes!

Both operators were summoned to appear before a Special Health Committee meeting on 3rd July, when the whole saga was revealed. Both refused to reduce the fares,

saying they could not do so and remain solvent. The Chairman admitted that the fixing of fares was outside the Council's jurisdiction but he stated that Jackson's licences were granted on the submission that fares would be lowered. In August Jackson was granted licences for two 20-seaters for a service between Wistaston and Crewe Square via Valley Road and Wistaston Road.

Fleet Replacement

It is of interest to note the composition of the Crewe-based fleet at that time. One of the latest Leyland PLSC1 Lions, No. 207, had been licensed in September 1926; it set a new standard of comfort and appearance and thereafter the Crewe Council tended to license the old buses for only short periods. In December 1927 the company announced their intention of converting the town services to Lion operation as soon as possible and requested that the licences for five Leyland GH7s and four Daimler CKs be extended. After at first refusing, at least four of the GH7s and one of the CKs (FM 1092) were relicensed. In March-April 1928, Crosville placed 17 new dual-door 32-seat Leyland PLSC3 long Lions in service, most of which were to stay in Crosville service for 20 years. Never satisfied, the Council suggested that passengers should enter by the rear door and leave by the front but this was rejected by the company as being impractical, having been tried in another district.

In September 1928, Crosville were still operating nine Daimlers, the oldest four (DU 2007, FM 603, 641 and 703) dating from 1913, albeit with 1924 Leyland-style bodies and pneumatic tyres; these were licensed for six months only. Five more Daimlers were soon drafted in, all licensed only to March 1929. Crosville appealed against the short terms of the licences, stating that the Daimlers were used on the country services and rarely worked in Crewe Town but the the Council stuck to its policy.

By March 1929 Crosville still had 11 Daimlers in the Crewe area and applied to license two more. The Council refused to renew the licences on the 11 or grant the other two. By the end of the month Crosville had reduced the request to just five Daimlers but this was still turned down. Eventually, in April, licences for six months only were granted for a solitary Daimler, FM 1386 of 1920, together with Leyland GH7s FM 2624, FM 2818-9, and PLSC1 FM 3710. The company agreed not to send any more Daimlers to Crewe. One concession won, however, was that a bus brought in as a temporary replacement to cover for one broken down or under repair could operate with the permission of the Council's inspector until the next Committee meeting, if applied for in writing.

On 15th April 1930, councillors inspected and were taken on a trial run in a new Leyland Titan TD1 double-deck bus No. 355 which Crosville proposed to use on the Chester-Crewe service. The bus was licensed temporarily in time for Easter but the Health Committee, at their May 1930 meeting, gave the application for licences for three double-deckers a very rough ride but their refusal was overturned by the full Council in June though standing passengers were disallowed. In March 1931 Crosville exchanged licences for eight single-deckers for a similar number of 48-seater double-deckers, bringing a total of 11 TD1s to the area, all from the batch FM 5882-95. With the Road Traffic Act, 1930 now in force, the Council's influence over bus operation in the borough was clearly on the wane and, on 12th March, a

heartfelt plea went out to the operators to notify the Council of any alterations in their services that affected the borough. They were not going down without a struggle, however, and on 2nd April the Council received a letter from Crosville explaining that they were still operating the SG9s, whose licences had expired at the end of March and would continue to do so, as was their new right, until such time as the Traffic Commissioners had granted or refused new licences. The Town Clerk complained to the Traffic Commissioners who confirmed Crosville's position.

It was not all one-sided, however, and on 16th April Crosville wrote to the Council complaining about Warburton and Sons running buses between Sandbach and Crewe via Coppenhall and Ettiley Heath and via Haslington and asking their assistance in the matter of protesting to the Traffic Commissioners. They were told to do it themselves! The old order was finally buried when, on 11th June, Crosville returned 77 drivers' and 78 conductors' badges to the Council and asked for their 1s refund for each. The sum of £7.15s.0d was duly returned to them.

The Company convinced the Crewe Watch Committee that double-deckers were acceptable after prolonged battle. The first vehicles allocated were from the 354-68 batch. Number 354 (FM 5882) is representative of these although in this view, it is seen at Heswall through the camera of David Deacon. These vehicles, dating from 1930, were the first double-deckers in the fleet with enclosed stairs, which had become usual on the standard Leyland body for the TD1 by then.

THE WELSH DEPOTS
1919-29

1. Mold

On 10th July 1905, the London and North Western Railway inaugurated a daily service between Mold, Northop, Flint, Oakenholt Paper Mill and Connah's Quay to which, within the next year were added a daily feeder between Holywell station (later re-named Holywell Junction) and Holywell Town and another route between Holywell, Halkyn and Mold. The services, worked by Milnes-Daimler buses which also carried mail and parcels, underwent various vicissitudes. In August 1908, a new service between Mold and Loggerheads was started; this was extended to Llanferres the following year. The Holywell station and Town service was replaced by a railway from 1st July 1912, the bus being used on a new route between Mold, Northop, Ewloe, Queensferry and Connah's Quay, which ran only until 31st December 1912, when it was replaced by a service between Mold, Flint, Connah's Quay and Queensferry. This itself had gone by May 1913. A final new service began on 1st October 1913 between Mold and Buckley. The Loggerheads to Llanferres extension ceased after 30th September 1914 and remaining operations in the area ended after 17th April 1915, when the bus chassis were commandeered by the War Office.

Crosville saw Flintshire, one of the more populous areas of North Wales which had a considerable community of interest with Chester, as a potentially profitable area for expansion. Its first approach to the County Council in September 1918 for permission to run a service linking Shotton, Connah's Quay, Queensferry and Garden City was unsuccessful but a door-to-door petition attracted 516 signatures, the only people not signing being two County Councillors and a handful of tradesmen, fearful that a bus service would drive trade away. After some trouble in agreeing terms, an agreement was signed on 1st March 1919 for a circular service, which had actually started on 22nd February. The problem areas were the restriction of laden weight of vehicles to six tons (this was eventually relaxed to seven tons, Crosville having informed the County Council that vehicles used on the Queensferry munitions factory services were eight tons laden) and the fact that Crosville wanted a specific charge quoted in the agreement for the use of County Council roads. This was agreed at 2d (0.83p) per vehicle mile, payable every six months.

The route which required one vehicle for each direction ran from Mold, via Buckley, Hawarden, Queensferry, Connah's Quay, Flint and Northop, back to Mold, buses connecting at Queensferry Cross Roads with a Connah's Quay-Chester service via Sealand church, Great Saughall and Mollington, using a Chester based vehicle. A second route from Mold to Pentre Halkyn via Northop, was agreed with the Council in May on the same terms. This was extended from 27th August 1919 as another circular via Holywell, Greenfield, Bagillt, Flint and Northop back to Mold, the mileage charge being increased to 3d (1.25p) per vehicle mile, payable every three months. In the meantime, in July, Mold was linked with Ruthin via Loggerheads. Most of the earlier railway network had thus been recreated and extended. Fares were based on 1½d per mile (0.625p) with a surcharge in Flintshire to cover the roads levy. For the quarter 1st July to 30th September 1920 Crosville paid £342.18.0 (£342.90) to the County Council for its four routes, made up as follows:

Connah's Quay 660	journeys	@ 4 miles		£22. 0.0
Mold-Ruthin 2104	"	@3	"	£78.18.0
Mold circular 660	"	@18	"	£148.10.0
Holywell circular 330	"	@20	"	£ 82.10.0

The Wrexham and District Transport Company's 1913 services between Chester and Mold and Chester and Flint had fallen victim to wartime restrictions and were not reinstated, that company concentrating its efforts on Wrexham and Oswestry. In October 1921, it commenced a service between Ellesmere and Mold, via Overton-on-Dee, Wrexham and Caergwrle and that was the full extent of its activities in the area.

In 1921 Crosville's Chester-Connah's Quay service was extended to Holywell and a direct route introduced between Chester and Mold; in 1922 new routes were established between Chester and Caergwrle and between Mold and Denbigh, while the following year saw the start of a new service between Holywell and Afonwen. There was more expansion in 1924, particularly in the Mold area, where a depot had been opened at Ponterwyl and new routes started to Halkyn, Pantymwyn and Coed Talon. By autumn 1925 a complicated network had evolved covering all the principal roads. However, on the coast road, Crosville could not get beyond Greenfield where Brookes Brothers' White Rose buses connected for Prestatyn and Rhyl. Llay Main Colliery, opened in 1922, was served by a new Chester-Caergwrle service via Dobs Hill, Penymynydd and Hope.

Links with Merseyside had already been forged by New Ferry-Mold-Loggerheads and Birkenhead (Singleton Avenue)-Ruthin-Denbigh services. There were also links between both Holywell and Mold and Denbigh via Caerwys, Afonwen and Bodfari with connections to St. Asaph and Rhyl, again by White Rose. Many of the more rural services ran on certain days only, usually related to local market and Fair Days.

A popular leisure spot was the Loggerheads Estate, some three miles from Mold on the Ruthin road and Crosville was quick to realise the potential of providing a regular service to the site, not only from nearby Mold, but also from the larger towns within a 30-mile radius. The place took its name from a tiny public house, We Three Loggerheads which was quite inadequate to cater for the

The Loggerheads Estate was acquired in 1926 and developed over the next years. These two views dating from the 'thirties show the bandstand and one of the kiosks. Some idea of the scope of the entertainment offered and the crowds attracted can be seen in the lower view. The crowds may have been expected to have come by Crosville bus – one is just visible on the right of the lower view.

needs of the huge number of trippers and showed no inclination to try. The Crosland Taylors realised that the inability to obtain refreshments limited the popularity of the place and they considered setting up some sort of facility if it could be done without spoiling the place. When the estate was sold by auction in 1926 Crosville acquired part of it for £1,600 and soon developed the site, erecting a tea-house with accommodation for upwards of 100 people and a bandstand; the Leete woods were thrown open to the public. The company claimed never to have made money from the catering facilities but thousands of new passengers were attracted to the summer services which ran from Birkenhead, Liverpool, Chester, Runcorn and Warrington. This was a classic example of a transport undertaking creating a demand for its own services.

To try and boost patronage of the catering facilities, combined travel and meal tickets were issued, not only on the direct buses but also, by connection, from Newcastle-under-Lyme, Crewe, Nantwich and Ellesmere Port. By the summer of 1928, the most popular service, from New Ferry, was running hourly with two express journeys at a premium fare of 6d above the ordinary rate.

The next few years saw a consolidation of the network and the inauguration of new services such as the Holywell-Brynford-Carmel circular, Shotton Steelworks specials and Mold-Rhesycae-Lixwm-Holywell.

An outstation was opened in Denbigh on 3rd October 1928, and the Denbigh-Ruthin service was increased. On market days, it was customary to use buses from other depots to augment this service during their layover.

2. Llanrwst

Crosville first put down roots in the Conwy Valley in May 1922, when the Betws-y-Coed-Abergele service of W H Roberts of Llanrwst (Roberts' Blue Motors) was acquired. For a year the service was run from Betws-y-Coed but a base was set up at the Victoria Hotel garage, Llanrwst in 1923. At first, there were two buses, one for the Abergele service and the other for the Llanrwst-Betws-y-Coed-Cerrigydrudion-Clocaenog-Llanfwrog-Ruthin service; the second bus also worked trips between Ruthin and Denbigh. By May 1923, a third vehicle was needed to run short journeys on both routes, particularly on Llanrwst market and fair days. The Ruthin service connected at Betws-y-Coed with trains on the Conwy Valley line between Llandudno and Blaenau Ffestiniog. The Abergele service was in the charge of driver Tom H Nurse with a regular bus, No. 80, (CC 1024), a Leyland GH6B 32-seater saloon, acquired from Roberts.

Developments through the 1920's were based on these two corridors, plus a service between Llanrwst and Blaenau Ffestiniog, operated from the Blaenau Ffestiniog depot, described below. A second bus was assigned to the Abergele service by 1924, and a third in 1926. A new service, from Llanrwst via Betws-y-Coed to Penmachno and Cwm Penmachno commenced on 1st December 1926 and the business of Hugh Jones of Penmachno was acquired on 10th February 1927. Traffic increased rapidly and two more buses were in use on the service by 1928. The main roads in the area were already served by other operators – Conwy and Llandudno to the north by the Llandudno Coaching and Carriage Co Ltd (Royal Blue) and Bangor to the north-west by Bangor Blues, who were bought out by Royal Blue in April 1928.

Royal Blue opened a new depot in Betws-y-Coed Road, Llanrwst, in 1929, and Crosville moved in to share the premises. The terminus moved to Llanrwst Square, with some trips extended to and from the railway station.

3. Barmouth and Dolgellau

E R (Evan) Edwards joined Crosville in 1921 as a conductor at Mold. In April 1923 he was sent to open a depot at the Min-y-Mor Laundry garage, Barmouth, with driver Rob Owen, of West Kirby. The bus was new Leyland GH7 No. 93, (FM 2480). The first service, to Harlech daily, was started on 1st May 1923 and a second service, to Dolgellau, commenced in 1924; this required one bus in winter and two in summer. A second bus was added to the Harlech service in May 1925 and a third in 1929.

A depot was opened in Arran Road, Dolgellau, in 1924, initially to work a summer service between Dolgellau and Tywyn, followed, in July, by a twice-daily service to Bala,

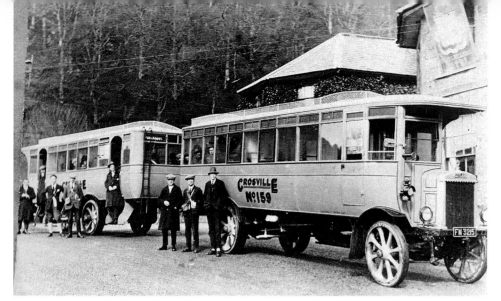

Crosville's progress through North Wales was achieved by a mixture of organic growth and acquisition. Typical of the former is this all-Leyland 40-seat 40SG9 seen at the Oakeley Arms on the Portmadog Road. It is believed that the picture was taken in 1927, and the use of a rear destination blind in the vehicle to the rear is something sadly lacking today. A few vehicles were fitted with the higher power engine to cope with the Welsh terrain.

with a short working to Drws-y-Nant on Saturday evenings. From 25th September 1924 for about a year, this bus also worked a Bala-Corwen service. From 11th March 1925 Dolgellau contributed one bus to the Dolgellau-Blaenau Ffestiniog service.

4. Blaenau Ffestiniog

This depot was opened in 1924 at Bodwydd Buildings, High Street, Blaenau Ffestiniog to cover services to Dolgellau, Llanrwst and Porthmadog. On the Dolgellau service, the nine miles between Trawsfynydd at 650 feet above sea level and Blaenau Ffestiniog at 1,000 feet took 55 minutes going up and 45 minutes going down, the route negotiating a hill of 1 in 8. Similar allowances were made on other services in the area. To help cope with the hilly terrain, several of the Leyland GH6Bs and GH7s were fitted with 45hp engines instead of the more usual 36hp. A local service was quickly established between Blaenau Ffestiniog

and Tanygrisiau and, by 1930, the frequency had increased to hourly during the day and half-hourly in the evening, but with only two journeys on Sunday.

A second Porthmadog bus was added in November 1924 and a third in July 1925, both based at a sub-depot at the Sportsman Hotel in Porthmadog. From May 1925 two or three return journeys served Harlech, diverting at Maentwrog and connecting with buses for Barmouth. A short-lived service linked Porthmadog with Pen-y-gwryd via Beddgelert between 1926 and 1927 and was later operated by Criccieth depot; from 22nd February 1928, new services were commenced between Porthmadog and Morfa Bychan and Borth-y-Gest. Workmen's buses from Blaenau Ffestiniog served Talsarnau from 24th November 1926, later being extended to and from Harlech, Maentwrog and eventually Tanygrisiau. A third bus was allocated to the Dolgellau service from 1927.

Blaenau Ffestiniog had been brought into the fold by 1924 and this building was to serve the Company until 1962. Even then the tourist boom had not come to the area and the depot was to remain in Company ownership well into the 'seventies. The vehicle facing outwards is KA 97, Leyland TS8 of 1938 but the one facing inwards enables the photograph to be dated around 1950. The building had scarcely changed however. The vehicle is KA 232, one of the Tiger PS1/1s diverted from Midland General and operated for a short while in an all green livery when new.

Earlier expansion northwards from Pwllheli had come with the business of Richards (Busy Bee) of Caernarfon acquired in 1926. One of the vehicles acquired was this 1926 Strachan & Brown bodied AEC 505. It is seen here when new. Erroneously the Company fleet list showed this vehicle as having a Hall Lewis body. Its rightful builder's transfer is visible on the waistrail on the original print.

Another vehicle used in the area was this 1927 29PLSC1, again with Leyland bodywork. The notice in the window of the bus towards the rear, 'begs to announce that the Crosville Motor Company has taken over the bus service between Pwllheli, Criccieth and Portmadog', which would place the view around October 1927 when A and R Motors was acquired.

5. Caernarfon

Richards' Busy Bee service of Caernarfon was acquired by Crosville on 9th November 1925. Richards operated a local service in the town, which was soon discontinued, and between Caernarfon and Porthmadog via Garn and to Llanberis and Pwllheli. The Porthmadog service required two buses, one stabled at each end of the route while the Pwllheli bus was out-stationed there, though a second, Caernarfon-based bus was used in summer. The Llanberis route was augmented by three additional buses in 1927. A service linking Llanberis with Beddgelert via Pen-y-gwryd ran only until 1926, with a shorter route, to Pen-y-gwryd only, in the summer of 1927. A new route, Caernarfon-Dinorwic, started on 17th November 1926 and was increased from one to three buses within a year, the then thriving slate quarries providing much traffic

With Busy Bee came Jack Griffiths, who was soon promoted to inspector. He became depot superintendent at Criccieth in 1933, moving to Pwllheli in 1940, where he remained in charge until he retired in August 1963.

5. Criccieth

On 1st October 1927 Crosville acquired the business of

A & R Motors, (Avery and Roberts) of Criccieth, who ran a two-bus Porthmadog-Pwllheli service. A summer service between Criccieth and Caernarfon was introduced on 5th April 1928 with a third bus for the Pwllheli service. Criccieth also supplied a bus for the Porthmadog to Pen-y-gwryd service in 1928.

6. Aberystwyth, Aberaeron and Cardigan

Services in this district were pioneered early in the century by the Great Western Railway, initially to work up sufficient traffic to justify the construction of a branch line from Lampeter to Aberaeron which was eventually opened in 1911. Originally the crews came from England and were housed in tents in Aberaeron, but resentment at this invasion by foreigners, coupled with the claim by the horse bus proprietors that the motor buses were taking their trade, soon led to the recruitment of local men for the work. A second route was inaugurated between Aberaeron and Aberystwyth, in November 1906 followed, on 1st May 1907, by a service between Llandyssul, on the Newcastle Emlyn branch line, and New Quay, using two new Milnes-Daimler buses. With the exception of the

Llandyssul service, which continued until 31st July 1929, operations finished on different dates during the 1914-18 war.

Aberystwyth Council had always expressed a preference for 'local' businesses to run local transport and so, when, in 1923, Crosville and the Corris Railway applied to run buses from Aberystwyth to Machynlleth, Tywyn and Devil's Bridge, the Council deferred making a decision until the GWR, whom they obviously considered to be 'local', had also applied. Permission was granted to the GWR for a service to Machynlleth, which commenced on 29th November 1923, and the other two applicants were refused. They appealed to the Ministry of Transport, who met a deputation from the Council to hear their reasons for local preference. The Council was persuaded to meet the three operators on 15th April 1924 and, as a result, agreement was reached for the operation of several bus routes as follows:

Aberystwyth-Machynlleth: GWR and Corris
Aberystwyth-Devil's Bridge: Crosville and Corris
Aberystwyth-Ysbyty Ystwyth: Crosville
Aberystwyth-Cardigan: GWR

However, a meeting convened to discuss purely local matters had far-reaching consequences as, from 8th May 1925, the GWR concluded a three-year agreement with Crosville, agreeing not to compete at Barmouth, Blaenau Ffestiniog or Llandrindod Wells or on any route south of Aberystwyth, except where competition already existed. The railway company could run through Devil's Bridge on its proposed service to Llanidloes via Llangurig and could extend its Corwen to Cerrigydrudion service to Betws-y-Coed and Porthmadog, both of which would be operated only in summer. It reserved the right to provide a service between Montgomery station and town centre. This was all good news for Crosville who, for their part, agreed to keep out of the Oswestry and Welshpool areas, to give up their services between Corwen and Llandrillo and between Brecon, Talgarth and Hay-on-Wye and not to compete along the GW 'line of railway' without prior discussion, nor to reduce fares. They also undertook to reroute their proposed Lampeter-Aberaeron service to avoid direct competition with the railway. The conciliatory attitude of the GWR was born of a letter sent by the London and Provincial Omnibus Owners' Association pointing out that the railway's bus operations were *ultra vires* though

they did not wish to take the matter to law. The implied threat was nevertheless there.

Crosville established a base of sorts at Pen-yr-anchor Kiln, Aberystwyth, and started, on an undisputed route to Llanilar, on 21st March 1924. This was followed in June by two routes to Devil's Bridge, to both the north and south of the Ystwyth River. In the meantime, on 14th March, a service was started between Lampeter and Aberaeron, using a bus outstationed at Lampeter. Before the GWR was able to get started on the Aberaeron-Aberystwyth route, Crosville bought out D M Jenkins of Aberaeron on 21st February 1925, for £900. Jenkins operated between there and Aberystwyth and New Quay. The GWR did not finally start until 22nd July. Later in the year, Crosville acquired Hooker's service between Aberaeron and Cardigan, a depot being established at the Aeron garage, Aberaeron, with a vehicle outstationed in Cardigan.

7. Llanidloes and Llandrindod Wells

A base was established at the Trewythen Arms Hotel in Llanidloes and a daily service to Newtown commenced on 8th October 1924. Two return journeys on Saturdays linked Llanidloes with Llangurig. From 2nd October 1925, a bus was outstationed in Montgomery where it worked a weekday service to Garthmyl, Abermule and Newtown but it ceased after less than four months' operation. A service from Rhayader to Llanidloes commenced on 5th October 1926, being extended to Newtown from 12th January 1927. It was a failure, being withdrawn altogether a month later.

Crosville decided to close down in Llanidloes and move to Llandrindod Wells in November 1924, establishing a base at the Llanerch Hotel. Hotels were a very popular source of accommodation for motor buses at this time, doubtless because many were old coaching inns with courtyards and stabling for horses, which made acceptable

Calmer times in the Square at Llandrindod Wells on market or Fair day. From left to right Nos. 116, 129, 110 (FM 2852, 3002, 2815) stand waiting departure for Rhayader, Howey/Builth Wells and New Radnor and Kington. The crews leaning on the vehicles have yet to be provided with uniforms, but nonetheless are reasonably smartly turned out with ties and jackets.

garaging and offices. In addition they tended to be focal points in towns and in many cases served a dual role as depot and terminus. The first service, to Builth Wells, commenced on 29th November followed by a second, to Kington, on 19th December; a third service, to Rhayader, was commenced on 2nd October 1925. There was no Sunday operation. It seems that a service was planned between Llandrindod Wells and Newtown but it is likely that it never started as there were already three other operators working this sparsely populated corridor. On 29th January 1925, the company started running on an isolated route between Brecon and Hay-on-Wye, but this route was handed over to the GWR on 13th July, in accordance with the agreement previously mentioned.

In 1928 Crosville moved into a depot in Oxford Road, Llandrindod Wells. Apart from occasional fleet changes and time table adjustments, this area remained remarkably unchanged and completely detached physically from the rest of the system until 1956. Even the depot superintendent, Seymour Lawson, was there from the start of operations to finish, being promoted from driver-in-charge in 1932. This episode can only be described as a manifestation of the Crosland Taylors' irresistible urge to start up services in remote places; it seems certain that, if the true costs had been calculated, it never made any money at all.

Another view taken in Llandrindod Wells shows 135 standing awaiting service in the 'Trewythew Yard'. The happy conductor is the same fellow that can be seen leaning on the mudguard of FM 3002 in the photograph above. Curiously a contemporaneous note on the back of the print suggests that this bus is cleaned and ready for SUNDAY service. The man is named as relief Conductor E. T. Higgs; one wonders if he has any surviving relatives in the area today.

ASSOCIATED WITH
LONDON MIDLAND and SCOTTISH RAILWAY COMPANY
TILLING AND BRITISH AUTOMOBILE TRACTION LTD.

CROSVILLE MOTOR SERVICES LIMITED

DIRECTORS:
W. S. WREATHALL, *Chairman.*
G. CARDWELL,
ASHTON DAVIES,
O. GLYNNE ROBERTS,
C. D. STANLEY,
C. CROSLAND TAYLOR, *Managing Director.*

CHESTER PRIVATE HIRE DEPT.
AND CITY ENQUIRY OFFICE:
MARKET SQUARE.
TELEPHONE - 1123i

HEAD OFFICE: CHESTER.
TELEPHONE: 1123 (3 LINES).
TELEGRAMS:
CROSVILLE - CHESTER.

ALL COMMUNICATIONS MUST
BE SENT TO THE HEAD
OFFICE AT CHESTER AND
ADDRESSED TO THE COM-
PANY AND NOT INDIVIDUALS.

Offices and Depots :

	Tel. Nos.		Tel. Nos.		Tel. Nos.		Tel. Nos.
LIVERPOOL—		HOYLAKE -	991	FESTINIOG -	59	LLANGEFNI -	4
WATER ST.	CENTRAL 2604	NEW FERRY -	664	CAERNARVON -	141	RHYL -	437
EDGE LANE	OLD SWAN 1308	ELLESMERE PORT	131	BARMOUTH -	77	PRESTATYN -	371
BIRKENHEAD—		NANTWICH -	5457	CRICCIETH -	19	DENBIGH -	124
PARK STATION -	1914	CREWE -	2420	ABERYSTWYTH -	221	LLANDUDNO-JUNC.	-81226-7
SINGLETON AVENUE	1980	WARRINGTON -	570	ABERAYRON -	19	OXFORD RD. -	6202
WOODSIDE -	2295	RUNCORN -	257	LLANDRINDOD -	111	CLONMEL ST. -	6201
LISCARD -	3952	MOLD -	23	BANGOR -	416 & 148	QUEEN'S ROAD -	6472
HESWALL -	280	LLANRWST -	51	HOLYHEAD -	2	COLWYN BAY -	2330
WEST KIRBY -	1471					BEAUMARIS -	43

(HEAD OFFICE):

OUR REF. **Eng. Dept.**

YOUR REF.

CRANE WHARF,

CHESTER,

16th July, 1931.

To the Managing Director.

With reference to your enquiry, the following passenger vehicles were among those I was asked by you to take over in the Colwyn Bay area on August 1st, 1930:-

E.H. 6070
R.F. 1096
O.N. 1184
E.H. 2559
E.H. 6314
C.C. 2287 (described in licence as E.H.2287)

The whole of these vehicles were running in Colwyn Bay either during the Summer or at some time during the year and composed the majority of the fleet being operated by the Silver Co. between Colwyn Bay and Llandudno.

These vehicles were in such a dangerous condition that, as an example, the side of the body of one of them opened up as the vehicle was going along the road and a gap appeared through which it would have been easy for a passenger's leg to slip or fingers to be trapped.

The brakes of all of them failed to work and the drivers had difficulty in bringing the buses to a standstill and there were several accidents. In every instance I found the woodwork rotten and falling to pieces. The bodies were completely worn out and unsafe although fully licenced by the Local Authorities for the area.

I had these buses broken up as soon as new vehicles could be obtained from the manufacturers.

I also had to scrap one or two Royal Blue vehicles as being in an unsafe condition and one of these was C.C. 147 running in Colwyn Bay on a local service.

In addition to the above list there were a number of other buses licenced in Colwyn Bay formerly belonging to the Silver Co. which I withdrew from service at once owing to their unsafe condition. It was considered however that if these vehicles were rebuilt they might be rendered temporarily capable of service. This work of rebuilding was carried out to enable these vehicles to be used.

Fuller details of the condition of the vehicles can, if necessary, be furnished but I think the above will give you some idea of the state these vehicles were found in and I was surprised they had been allowed to be on the road at all.

Signed.

Walter. George Wright.

ENGINEER.

A vivid indication of the poor condition of some of the buses taken over in North Wales, particularly from North Wales Silver Motors, is given by this letter in which Crosville's Engineer, Wally Wright, reports on his actions. The vehicles he lists were all from that fleet, including two Dennis 2-ton models, a Guy B and a Karrier HH dating from 1925, another Dennis 2-ton of 1921 and a Daimler CK of 1920. The last were thus quite old, but even on five-year-old buses, wood-framed bodywork, especially if made from poor-quality timber, could rot quite severely and of course brakes, especially in those days, required regular maintenance to remain effective. The Royal Blue CC 147 he also mentions does not appear among vehicles taken over and it seems it may have been an error as this number suggests something very old, the CC series having begun in 1904.

4 NORTH DEVON INTERLUDE

It is pure speculation as to why the Crosland Taylors should have looked towards North Devon as part of their expansion plans at a time when every pound of capital was needed to establish services in their core operating area. Perhaps the warmer climes of the south-west attracted them and, if the financial rewards had been greater, they might never have continued their efforts in Cheshire and North Wales.

Colwills (Ilfracombe) Limited

Sam Colwill began operating horse drawn coaches in the 1880s; his first coach, named Benita, was used on a daily excursion from Ilfracombe to Lynton. His second coach 'Magnet' was driven by his son, Tom, who took over the business in 1894. By 1900, Tom was providing a network of horse bus services based on Ilfracombe, known as 'Colwill's Greys', the colour of all his horses. Some years later Tom met an untimely death in an accident involving his coach and the business was continued by his sister, Laura Squire Colwill.

In 1919, Laura decided to modernise the operation after she was approached by a motor charabanc proprietor, Captain Geoffrey Cecil Shiers, of 'Rockland', Ilfracombe. It appears likely that she hired Captain Shiers's AEC charabanc. Around this time members of the Crosland Taylor family were visiting the area and chanced to meet Captain Shiers. This meeting resulted in an agreement dated 17th November 1919 between Laura Squire Colwill and Claude Crosland Taylor by which the firm of Colwills (Ilfracombe) Limited was formed on 17th January 1920, with an authorised capital of £25,000 of which £17,450 was issued, to take over the goodwill of Laura's business

as a horse and carriage proprietor. Among the long list of objectives for which the company was established were 'to carry on the business of motor car, omnibus, van, motor plough, tractor and cab proprietors, and carriers of passengers and goods', etc. The company paid Laura £3,600 for the business, probably about £70,000 in today's values. The shareholders were Captain Shiers, three local Ilfracombe investors and George, Claude and James Crosland Taylor. The directors were Captain Shiers, Claude Crosland Taylor and Henry Hill Coleridge. The registered office was at 107 High Street, Ilfracombe and the garage was in Marlborough Road. It would appear that Daimlers from Crosville in Chester were used to start the first motor bus service, between Ilfracombe and Barnstaple via Braunton, in December 1919. There were three return journeys on weekdays and two on Sunday. Crosville tickets were used and at least one Crosville bus stop sign has been located, at Fremington. Bus services and coach excursions were expanded in the Ilfracombe area and new services established around Barnstaple and Bideford. Two businesses were acquired, the excursion business of Thomas Lavin Thorne, of Ilfracombe, and the bus service of W H Dyer, of Braunton. In Barnstaple, a small garage was acquired in Buller Street. By 1923, services had been started as far away as Bude and Wadebridge, in North Cornwall.

The sparse population of the district and the seasonal nature of much of the traffic led to poor financial results and in the year ending 31st March 1923 the profit was only £785, against a bank overdraft of nearly £5,000. A resolution was passed on 23rd June 1924 that Colwill's (Ilfracombe) Ltd. should go into voluntary liquidation and on 12th July the sale of the company was confirmed to the Hardy Central Garage Ltd., of Minehead, for £28,339.13s, being

FM 652 was a Daimler CD with Eaton body of a type being delivered to Crosville at Chester around 1915, some few years before the Devon interlude. There is no record of this specific vehicle in the Crosville listing. However, registration numbers were reissued, for example, numbers as low as FM 224 appearing on new vehicles in 1919. Quite how its identity might have been altered cannot therefore readily be established.

Another pair of mysteries are illustrated here. The upper view shows Colwills No. 13 (FM 1873), a Crossley tender X in series with a Chester based example FM 1874. The lower view is another Daimler, this time a CK with Bartle body which follows on from the above as well as tying in with Crosville series of similar buses in the range FM 1881 upwards. Note the 'corporate identity' effect in conformity of fleetname, fleet numbers and livery style.

the issued capital of the company, plus its debts. The new directors were Messrs John Priscott and James Hardy, of Hardy Central Garage, J H C Goodban and Albert Venn. The trading name became Hardy-Colwills Motor Service and the registered office was moved to The Strand, Barnstaple. Besides a bus operation in Somerset, based around Minehead, the Hardy-Colwills empire spread down the Atlantic coast of Devon and Cornwall as far as Newquay, with a service between Newquay and Truro. With the fleet in need of replacement and a lack of the necessary resources, the undertaking sold out to the National Omnibus and Transport Co. for £48,500 in February 1927.

Croscol's Limited

During 1920 the Crosland Taylors formed another company, based in Tiverton as a wholly-owned subsidiary of Colwills. This was Croscol's Limited, the name being derived from Crosland (Cros) and Colwill's (col). The first bus, registered in Chester, was delivered in November 1920 and a service was started on 5th April 1921 from Tiverton to Dulverton via Bampton, on Tuesday only.

This was followed, from 6th May, by a service between Tiverton and Exeter with three return journeys daily. Later, services ran to Uffculme three times a day and Cullompton four times. Captain Harold Youlton was sent from Chester to organise the company, becoming Managing Director, the other director being Home C Smith. Road staff were recruited locally, it is thought from unemployed ex-servicemen. The company was not registered until 7th July 1921, with an Authorised Capital of £10,000, of which £6,400 was issued. The registered office was 8A Fore Street, Tiverton.

Later on, the company started to operate in the summer as far afield as Budleigh Salterton and Exmouth. Again, all tickets used carried the Crosville name. A garage in Chapel Street, Tiverton was obtained as a result of purchasing the small charabanc business of F G Eastmond, who joined the board. With the combination of poor receipts from the Devon subsidiaries and the competition from the Devon General Omnibus and Touring Co Ltd, Croscol's was sold to Devon General on 24th May 1924. Home C Smith, who had become Chairman, joined the Devon General board.

5 THE CIRCLE OF COMPETITORS

By 1929, Crosville had consolidated an operating area consisting of the Wirral peninsula, Lancashire south of a line between Liverpool and Warrington (the territory to the north being served by a network of tramways and feeder bus routes), the western half of Cheshire, and Flintshire south of a line from Greenfield to Holywell. In Wrexham, Ellesmere and Oswestry, with tentacles stretching out to the south west, were the Wrexham & District Co and the services of the Great Western Railway, the mutual pact of May 1925 precluding any expansion by Crosville. Further west in Wales, though connected on the map, services in the districts then known as Denbighshire, the Lleyn peninsula, Merioneth and Cardiganshire were scattered and sparse. There was also the strange little disconnected outpost at Llandrindod Wells.

In other words, the most populous and potentially most profitable coastal and industrial areas of North Wales remained unpenetrated because of the presence of a number of old established operators with comprehensive networks of services. The same applied to Anglesey, though the traffic potential there was considerably lower.

Royal Blue

The scenic jewel of the North Wales coast was undoubtedly Llandudno with its impressive bay dominated by the Great Orme's Head. There, the Llandudno Coaching and Carriage Co. Ltd., registered on 29th December 1897, was formed to acquire the coaching and carriage businesses of C A Hartley, H J Pell, Charles Clements and Captain Wilson, all of Llandudno. The registered office was The Coaching Office, Queens Hotel Gardens, Clonmel Street, Llandudno.

In 1915, the British Automobile Traction Co Ltd took a financial interest and the Authorised Capital was increased from £15,000 to £17,000 in 1916 but later reduced to £13,700, of which all had been issued by 1923. Growth was rapid through the remainder of the 1920s, and capital was increased to £100,000 in 1923 of which British Automobile Traction (BAT) held £61,581.

The original managers were John Jarvis and George Woodyatt, who were partners in the company until 1924. They were succeeded by a General Manager, A C Clifford, who was himself replaced by Claude R. Taylor (no relation to the Crosland Taylors) by 1926. Chairmen during the 1920s included S E Garcke and W S Wreathall of the BAT. In December 1929, the LMS acquired an interest in the company, offering £1.5s per Ordinary Share.

The growth of the company is illustrated by the passengers carried and miles run in the years ended 31st October 1923-29:

Year	Passengers	Mileage
1923	763,383	Not Recorded
1924	1,159,926	436,298
1925	1,864,568	571,272
1926	2,488,560	832,896
1927	3,587,693	1,045,130
1928	6,082,193	2,055,108
1929	7,444,053	2,824,688

Thornycrofts were favoured for the early rolling stock which included charabancs and single- and double-deck buses. Later, the Dennis marque found favour and, under

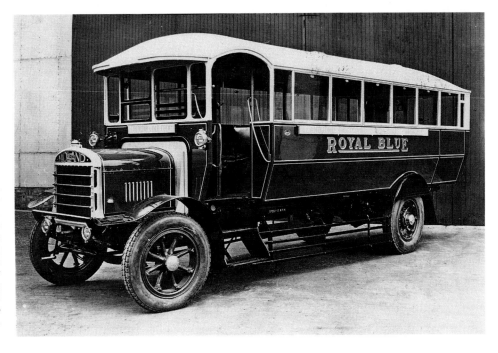

The 'Standard SOS' of the Birmingham and Midland Motor Omnibus Co Ltd was built from 1923 to 1926 and demonstrates the Midland 'Red' company's influence on the engineering policy of the Llandudno Royal Blue company. It was a relatively lightweight design powered by a 4.332-litre 4-cylinder petrol engine. The bodywork also to Midland Red's standard pattern, was by Ransomes.

BAT influence, Birmingham-built SOSs became the standard purchase, with a few Leylands.

The company started by operating seasonal excursions in and around Llandudno, but by 1919 some excursions were being operated throughout the year. Motor bus services started in January 1921, under the name 'Royal Blue', and by 1923 there were five quite frequent main routes, reaching Colwyn Bay, Conwy, Llanrwst (by both sides of the valley) and Penmaenmawr. Some competed with North Wales Silver and J Fred Francis and, of course, with the trams of the Llandudno and Colwyn Bay Electric Railway.

An early depot in Mostyn Street, Llandudno had gone by 1921, others being situated in Oxford Road and Queens Road; Llandudno Junction depot at Imperial Buildings, Glan-y-Mor Road, was opened in 1924, became the registered office in 1928 and is now the headquarters of Crosville Wales Ltd. The Llanrwst depot, in Betws-y-coed Road, opened in 1929, was shared with Crosville, as already mentioned.

In 1925 the company acquired the bus but not the coach business of J Fred Francis and Sons Ltd, of Colwyn Bay. This company originated on 16th April 1920 and initially ran a fleet of motor coaches known as the 'Grey De-Luxe Motors' on excursions to 'Snowdon, Llanberis and all beauty spots in North Wales'. One director, A Lynn, joined the Royal Blue board, remaining also on the Francis board.

Their local services, worked by four 32-seat Leyland saloons, ran between Old Colwyn, Colwyn Bay and Llandudno and Colwyn Bay, Old Colwyn and Abergele. Royal Blue amalgamated them with their own Llandudno-Colwyn Bay route to form a new through route between Llandudno and Abergele and opened up new routes between Llandudno, Colwyn Bay and Conwy and between Llandudno, Colwyn Bay, Llanberis and Caernarfon. In addition a Llandudno local service was commenced.

In 1927, Royal Blue bought the bus operations of Robert Unsworth and Co of Colwyn Bay. This company, with origins in the early 1920s, ran one 20-seat Renault bus on two local services to Rhyd-y-Foel and Betws-yn-Rhos and to Llysfaen.

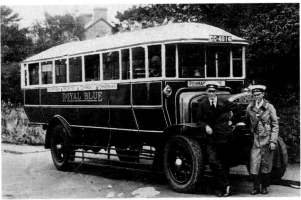

Amongst the other vehicles to be taken over later were EY 2741, the future 578. This slightly ungainly vehicle was a Bristol O type 2-tonner with seats for 20. Brush was the bodybuilder on CC4816, an SOS S type to be numbered 504.

Bangor Blue

In April 1928, the business of Bangor Blue Motors Ltd, of 263 High Street, Bangor was purchased by Royal Blue. It was originally registered as a private company on 17th March 1921 with a nominal Capital of £2,000. On 19th January 1922 the Authorised Capital was increased to £15,000 and the following month there was an amalgamation of interests embracing the motor section of Tourist Hotels Ltd, Lancashire United Tramways Ltd (LUT) and A & R Motors Ltd who together acquired a controlling interest in the company and took over the management. There were two LUT directors, E. H. (Ned) Edwardes, the LUT General Manager and Harry England.

Initially, vehicles were based at Bangor, Menai Bridge, Llanfairfechan and Penmaenmawr but by 1928 the depots were at Bangor, Beaumaris and Llangefni.

The principal Bangor Blue bus services extended to Menai Bridge, Caernarfon, Penmaenmawr, Bethesda, Betws-y-coed, Deiniolen, Llangefni, Holyhead, Amlwch and Malltraeth Bay with market services to Llanrwst and Llandegfan and various routes within Anglesey to Beaumaris, Llangoed, Llandegfan and Llanerchymedd. A full programme of full-day, half-day and evening tours was operated from Bangor and Llanfairfechan.

This acquisition gave Royal Blue an extensive territory and the fleet at the time of acquisition by Crosville numbered 80 vehicles. The company had good relations with Crosville and there was interavailability of return tickets between Caernarfon and Llanberis and between Betws-y-coed and Llanrwst as early as 1928. They also shared a garage at Llanrwst as previously mentioned. In 1929, Crosville advertised a joint Grand Circular Tour from Caernarfon, visiting Llanberis, Pen-y-gwryd, Beddgelert and Waunfawr, all by ordinary service buses for 3/6d (17½p). There was another all-Crosville circuit from Caernarfon via Porthmadog, Criccieth and Pwllheli which cost 4/- (20p) midweek and 5/- (25p) at weekends.

Bangor Blue placed this Dennis E in service in 1927. Its Ransomes body is to BET Federation style of the time, with distinct echoes of the Midland Red SOS in its rear-end styling. In 1928 it passed to Llandudno Royal Blue and when the latter was taken over by Crosville in 1931 briefly entered the latter's fleet as No. 566.

43

North Wales Silver Motors had the usual varied selection of vehicles: This 1921 32-seat Dennis, CC1807, was later numbered 115 and this Buckingham-bodied Tilling Stevens B10A, CC8610, was the future 103.

North Wales Silver Motors Ltd.

Registered on 23rd May 1914, this company was formed to take over the business of an earlier company, the Llandudno Automobile Touring Co Ltd, registered on 8th May 1911. The offices and depot were in Mostyn Broadway, Llandudno. At its inception the company had an Authorised Capital of £35,000 but this was later reduced to £18,000, of which £16,224 was eventually issued. The Chairman was Joseph Dicken, the Secretary, H F Cunningham and the General Manager (from about 1926), W M Wynn.

The company operated buses and charabancs in and around Llandudno and longer-distance tours in North Wales. The main routes were all competitive with other operators – from Llandudno to Penmaen Head and Abergele; to Conwy and Penmaenmawr and up the west side of the Conwy valley to Betws-y-coed (later truncated at Llanrwst). The company also had an interest in the Chester Silver Motors Company mentioned in Chapter 1.

The fleet, which included double-deckers, grew from about 15 in 1914 to 27 in 1930.

Competition was fiercest between coach operators; in 1927, for example, there were some ten firms operating day, half-day and evening tours from Llandudno, half of whom were fleet operators and the rest single vehicle owners. North Wales Silver at this time owned seven coaches.

White Rose

Rhyl, a brasher holiday resort, had the advantage of being nearer England and thus potentially more accessible. It attracted thousands of holiday visitors while its neighbour, Prestatyn, was favoured by a more discerning minority and as a retirement place.

The Brookes brothers, Joseph, Daniel and Thomas, had started in business around 1900, operating 'four-in-hand' horse-drawn coaches on excursions further into

The Brookes Brothers, proprietors of The White Rose Motor Services tended to dominate many areas of Rhyl's commercial life. Despite this apparent respectability, they seemed to have scant regard for certain aspects of the law as Crosville found when it was discovered that certain vehicles were nearly eight feet wide. It is difficult to do proper justice to this fleet in the space available but a few of the interesting vehicles can be shown. Crosville 496 (DM 2128) was an 8-seater Fiat which appears to have been used for the guests of one hotel.

North Wales from Rhyl. Motor vehicles were introduced in 1911, the first motor charabanc being a Lacre, (DM 472). The following year brought five more charabancs and two open-top double-deck buses, all Leylands and running under the name White Rose. Most of the chassis were commandeered by the War Department in 1914 and the bodies stored, but by acquiring three Leyland S4 chassis and fitting them with double-deck bodies, Brookes Bros. were able to maintain a limited local service, mainly for troop transport between Kinmel Camp, Bodelwyddan, and Rhyl.

After the end of the war, they began to rebuild the bus and charabanc fleet and charabanc trips were soon operating again. Rhyl Council had a policy of prohibiting loading and unloading passengers on the streets so Brookes Bros. built a bus station at the White Lion yard, in High Street, and enjoyed a monopoly in operating local bus services. This monopoly was threatened in 1924 when a rival coach proprietor and motor engineering firm, the Rhyl and Potteries Motor Co, acquired eight vehicles and applied to Rhyl Council for licences. The Council turned down the rival application, leading to the resignation of the Chairman. A public meeting decided to demand that the Council reconsider its decision, as many people felt that it was not in the public interest to stifle competition. The Council remained unmoved, however, and still refused to license the Rhyl and Potteries buses. However, eventually the Rhyl and Potteries buses were licensed and ran in

This Leyland Lion 29PLSC1 was new in 1927 with Leyland bodywork. In common with many native Crosville Lions, it was rebodied during 1935/6 and survived until after 1945. The White Rose livery gave a 'different' look even to standard Leyland types. The '29' prefix to the PLSC refers to the horsepower and appears to be a Crosville designation as opposed to an official Leyland one.

We do not accept Liability for any Loss or Damage from Fire or Other Causes to any Property entrusted to us for any purpose.
Customers' Cars are driven at Customers' Risk only.

TELEGRAMS: "POTTERIES," RHYL.   ...THE...   PHONE: RHYL 181.

RHYL AND POTTERIES MOTORS
Proprietors: ROBINS and ROBINS.

CHAR-A-BANCS, TAXIS and
BUS FOR HIRE.

**MOTOR ENGINEERS . BODY BUILDERS
TRIMMERS AND PAINTERS.**

RHYL.

NORTH WALES AGENTS
...for...

Commercial Motor Vehicles.

Office and Showrooms—
Queen Street.

HAULAGE CONTRACTORS.

Garage - Westbourne Avenue.

...Proprietors of...

THE PRIMROSE MOTOR COACHES.

All Communications to be addressed to QUEEN STREET.

June 25th. 1925.

J. Lloyd Hughes Esq.,
Clerk to Prestatyn Urban District Council,
PRESTATYN.

Dear Sir,

We beg to apply for Licences for 8 (eight)
Motor Omnibuses, particulars as below –

	Seat:Cap:	Reg:No.	Make.	Licence No.
1	32	X.B.2247	A.E.C.	J. 292169.
1	32	X.B.9098	"	J. 292166.
1	32	D.M.2492	"	J. 292170.
1	32	D.M.3740	"	J. 292168.
1	34	D.M.3647	"	J. 292185.
1	34	D.M.3648	"	J. 292186.
1	34	D.M.3649	"	J. 292165.
1	54	D.M.3850	"	J. 292187.

We also beg to apply for Licences for Drivers
and Conductors as list herewith, should this staff be
altered or added to, we will immediately notify you.

Trusting you will find the foregoing in order,
We remain,
Yours faithfully.

p.p. RHYL & POTTERIES MOTORS.

In June 1925 Rhyl and Potteries Motors applied to Prestatyn for renewal of the licences for their eight vehicles. Four of these (the last four listed in the application) would eventually pass to Crosville via Brookes Brothers. The double-decker, listed here as having 54 seats, is recorded as having gained a further two seats with White Rose, being a 56 seat open-topper by the time it came into Crosville hands as their number 480.

Below: Whilst many vehicles came into the Crosville fleet after passing through another operator's hands this Dennis from the New Blue Bus Company, seen lettered for service in the Llandudno and Colwyn Bay area, passed directly to become Crosville U43 in 1935 when it was acquired with the Owens business. It was renumbered W5 before withdrawal in 1936.

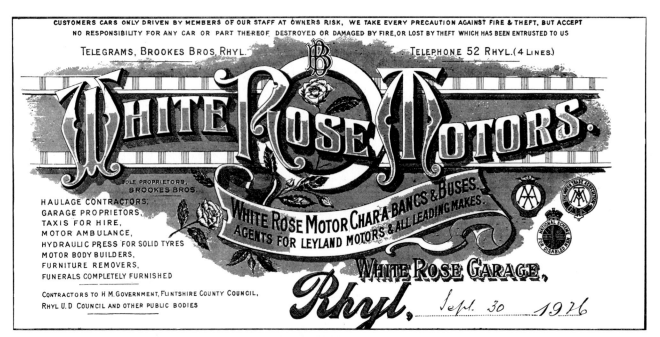

This was White Rose's flamboyant letter head as used in 1926. Note that the concern held a Leyland agency.

Brookes Brothers will probably be best remembered for introducing the toastrack fleet to Crosville service; here DM 4833 is seen as Crosville 493. The tradition was maintained with further deliveries of toastracks later in the 'thirties.

competition with Brookes Bros. on their main routes. Eventually the competition became too hot for Rhyl and Potteries and they sold out the local bus side of their business to Brookes Bros. in 1926. They retained their coach business, however, which was run under the title 'Primrose Motor Coaches'.

Brookes Bros. expanded their business through the 1920s, opening depots in Prestatyn and Denbigh. They carved out for themselves an exclusive operating area along the coast from Greenfield to Abergele, with significant penetration inland from their Denbigh depot. Neither Crosville nor the Llandudno operators had been able to gain a foothold in this stronghold though Crosville negotiated an Agreement for the exchange of traffic at boundary points. Several of the Rhyl routes were very frequent and some summer routes were run with SD Freighter toastracks.

Services ran between Rhyl and Prestatyn, Rhuddlan, St. Asaph, Llanfair Talhaearn, Denbigh, Rhuallt, Caerwys, Kinmel Park, St. George, Abergele, Tremeirchion, Meliden, Dyserth, Ochryfoel, Greenfield and Holywell. From Prestatyn buses ran to and from Ochryfoel,

Trelawnyd, Llanasa, Trelogan and on some town services. The Denbigh services operated frequently to Henllan and the Sanatorium and to Llangynhafal and Ruthin, Llannefydd and Plas Harri, Bylchau, Tremeirchion, Bodfari, Nant Glyn and Groesffordd Pant Glas. There was also a service from Ruthin to Bontuchel and Cyffylliog. Several of the Denbigh services ran only on Wednesdays, the market day.

There were a number of express journeys between Rhyl and Greenfield, connecting with Crosville buses for Flint and beyond. Another popular service advertised as 'Through the Switzerland of Wales' covered a circular route from Rhyl, outward via Abergele, Llanfair Talhaearn and Henllan to Denbigh, returning via St. Asaph and Rhuddlan.

By 1930, the fleet comprised some 89 buses, coaches and charabancs, mainly of Leyland manufacture. There were also taxis, hire cars and furniture removal vans. Depots were located at Crescent Road and Albion Works, Rhyl, White Rose Buildings, and Sandy Lane Garage, Prestatyn and at Lenten Pool, Denbigh.

The presentation of this vehicle might best be described as confusing! DM 4016 was a 1926 Leyland C7 with London Lorries bodywork new to Brookes Brothers. It is seen here bound for Caernarvon (sic) in Crosville livery and side fleet names but carrying a Royal Blue headboard above the cab.

Red Dragon

W Edwards ran a fleet of about a dozen buses from the Abbey garage on the main Denbigh to Rhyl road, competing with Brookes Bros. over certain sections of route. Less than a month before Edwards sold out, he had acquired the local services and two vehicles from Robert Smith of 58 Love Lane, Denbigh.

Edwards was a typical market service operator but he was a sworn enemy of Brookes Bros. whom he regarded as interlopers. His main route was between Denbigh, Pen-y-cefn and Llansannan via Deunant and Bylchau, others extended to Penniel, Nant Glyn, Henfryn; Henllan, Llannefydd, Moelfre and Abergele; Prion, Saron and Brynglas; Tremeirchion.

Ruthin-Hiraethog was served every weekday with extra market day and Saturday trips between Ruthin, Clocaenog and Tai Teg and to Rhewl.

The combined fleets of the above-mentioned operators in 1929-30 which subsequently came into the Crosville fold, totalled about 200 vehicles which compared with the Crosville fleet of about 350 vehicles at the time.

Wrexham and District Transport Co Ltd

Registered on 26th August 1901 as Wrexham and District Electric Tramways Ltd, this BET subsidiary laid down a narrow gauge electric tramway between Wrexham, Rhostyllen, Johnstown and Rhosllanerchrugog (usually contracted to Rhos), which opened to the public on 4th April 1903, replacing an earlier horse tramway between Wrexham and Johnstown which dated back to 1876. There were ten open-top double-deck tramcars, housed in a depot at Johnstown, providing a service which, at the busiest times, ran every ten minutes. Arthur A Hawkins came from Greenock Tramways in 1906 to become general manager and remained in the post until the 1933 Crosville takeover.

The first bus service started on 23rd September 1913, using a Daimler CC saloon (FM 614) and, within six months, the company had six Daimlers and two McCurd buses. Services were operated from Wrexham to Chester, Coedpoeth and Brymbo from a depot in Lord Street, Wrexham and an outstation in Castle Street, Chester. The

Wrexham Tramways was the predecessor of Western Transport taken over in 1933 and here the first bus, a Daimler, is seen complete with bowler-hatted general manager A A Hawkins looking on.

company had grandiose expansion plans as mentioned in Chapter 1 but the war intervened.

On 19th March 1914 the company's name was changed to the Wrexham and District Transport Co. Ltd. and was marketed as 'Transport Red' with a fleetname Transport. By August 1914 the bus fleet had grown to 16 of which nine Daimler B-type chassis were soon commandeered by the army, the bus bodies being stored. Several drivers joined the army with the chassis and one, S N Jones, on arrival in France, found himself allocated former Wrexham and District Daimler FM 654!

By June 1915 ten buses a day were running between Wrexham, Gresford, Rossett, Pulford and Chester at a through fare of 1/- (5p) single and 1/6 (7.5p) return. Occasional services from Wrexham served Ruthin fair on the first Tuesday in the month, Ellesmere on alternate Tuesdays, Oswestry every Wednesday and Whitchurch every Friday. Services were also commenced between Wrexham and Overton, via Bangor on Dee, and Wrexham to Gwersyllt, via Rhosddu and Rhosrobin, but these petered out during 1916 due to loss of vehicles, leaving just a skeleton service between Wrexham and Chester and Wrexham and Acrefair. In 1916, a small garage was built at Maesgwyn, Mold Road, Wrexham and in 1920 a brick tram shed was added.

After the war, the stored bus bodies were mounted on ex-War Department Daimler Y-type chassis and curtailed services were gradually restored. The Wrexham-Overton service was recommenced and in 1920 an outstation was opened at the Queen's hotel yard in Oswald Road, Oswestry, initially to operate part of the trunk route to Wrexham. Oswestry's first allocation was Daimler FM 1298. By May 1921 services were in operation between Wrexham and Chester, Acrefair, Oswestry, Caergwrle, Holt, Farndon, Whitchurch, Mold, Southsea, Brymbo, Marchwiel, Ruthin, Pen-y-cae and Ifton Heath. Many of these were market services which worked only on certain days of the week and it was the practice for buses to run local trips from the market town to fill in their time there. Thus there were Mold-Buckley, Whitchurch-Malpas, Oswestry-Ifton Heath and Ruthin-Llandegla trips on market days only. A local network, based on Oswestry, served Knockin, Four Crosses, Gobowen, Preesgweene and Weston Rhyn.

The tramway was operated on a basic 15-minute headway on Monday, Thursday and Saturday, and 20-30 minutes on all other days, including Sunday. Workmen's trams operated between Johnstown and Wrexham from 4.50 to 6.30 am on weekdays.

Wrexham's premier market day was Thursday but smaller markets were held on Mondays and Saturdays each week. Most services operated into Wrexham on these three days, leaving buses available on Wednesdays to serve markets in Mold and Oswestry and on Fridays, to serve Whitchurch market. Tuesday was a very quiet day. Sunday was the day for recreation and such services as did run were for making family visits or for trips to chapel, into England, to Farndon, Chester or Oswestry, to sample liquid refreshment not then available in North Wales on Sundays.

By August 1922, there were new routes from Wrexham to Bangor and to Hawarden, Queensferry and Connah's Quay, both on Mondays, Thursdays and Saturdays only. The Wrexham-Chester and Wrexham-Acrefair services were combined and extended to form a through service from Chester to Llangollen. The Wrexham-Caergwrle and Wrexham-Overton services were extended at both ends to form a through service between Mold and Ellesmere, still running only on Monday, Thursday and Saturday, except for two Sunday evening Wrexham-Ellesmere trips and one market journey on alternate Tuesdays. The Wrexham-Farndon route was extended to Broxton on Monday and Thursday (two return journeys) and Saturday (three return journeys).

Between 1922 and 1927 new services were commenced from Wrexham to Oswestry via Llangollen; Chester via Llay; Coedpoeth via New Broughton and Talwrn; Minera; Pentre Broughton and Ponciau. Oswestry-Four Crosses was extended to Llandrinio Bridge and Wrexham-Farndon to Broxton. On Sunday the 11.30am departure from Wrexham connected at Farndon with the 1.0pm river boat service to Chester.

A bus service was commenced early in 1924 between Wrexham and Rhos on a 15-minute headway and this had a devastating effect on the tramway which, by now, was in a poor condition. Local taxis also suffered, with some taxi drivers joining Wrexham and District as bus drivers. By 1926 the tram service had been reduced to hourly, maintained by a single car, and gave way entirely to buses on 31st March 1927, the last trams being cars 2 and 9. Johnstown depot was now used for buses; initially these were the ex-W-D Daimlers which were used on the colliery services. Ten buses were required for the day shift and three for the night shift, carrying miners from Penycae, Rhos, Ponciau, Wrexham and Cefn Mawr to Hafod and Bersham collieries. To increase the seating capacity of these vehicles each row of seats had an extra hinged seat which was let down into the gangway space! Tram driver Albert Davies was appointed Inspector to supervise the colliery buses. He was stationed at Broad Street, Rhos, and was provided with a wooden hut sited in front of the Bull's Head public house. Crews would travel out to Johnstown from Wrexham on the first colliery bus at 4.30am and return on the last bus from Johnstown. Several other services were also worked from Johnstown which now participated in the Wrexham-Rhos and Oswestry services, reducing dead mileage. New circular services were commenced from Johnstown, via Rhos, Copperas, Plas Bennion, Acrefair, Cefn Mawr and Ruabon and in the reverse direction. They were not well supported and were soon reduced so that one bus could operate both directions. Wynne Bowyer, clerk at Wrexham, took charge of the Johnstown office and Harry Hughes became fitter-in-charge.

No doubt because of the success of the Sunday evening services from Wrexham to Ellesmere, in 1924 a regular Sunday evening excursion started, leaving Wrexham High Street at 5.30pm and running via Ellesmere, Whitchurch, Malpas and Bangor-on-Dee, returning to Wrexham at 10pm. Half-hour stops were made at Ellesmere, Whitchurch and Malpas, all in England and therefore 'wet'. Wrexham at this time was 'dry' on Sundays and the excursion was a veritable pub-crawl. The fare was 2/6d (12.5p) and as many as five or six charabancs were regularly filled.

With expansion in the Oswestry area, the Queen's Hotel out-station was replaced by a rented garage in Lower Brook Street in 1925; this, too, was outgrown within five years, the old drill hall in Oswald Road being adapted in its place. It is now occupied by Midland Red North. Bert Smithers was promoted from driver at Wrexham to inspector at Oswestry; he was replaced about 1930 by George Inman, who became depot superintendent in 1933, with the Crosville takeover.

During the mid-1920s summer express services were inaugurated between Wrexham, Rhyl and Llandudno via Rhyl (later also from Rhos and Johnstown) and to Blackpool. Half-day excursions were run to Rhyl and to New Brighton and full-day excursions to Blackpool illuminations.

The bus fleet had grown to 30 by 1925 and reached a maximum of 86 by 1930. A new depot was built in Mold Road, Wrexham, in 1928, on land purchased with the Maesgwyn Estate. The General Manager lived at Maesgwyn Hall.

The growth of the company between 1924 and 1929 is demonstrated by the following mileage and passenger statistics for the years ended 31st December:

Year	Bus Passengers Carried	Bus Miles Run
1924	1,357,287	601,083
1925	2,398,681	911,106
1926	3,519,299	1,202,474
1927	5,330,968	1,635,129
1928	6,860,405	1,827,324
1929	7,224,780	2,111,195

Great Western Railway Road Services

The Great Western Railway was the first motor bus operator in Wrexham with a service to Farndon which commenced on 11th October 1904 and ran until 30th April 1919; between July 1905 and August 1914 it was extended in summer to Aldford. By 1925, the Wrexham and District buses were affecting railway traffic seriously and the company began predatory competition on 24th June 1925 with services from Wrexham to Pentre Broughton, to Llay and to Brymbo. From 25th April 1927 the GWR attacked the former tram route between Wrexham and Rhos. The Llay route originally was extended via Rossett and back to Wrexham as a circular but was curtailed to Llay on 10th July 1926.

One of the Western Transport vehicles to be rebodied was UN 1916, a Tilling Stevens B10A; new with Alexander charabanc body it gained this Brush 34-seat bus body in 1934.

Buses were kept on Wrexham General station forecourt, where there was a galvanised shed between the two railway bridges. Ticket boxes were kept in the station office. Ticket inspector F W Averill was transferred from the railway section to the bus section.

In Oswestry the GWR started three services on 27th July 1925, to Gobowen (extended to St Martins from September to November 1925), to Llansantffraid, Meifod, Llanfair Caereinion and Welshpool, and from Welshpool to Garthbeibio via Llanfair Caereinion and Llanerfyl. From 21st September 1925 a service ran from Oswestry to Welshpool via Llanymynech, Arddleen and Guilsfield. From May 1926 a summer service linked Four Crosses (later Llanymynech) with Llangollen via Oswestry, Gobowen and Chirk. In the winter months, the service ran between Llanymynech and Gobowen. Finally, a weekday service commenced on 11th November 1929 between Llangynog, in the Tanat valley, and Oswestry via Llanrhaeadr-ym-Mochnant. Buses were garaged on railway property near the station and leading driver Fred Page was in charge.

The first GWR road service out of Corwen, to Cerrigydrudion, started on 15th August 1907 and two days later a service was commenced to Pentre Foelas. From 1st May 1908 a service ran to Betws-y-Coed and was extended from 4th July 1910, perhaps for a few days only, to Capel Curig. Most of these were war casualties though the Cerrigydrudion service continued in modified form.

In post-war years, a weekday service from Corwen to Llangollen via Bonwm, Carrog, Glyndyfrdwy and Berwyn commenced in October 1922, following the company's railway line. From 20th July 1925 the Cerrigydrudion service was once more extended, during the summer only, to Betws-y-Coed and on to Swallow Falls and, following the agreement mentioned earlier, from 1st October 1925 GWR buses took over the Crosville service between Corwen and Llandrillo which was extended to Bala and Dolgellau in July 1927.

From April 1926 a service operated on Corwen fair days (third Tuesday) to Bryneglwys, was extended from July 1928 via Llandegla to Llangollen. Between April and November 1926 a service was operated between Corwen and Glan-yr-Afon; it recommenced on 14th July 1927, extended to Bala. From the same date a separate service linked Bala with Cwmtirmynach; this was extended in stages, to Gellioedd, Pont Moelfre and Cerrigydrudion.

By the end of 1927 a Corwen fair day service was operating from Llangwm village and finally, from 8th July 1929, a service operated between Corwen and Llanrwst via Cerrigydrudion and Nebo on Saturdays and Llanrwst market and fair days. Buses were housed in a corrugated iron garage on Corwen station forecourt and were under the control of leading driver Jim Corbin.

GWR buses began operating from Dolgellau on 2nd September 1924, with a service to Dinas Mawddwy. In January 1925 a service was commenced to Drws-y-Nant, which ran until 9th July 1927 when it was absorbed into the Corwen to Dolgellau service. Crosville was also operating on this route (see Chapter 3). Just before this, on 4th June 1927, a second route was established, between Dolgellau and Llanfachreth via the Precipice Walk. The leading driver was Jack Martin.

On the Lleyn peninsula a route was established on 1st September 1925 between Pwllheli and Hebron via Nefyn, Edeyrn and Tydweliog, rerouted to Llangwnadl from 21st December. A second route, Pwllheli to Nefyn and Glanrhyd, was started on 23rd December, operated on Wednesday and fair days only. The leading driver was Arthur Jones.

Finally, in the Aberystwyth area, the GWR re-commenced service on 29th November 1923 on the Aberystwyth to Machynlleth corridor. From 3rd September to 4th October 1924 a service operated between Machynlleth and Aberllefenni via Corris, later taken on by the Corris Railway. On 22nd July 1925 the railway company finally started operating again between Aberystwyth and Cardigan, in competition with Crosville. The railway buses stopped temporarily in May 1926 and recommenced on 27th September rerouted via New Quay. The route was transferred to the Western Welsh Omnibus Co Ltd on its formation on 1st August 1929. One other route, between Aberystwyth, Llandre, Borth and Ynyslas, commenced on 21st May 1928. The leading driver was Charles Kent, later to become a Crosville inspector and the recipient of the BEM. Other bus services were operated by the GWR south of Aberystwyth but had no connection with Crosville until 1972.

Corris Railway

The Corris Railway was owned by the Bristol Tramways & Carriage Co Ltd so it was perhaps natural that this little railway had aspirations towards operating motor bus services and, in fact, introduced the Bristol marque of chassis to the area a quarter of a century before the Crosville fleet standardised on that make.

Its first venture into road services commenced on 8th July 1911, with a series of summer tours to Talyllyn Lake. Local motor buses were introduced on 13th February 1922 on a service from Machynlleth to Aberhosan via Forge on Wednesdays and stock sale days only. This was followed, in February 1924, by a weekday service between Machynlleth, Aberdyfi and Tywyn. Three months later, three new routes were opened up from Machynlleth, to Aberystwyth in competition with the GWR, to Newtown via Cemmaes Road, Talerddig and Caersws on Fridays and to Dinas Mawddwy via Cemmaes Road, Cemmaes and Mallwyd. Finally, from 1st May 1927, a service connected Dolgellau with Corris, Abergynolwyn and Tywyn, extended in summer to Aberdyfi. Although provided for in the Aberystwyth agreement (see Chapter 3), there is no record of the Corris Railway operating between Aberystwyth and Devil's Bridge.

There were garages at both Corris and Machynlleth. Inspector Edward Hughes of the Corris Railway became inspector-in-charge and later transferred to Caernarfon when Crosville took over.

6 THE NEW CROSVILLE – the 1930s

RAILWAYS (ROAD TRANSPORT) ACTS 1928

The loss of both passenger and goods traffic by the railways to road transport during the 1920s was very serious and the four main line companies created in 1922-23 were further handicapped by seven years' wrangling over a new charging system which, when it was finally announced, had most of the drawbacks of the 19th century tariff which it replaced. The railway companies could see that there were certain circumstances in which road would always be superior to rail and felt that, as they were burdened with statutory obligations which detracted from a purely commercial approach, they were entitled to the freedom to engage in road transport which was not totally ancillary to rail services when circumstances made it desirable to protect their interests. Their first attempt was unsuccessful but their right was conceded by Parliament and the Railways (Road Transport) Acts, 1928 which granted the necessary powers.

This development was viewed with considerable alarm in road transport circles, not least by Crosville whose staff accepted a 5% cut in wages to enable a fighting fund to be built up. But the railways realised that outright competition with well-established existing operators would be expensive; furthermore, while some junior managers thought that buses could be run by traditional railway methods, the senior people recognised that they lacked the expertise to handle a completely different discipline. The Great Western Railway was already running buses in North and Central Wales and elsewhere but, to a great extent their network was fragmented. They did run their buses like a railway and perhaps some clear-thinking people at the top realised that it might be much more profitable if run on different lines.

The railway strategy was, therefore, to buy into existing companies either by outright purchase or by investment. The Crosville Motor Co Ltd, a large, thriving family-managed business but publicly quoted, was one of the obvious targets and in *The Sowing and the Harvest*, James Crosland Taylor tells how the LMS Railway made an approach early in 1929. Bargaining started with an all-day meeting at Euston on 5th February 1929, but there were then discussions between the LMS and GWR who, in August 1929, offered to pay £398,750, the equivalent of £1-7-6d (£1.37½p) per share, compared with the quoted price of £1-6-0d (£1.30). In November 1929, the Crosville Motor Co. Ltd. went into voluntary liquidation, Claude Crosland Taylor becoming manager for the LMS, the GWR having dropped out at this stage, probably to give itself time to consider their interests in the Wrexham-Oswestry area. The railway wisely decided to retain the name and the business operated as LMS (Crosville). A new livery resembling the LMS maroon, as used on its passenger rolling stock, gradually replaced the Crosville grey or bright red liveries and an oval logo inscribed 'LMS Crosville' was applied to a few vehicles.

The LMS independently purchased Holyhead Motors (who traded as Mona Maroon) and UNU (U-Need-Us) Motor Services of Caernarfon, paying, according to *The*

The period of outright LMS ownership was very short and only a few vehicles were delivered with LMS in the oval fleetname. One such was No. 367, an all-Leyland Titan which is seen in a formal Leyland Motors view prior to being exhibited at the Commercial Motor Show in 1929 and subsequent delivery to Crosville.

Another delivery to the Company at this time was this Leyland LT1 Lion. When delivered, these vehicles had roof racks. The changes made over but a few years can be seen in the next illustration.

Sowing and the Harvest far more than they were worth. Mona Maroon had 18 buses and about four taxis based on three small garages in Holyhead. Routes ran to Amlwch by four different routes serving Llanerchymedd, Cemaes Bay and many intermediate hamlets; Benllech, Trearddur Bay, Valley, South Stack and Rhosneigr but the expansion of UNU was seen as a threat. As well as operating bus services, Mona Maroon had a busy taxi service which was retained for some years by Crosville, and a car repair and storage facility for travellers to and from Ireland. There was a steady revenue from parcels carried on the buses, the parcels and enquiry office being situated at Market Buildings, Stanley Street, Holyhead. The fleet of Albion, Chevrolet and Dennis manufacture was in a poor state.

UNU was started by George E Richards and was registered as a company on 30th March 1927 when there were five buses and one coach. Regular interval services were run, half-hourly between Caernarfon and Bangor and two-hourly between Bangor and both Holyhead and Llangefni. A twice-weekly excursion was run to Llandudno from Caernarfon. William Webster, having sold a business in Wigan to Ribble and Lancashire United, bought the company, then with four buses, on 20th April 1928, son Fred acting as manager.

The company operated from Penrallt Garage, Caernarfon and Bridge Street, Llangefni. The Websters brought with them four newish Leylands – two Lions and two Lionesses – and added 10 Vulcans to the fleet which eventually totalled 22 vehicles. Additional services were started from Llangefni to Bangor via Newborough and via Llanddaniel and from both Llangoed and Newborough to Caernarfon. An express service was put on twice daily between Caernarfon and Birkenhead though, as licences were refused in Birkenhead, only return ticket holders could be legally picked up there. This was the origin of the Crosville Merseyside-North Wales coastal express services.

Crosville was told by its LMS masters to integrate these businesses and, in the meantime, other important events were afoot.

The railway companies entered into agreements with the Tilling and British Automobile Traction (TBAT) Group to acquire 50% of its shareholdings in most of the companies under its control. They could never gain absolute control and the chairmen were to be appointed by the road interests. On their part, the railways sold half the shareholding in the businesses they had acquired to Tilling-BAT. In several cases of which Crosville was one, this entailed the formation of new companies. Crosville Motor

Number 342 was a 1929 delivery to the railway-owned Company. It is seen here in later years through the camera of David Deacon at Chester's Market Square outside the former King's School building, now Barclays Bank. Apart from the obvious change to the fleetname, in this case reverting to the style of the 'twenties, the roof rack was no longer fitted.

Normal deliveries to the fleet in the 'thirties brought in a wide variety of Leyland types as could have been expected. There were exceptions and this Daimler CH6 was certainly one. According to company records this vehicle was originally ordered by Edwards (Red Dragon) of Denbigh. It was fitted with a 35-seat United body before delivery in 1931. Fleet number was 606 and a Chester registration mark, FM 6472, help to complete the disguise. In November 1934, it received a Leyland four-cylinder oil engine and in the 1935 renumbering became J1, at the beginning of a series used mainly for oil-engined Leyland Lion buses.

Services Ltd. with a capital of £800,000, was registered on 15th May 1930, ending nine months of outright railway ownership and the display of the LMS name.

The railway company continued with their spending spree, targeting Brookes Brothers' White Rose Motor Services of Rhyl who held out for an even higher price than that offered. However, the railway had begun to realise that they were throwing money away and insisted on a valuation of assets as a result of which the price came down by 22%. White Rose was transferred to Crosville from 1st May 1930, followed by Red Dragon of Denbigh and Burton of Tarporley on 31st July and North Wales Silver Motors on 1st August. Llangoed Red Motors, with a service at Beaumaris, worked by one Renault, came in on 1st October.

The Llandudno Coaching and Carriage Co (Royal Blue) was one of the companies in which BAT sold a shareholding to the LMS and it was amalgamated with Crosville by a share exchange from 18th February 1931, thus completing the major consolidation of bus services in the North Wales coastal region. The total cost of these purchases was £751,218 (£632,468 in cash and £118,750 in shares).

Lest these seemingly paltry sums by modern standards should mislead the reader as to the size of the investments, it is interesting to convert them into present-day spending

power. Thus the railway offer for the old Crosville company would have been £9.87 million, the capital of the new Crosville company £19.8 million, and the cost of the various North Wales purchases £18.6 million.

Simultaneously with all this, the Road Traffic Act, 1930 was being applied, transferring the licensing powers of the local authorities to Traffic Commissioners. Most of Crosville's services were in the North Western Traffic Area, based in Manchester, but a few penetrated into the West Midland and South Wales Areas. Road service licences had to be applied for for every service, an enormous task complicated by the need to reorganise the recently acquired services and integrate them with Crosville's network.

While the larger operators had been consolidated into the enlarged Crosville company, there were still many small operators, especially in the excursion and tour business so competition was by no means dead.

The Merseyside Agreements

The railways saw the intransigence of the local authorities in Liverpool and Birkenhead as an obstacle to development and, in 1929, they made overtures to both councils; in Liverpool the London and North Eastern Railway was also a party by virtue of its two-thirds holding in the Cheshire

Number 359, photographed at Leyland before delivery, shows the maroon livery and oval fleetname together with the garter on the rear panel. The open emergency exit reveals that access to the driver's cab was from the lower saloon, whilst the thicker pillars on the third window of the upper saloon indicate the position of the upper-deck emergency exit. The rear upper-deck emergency exit had not yet been developed.

The Merseyside agreements were put into place in the early 'thirties and although superseded by the 1972 Agreements with the Merseyside PTE the area was to remain important to the Company until the industrial relations problems of the late 'eighties and re-organisation by the Company's new owners saw a withdrawal of Crosville from the area. In trouble on the 'A' route from Warrington to the Pier Head is this Leyland Titan TD2 of 1932. Number 737 (FM 7464) shows many of the typical features of a Crosville bus of the time – the Widd boards and obscured destination box, and the rear registration number illuminated solely by stray light from the lower saloon. Clearly, there had been quite a heavy side-impact causing four pillars of the normally sturdy Leyland wood-framed body to break in this collision with a timber lorry near Widnes. It would appear that the TD2 might have skidded on ice but the lack of tread on its rear tyres could have been more significant.

Lines Committee. The pattern of the settlements which the railways sought in many towns and cities was broadly similar. The local council services should be protected within an inner or 'A' Area beyond which there should be a 'B' area where both company and council should share services. Beyond that, in the 'C' area, the services should be company-operated.

Variations to this pattern had to be made to meet local conditions and Birkenhead was one of these. The Tramways Manager, Cyril Clarke, backed up by his Council, wanted mutual expansion with the municipal buses running further into the Wirral countryside in return for Crosville buses being allowed to reach their goal at Woodside ferry. There was to be no 'B' area as the peculiar geography of the peninsula, sandwiched between two rivers, made this impossible. The negotiations were conducted by Claude C Taylor, H H Merchant (the divisional manager) and Ashton Davies for the LMS. After many alternatives had been explored, it was agreed that Birkenhead Corporation buses would run out as far as Eastham, Heswall and Frankby in return for Crosville buses running to Woodside. This meant Crosville surrendering their New Ferry-Bromborough-Eastham local service and one of the ex-Pye routes between Birkenhead and Heswall via Irby, the least attractive of the three. The changes were brought in in two stages on 1st August and 1st October 1930.

The loss of these services was a blow and James Crosland Taylor argued that the Road Traffic Act would have given them the Woodside facility without surrendering any territory. However, the agreement also included an undertaking by the Corporation to assist in the development of long distance services and as, under the 1930 Act, these had to be up and running before the cut-off date of 9th February 1931, this was a most valuable concession as explained in Chapter 7. It also gave Crosville an advantage over the local excursion operators who complained bitterly to Birkenhead Corporation.

The Agreement led to an enormous increase in traffic as thousands of passengers crossed from Liverpool on the ferry to board Crosville buses for North Wales, Chester, Parkgate etc. It was renegotiated in 1938 but the changes were not major amounting mostly to adjustments found desirable in the light of experience. Crosville carried all the traffic from Park Station to Greasby and Frankby while the Corporation carried it from Woodside and there was some extension of the through bus and ferry tickets to Liverpool which were issued on both Corporation and Crosville buses and were interavailable between common points.

In Liverpool, the negotiations were much more protracted as the Corporation at first adopted the arrogant and contemptuous attitude which it considered appropriate to its perceived dignity. Ribble, too, was involved though it had agreed a boundary line with Crosville along the A57 which was to be available to both of them. Discussions with the railways started in October 1929 but it was not until 4th March 1931, after the Town Clerk had made it clear to the Council that the Road Traffic Act would give the bus companies most of what they wanted, that the parties were able to get down to serious business. The full details of the five-year Agreement, signed on 2nd July 1931, need not be set out here but suffice it to say that Crosville was able to extend all its services to the Pier Head from 24th February 1932 and the 6d minimum fare was reduced to 4d with graded fares close to the boundary. A toll of 30% was payable to the Corporation for traffic carried within the city boundary.

Furthermore, the Corporation was in difficulty with its own bus services and asked Crosville to run, on its behalf, a service between Pier Head, Mossley Hill and Garston and withdrew some of its services between Pier Head and Hunts Cross to make way for a new company service. The Prescot via Huyton services were also extended from Bowring Park to the Pier Head on 26th July 1933. A system of route letters, using A to H (and later F1 and K), displayed on Widd plates, was adopted to distinguish the various services.

A scene in Crewe at the Market Square during the 'thirties. KA 3 (FM 9967) is nearest the camera and the double-decker pulling out is M45 (AFM 499).

This was a notable victory for Crosville and the Lancashire services became very profitable. Despite the high minimum fares, traffic carried within the city was substantial, to the extent that regular duplication was needed between the Pier Head and Garston, and not only at peak hours. In this case the through fare was more than double the tram fare. In 1934, the company applied to extend its Loggerheads/Pantymwyn-Birkenhead service through the Mersey Tunnel to Liverpool, the police agreeing to a stand in Hotham Street, off London Road. The summer service via the Widnes-Runcorn Transporter Bridge was abandoned on 14th September 1935 as it was easier and cheaper to cross the river and go from Woodside. The Liverpool and Birkenhead Corporation transport undertakings opposed tunnel bus services because of the toll structure and the effect on the ferries and the application was refused, that decision being confirmed on appeal. A similar fate befell a joint Crosville-Ribble application for a Chester-Southport through service proposed in 1936. An almost identical service, but extended beyond Southport to Banks, was eventually started by Crosville and Ribble's successor, the new North Western company, in May 1987 and has been very successful.

When the Agreement expired in 1936, Liverpool Corporation asked for several extensions of time while it decided on its strategy and the bus companies consented to delay any plans for service changes until the new Agreement was signed. This was unfortunate as it was almost two years before an accord was reached, a new ten-year Agreement being signed on 10th June 1938. For Crosville there was very little change though administrative procedures were simplified and Liverpool's buses were able to compete between the city centre and Huyton village; the Corporation also took back their Garston via Mossley Hill service. The toll payable to the Corporation was reduced to 15%. Six years of collaboration had forged a bond of trust and relations between the parties were now much more relaxed.

The company now applied to the Traffic Commissioners for major improvements to its services through Huyton which had been expanded rapidly and found itself strongly opposed by its shareholder, the LMS Railway, who thought that the buses should feed the parallel railway line. Improved

services to Hunts Cross and on the Warrington via Prescot route were commenced in September 1938 but the Huyton proposals were refused. A second application was successful, authorising increased frequencies between Liverpool and Prescot via Huyton but the reinstatement of the Wavertree-Warrington via Cronton service – suspended since 1928 – had to wait until March 1939.

Chester Corporation Transport

Chester Corporation had replaced its trams by buses on 1st February 1930 and extended some routes beyond the tram termini, within the 3½ mile radius permitted by its Act. A conference, sponsored by the railway companies, was held in London on 5th June 1930, attended by representatives of the LMS, GWR, BAT, Crosville and Chester Corporation, the object being to ascertain whether the Corporation would be receptive to proposals for the purchase of its undertaking or, failing that, a co-ordination scheme.

Outright purchase was rejected but the Corporation was willing to consider co-ordination proposals. Proposed Heads of Agreement were set out in a letter from Claude Crosland Taylor to Chester Corporation dated 13th October 1930 but the matter was deferred as the city hoped to extend its boundaries. After much discussion, an Agreement came into force from 1st July 1932. Local services, except those in a segment of the city between Hoole Road and Liverpool Road, were to be run by the Corporation and, in addition, the Corporation handed over its services to Parkgate Road and Sealand Road in exchange for services to Eccleston and Saughall. In the long term there were benefits to both sides as Crosville gained from housing developments in Hoole, Newton and Upton and the Corporation gained from post-war developments in Blacon.

Cheshire

As already mentioned elsewhere, Crosville had consolidated much of its West Cheshire territory by 1931. H C Pascoe's Friday services between Tarporley and Northwich were acquired with a 14-seat Fiat for £50 in

Rebodying was not neglected in the 'thirties and this Leyland Lion PLSC1 received a new Eastern Counties 31-seat body in January 1933. The body was one of a batch of ten which began what was to be a major rebodying programme for PLSC models – Crosville was unusual in so treating this type on a large scale, most in other fleets retaining the square-cut Leyland bodies to the end. The main benefit was in the interior, much more up-to-date than the original.

February 1931 but it was five years before the company got round to recasting and integrating them with existing services from Utkinton, introducing weekend services and making them joint with North Western.

Common BET/BAT interests brought friendship with the Potteries company and a small Crosville unit was added to the PMT depot in Newcastle-under-Lyme in 1932, a great improvement on the out-station at Madeley. Stoke itself remained out of reach, however. It was 1934 before Crosville was able to achieve a near monopoly in West Cheshire with the acquisition of Jackson's Malbank Motor Services on 27th June, T Maddocks of Tattenhall on 1st July and H Lowe & Son of Audlem on 1st August. The latter served Market Drayton and Nantwich and his routes were to some extent abandoned, being duplicated by existing Crosville facilities. These purchases also brought valuable excursion and tour licences from Audlem, Middlewich, Sandbach and Tattenhall. Crosville at last had a monopoly of the Crewe town services which, with the establishment of new industries in the town, became busier than ever.

Runcorn, too, was expanding. Two small operators were running in the town, Frederick Watson with a Weston Point-Delph Bridge service and J W Garner, trading as Weaverside Road Services, with services to Weston Point, Helsby and Astmoor Works. Any relationship with Trevor Garner, whose Runcorn local service was taken over in 1927, is not known. The Runcorn locals were designed to connect with the town centre, the railway station and the Transporter Bridge and very frequent services were provided. Interurban services to Chester and Warrington were also increased in frequency.

Further down river, Ellesmere Port was of similar size and its oil and paper industries provided a great deal of traffic. A local service on Fridays and Saturdays was started in 1932 and, in 1934, the local council asked Crosville to provide facilities to their new swimming pool at Rivacre Valley. However, most needs were met by the through services to and from Birkenhead and Chester which were all double-decked. A two-hourly Ellesmere Port-Mold service, inaugurated on 4th June 1937, was short-lived. A service between the same points by a different route was eventually started in 1980.

North Wales

The integration of the acquired services was a mammoth task. Crosville systems had to be applied, running times corrected and duplication of facilities eliminated. Protective conditions were removed enabling buses to be used more effectively. As far as the businesses acquired in 1930 were concerned, it was important to make the necessary changes quickly as, after 9th February 1931, nothing could be done without the Traffic Commissioners' consent and the enormous volume of applications to be considered inevitably led to lengthy delays. An obvious need was to establish a Chester-Rhyl service by joining up the Crosville and White Rose routes at Holywell and Greenfield.

An Agreement was made with the Llandudno and Colwyn Bay Electric Railway on 18th December 1930 governing the frequencies of the respective tram and bus services between Llandudno and Colwyn Bay; following the various acquisitions in the area this agreement was modified from 12th August 1932. Crosville agreed to withdraw monthly contract tickets between common points.

Crosville introduced double-deck buses in late 1932 or early 1933 on the Llandudno-Colwyn Bay-Penmaen Head route. Colwyn Bay UDC demanded that the double-deckers turn at the junction of Cefn Road with Princess Road, Old Colwyn but the company contended that that was an unsuitable place and, even if the buses unloaded there, they would still have to travel on to Penmaen Head to turn. The Council also wanted 'hail-and-ride' facilities in the rural parts of the town. Crosville disagreed on safety grounds, inability to keep to a time table and increased mechanical wear and tear. The Council gave notice that when licences came up for renewal on 6th July 1933, it would object to Crosville operating any buses within the town. It wanted the banning of double-deck buses in perpetuity, the reinstatement of contract tickets and the 'hail-and-ride' facility. The objections were thrown out by the Commissioners and this was just one of many examples of local authorities having difficulty in realising that they no longer had the power to regulate bus services within their boundaries.

Western Transport

Following the events of 1928-29, the services of the Wrexham & District Transport Co. and the bus services of the Great Western Railway in north and central Wales were merged from 7th July 1930. The GWR purchased the Corris Railway Co on 4th August 1930, passing the bus services to the Wrexham company, though the buses went back to the Bristol parent. The Wrexham company was renamed Western Transport Co Ltd on 3rd November 1930, the GWR paying £87,710 for 76,916 shares. A proposal for the London and North Eastern Railway, who had a station in Wrexham, to join in the purchase was not pursued. The new company continued to use the 'Transport' fleet-name and was known everywhere as the Transport Red.

While Western Transport had a clearly defined area around Wrexham, Oswestry and Ellesmere, there were areas further west where Crosville and Western interests overlapped and Tilling and BAT, shareholders in both, revived the idea of a further merger. This was done on 1st May 1933 when Western was completely absorbed by Crosville whose shareholding now became Tilling and BAT 50%, LMS 37½% and GWR 12½%. Western's share capital of £155,000 was exchanged for Crosville shares on a one-for-one basis at par, a source of some dissatisfaction to the Crosland Taylors who thought the Crosville shares were worth more. Crosville also paid the winding-up expenses.

More Consolidation

Crosville now had control of most of the bus services in north and central Wales and the directors decided that every effort should be made to accelerate the process of acquiring the remaining independents, some of which found the discipline of the Road Traffic Act 1930 hard to come to terms with. Since the major acquisitions of 1930-31, Crosville had bought the businesses of Vincent Smith of Prestatyn with one local route; W J Williams (Bethesda Greys) with two Chevrolet 14-seaters and a mixed bag of Vulcans working routes between Bangor, Rachub, Gerlan

UN 187 was a Daimler CF6 with Brush bodywork in the Western Transport fleet. The vehicle is seen here in Wrexham, bound for Llangollen, a service which ultimately became Crosville trunk route D1, but which ceased for a period under the intense competition with another local operator, the Wright Company, at the end of the 'eighties. Today it is run by the successors to Crosville Motor Services, Crosville Cymru. Number UN 187 became No. 827 in the Crosville fleet and survived only until 1934. Although alleged to date from 1927, Daimler records show it to have been delivered in May 1929, perhaps taking the body and registration of an earlier bus.

Above: Perhaps the two most significant purchases were to be those of Brookes Brothers and Western Transport of Wrexham. As was quite normal both fleets were made up of a variety of makes but their sheer size ensured that many were to be operated for a number of years. UN 5896 was a 1932 Tilling Stevens B10A2 with Brush bodywork which Crosville had allocated fleet number 874. One of Crosville's less endearing customs was to put a paper sticker in the destination box showing its name and rely on a variety of window stickers or Widd boards to show the purpose of the journey. In this instance, the vehicle is engaged on a private hire for the 4th Battalion of the Royal Welch Fusiliers. The B10A2 was a durable machine, this one, like the rest of its batch, surviving until 1949.

Below: Two more Western Transport vehicles are seen in this view at Llanbadarn. As a railway inspired picture, the caption on the print 'Motor Traffic at Llanbadarn' is a poignant reminder that the private car was a seen as a nuisance even then. FM 3534 was a Daimler CM new in 1925 to Wrexham & District Transport, entering the Crosville fleet as No. 803 in June 1933 and leaving in the same year. YV1118 was a Maudslay ML3 with Vickers body new to the Great Western Railway in 1928, passing to Crosville briefly as No. 908 with the Western Transport business.

Above: Another ex-Western Transport bus was this Tilling Stevens B10A2, again with Brush bodywork. A 32-seater, new in 1931, it was to serve Crosville as No. 867 until 1938.

The stream of take-overs continued throughout the 'thirties although the subjects were perhaps less dramatic. Ten vehicles came from Seiont Motors of Caernarfon in 1934, several of which were rebodied later on. CC8531 became Crosville No. 970 upon acquisition. An all-Leyland Lion LT1 of 1929, this was not one of the rebodies.

and Bethesda and a Bethesda-Birkenhead express service; J W Hughes of Rhiwen with routes from Caernarfon to Rhiwlas and to Dinorwic and from Bangor to Llanberis; Caernarfon Bay Motors (Caernarfon-Dinas Dinlle) and Roses Tours of Rhyl.

On the same day as Western Transport was taken over (1st May 1933), Crosville acquired the business of Jones Brothers of Aberystwyth, which was in receivership. Services radiated to Aberaeron, Lampeter, Borth, Tregaron and Ponterwyd and the subsequent integration of the South Cambrian services was made that much easier. Acquisition of J D Davies' Aberystwyth-Tregaron-Lampeter service in July 1934 further aided consolidation.

The company now adopted a strategy of trying to make several purchases in the same area simultaneously, simplifying the licensing procedures and consolidation process. Applications for licences for takeovers were often opposed by the remaining operators and if they, too, could be taken over these problems were averted. Lleyn Peninsula was tackled in 1934, the most important purchase being John Evans' Seiont Motors, (named after the local river), which had its origins in 1912. Indeed, it is remarkable how many of the North Wales businesses had very early origins. The Seiont routes which were taken over on 1st January linked Caernarfon with Penygroes, Nantlle, Nebo and surrounding villages to the south-west and were worked mainly by good quality Leyland vehicles of which there were seven, backed up by an Albion and a Morris.

Next, a number of operators serving Pwllheli were acquired. The Tocia Motor Omnibus Co. Ltd. had been registered on 7th November 1911 and served the far west Lleyn area, linking Pwllheli with Aberdaron, Abersoch and adjacent villages. There were 14 assorted vehicles of which only one, a Morris, survived into 1935. Others were R J Harris' Nevin Blue Motors, running between Nefyn, Edern and Pwllheli; David J Williams' Mynytho Red Motors serving Pwllheli, Llanbedrog and Mynytho with a Lancia and a Maudslay; William J Jones with a Pwllheli-Rhiw service and John D Davies of Chwilog whose service appears to have been suppressed as redundant. Peripherally, Crosville absorbed William Morris of Bethesda with yet another Bangor-Rhiwlas service and R T Jones of Trefriw

running Llanrwst-Melin-y-coed.

The Lleyn clean-up continued into 1935 with the absorption of R Roberts (Pwllheli-Uwchmynydd and Sarn with a 14-seat Willys Overland), H O Evans (Pwllheli-Dinas Bodean), Tudor Evans' Cream Motor Services (Llithfaen-Pwllheli, Edern-Nefyn-Llithfaen-Caernarfon with a 26-seat Gilford) and, further south, A Richards with a Tywyn -Bryn Crug-Caerbellan route worked by two 20-seat saloons, a GMC and a Vulcan.

Further east, there were two important acquisitions. J Owen of Llandudno Junction traded as New Blue Motor Bus Service with routes from Conwy to both Llandudno and Colwyn Bay and Fforddlas Bridge to Colwyn Bay, all competitive to some degree with Crosville. There were eight Dennis saloons and the business was taken over on 11th April. Price's Motors of New Broughton was a force in Wrexham having started in August 1921 and built up a fleet of 10 assorted vehicles. In addition to services from Wrexham to Llay Main, Caergwrle, Tanyfron and Cymmau, he also had summer express services from Rhos to Blackpool and Rhyl and excursions and tours from Llay Main and Wrexham. His business was taken over on 15th April 1935.

On 1st May there was a clean up in Holyhead when no fewer than six tiny operators were bought out for nominal

Owens (New Blue) of Llandudno Junction provided CC 8249 upon take-over in 1935. Numbered into the miscellaneous category as U42, the vehicle bore a Jackson 32-seat body on a Dennis E chassis, being sold off, like most of this fleet in 1936.

How valuable this registration number would be today ! FM 9000 was a 1935 Leyland LT7 with Leyland bodywork, delivered shortly after the renumbering of the fleet and received fleet number H2.

figures, followed on 5th June by a seventh, Mechell Maroon who also had a Bangor-Cemaes service. There were three Williamses, two Roberts, a Parry and an Owen. All surrendered their licences, the services being integrated with existing Crosville facilities; the only vehicles taken over were a GMC, a Reo and a Commer – all 20-seaters-from W H Williams (Mechell Maroon).

In 1935, there was also a determined effort to mop up in Oswestry, four businesses being acquired on 18th March and two others late in the year. The March contingent were A W Reeves serving Bagley, Treflach and Leighton; D H Tylor of Trefonen, serving Nantmawr and Sychtyn; J B S Platt running to Trefonen and Bryn and William B Jones of Ifton Heath with services between Oswestry and New Marton, Sodylt Bank and Dudleston Heath and between Ellesmere and Dudleston Heath and Ifton. Four vehicles, two Bedfords, a Chevrolet and a GMC came from Jones but none from any of the others. Albert Mates of Rhosywaen, running between Chirk Green and Cefn Mawr and from Rhosywaen to Ifton Heath Colliery, was purchased from 30th November followed, on 21st December, by Iorwerth Evans with services between his home village of Llanrhaeadr-ym-Mochnant and both Oswestry and Llanfyllin. Two Chevrolet 14-seaters were taken over with this business.

Despite the many acquisitions, there were still two large operators and a host of small ones serving Caernarfon and Lleyn peninsula. One of the smaller fry, John Hughes of Groeslon had a Caernarfon-Cilgwyn route and local services to Carmel, run with two Maudslays and a Guy. He was taken over on 25th January 1936, followed by one of the more substantial firms on 1st March. This was DM Motors of Llanrug, started by D M Prichard, postmaster of Llanrug, in the mid-1920s. The business was run from the back room of the post office where the ticket stocks were kept. The main route was Caernarfon-Nant Peris via Llanberis, with short workings to Brynrefail, at the foot of Llyn Padarn. There was good all-year traffic, with the additional bonus of summer visitors. The route had been shared with Crosville and Royal Blue and after the acquisition of the latter in 1931, Crosville had introduced two double-deck Leyland TD1s, the only ones working

west of the Conwy river at that time.

Other routes were Caernarfon-Bethesda via Bethel and to Rhiwlas, and excursion and tours from Llanrug and Llanberis. Prichard's health was failing and his son was not too anxious to continue the business so he sold to Crosville. The fleet comprised ten vehicles of which nine were Leylands, the other being a GMC 20-seat ex-demonstrator. Three were second-hand Leyland PLSC3 Lions, one from Todmorden Corporation and two from Birkenhead Corporation, the latter still displaying their fleet numbers 75 and 76 inside. Most were quickly repainted but two Leyland TS4s retained DM's red and white livery with the name painted out and Crosville fleet numbers K112-3 added. They continued to run in the area but mostly worked on the Caernarfon-Penisarwaen-Dinorwic route, which passed Llanrug post office but had never been a DM route. The depot alongside the post office was retained and continued to house ex-DM buses. The two TS4s were renumbered K42 and K43 in 1937 and rebodied with dual-purpose ECW bodies in 1939, surviving until 1951-52.

On the same day, the Caernarfon-Bethel service of W D Humphreys was taken over, his blue Bedford WLB 20-seater continuing to operate unrepainted but with fleet number U17 added. This was a common practice at the time based not only on economy but on retention of goodwill. It would have been wasteful to repaint many of the vehicles acquired which had to be run for a time until new replacements – usually Leyland Cubs for the thinner country routes, were delivered.

There were a few further takeovers in Caernarfonshire and Anglesey. E J Hughes of Penygroes, with an unimportant route thence to Dinas Dinlle, and David Jones with a Llangefni-Newborough service, both sold out on 15th June 1936. L J Jones of Llanrug with a Caernarfon-Ceunant route on Wednesdays, Fridays and Saturdays continued running until 30th June 1939. Other operators just did not want to sell. The largest was the Clynnog and Trefor Motor Co, running on the Caernarfon-Pwllheli service with a co-ordinated timetable with Crosville who came to an arrangement whereby through bookings to and from the Liverpool-Caernarfon service were accepted on

Vehicles taken over from independents were sometimes retained in the Crosville fleet for extended periods. J R Lloyd of Bwlchgwyn had this Leyland SKP3 with Spicer 26-seat bodywork which was to survive until 1950. Similar chassis with bus bodywork were used for the services over the Menai Suspension bridge as mentioned on page 64.

Clynnog and Trefor buses. Others were Express Motors and Silver Star of Rhostryfan and O R Williams & Son's Whiteway Services of Waunfawr.

Most of the Wrexham area independents elected to stay in business. James Rothwell of Holt had sold his Wrexham-Holt-Broxton services from 1st January 1934 with three Maudslays, a Crossley Eagle and a Reo. It was 1936 before further progress was made, the Wrexham-Bradley service of George Roberts of Southsea, who also had a Wrexham-Rhyl summer route, being taken over with five Dennises and a Bedford in January followed in February by George A Williams of Cefn Mawr, running thence to Chirk, Ellesmere and Llay Main with excursions from Froncysyllte. Sarah Williams and Sons, Pentre Broughton with services from Wrexham to Pentre Broughton and Moss worked by four Dennis saloons was acquired in June. This business yielded Crosville's only Dennis Ace.

May 1938 saw the acquisition of the Wrexham-Bryneglwys and Gwynfryn services of J R Lloyd taken over together with some Llay Main colliers' services and three Dennises, two Bedfords and a Leyland Cub but Peters of Llanarmon continued to run in that area. Alfred Wright of Rhosymedre, working Chirk-Cefn Mawr and Glynceiriog routes, followed in March 1939. A consortium of three operators working between Wrexham and Coedpoeth, H Hooson, D S Rogers and I T Roberts, sold their services in May 1940, perhaps because fuel restrictions made their businesses non-viable or because the proprietors were called up for war service.

In Flintshire, the independents were thinner on the ground. R Jenkinson of Buckley who ran thence to Chester Infirmary, Mold and Connah's Quay and between Mold and Alltami sold out in September 1934. Phillips of Holywell was not on the market and Crosville made a joint working agreement covering the Mold-Holywell service.

Body styling had marched on by the 'thirties and, in 1934, Leyland had produced this attractive 52-seater on a Titan TD3 chassis. Number 916 (FM8149) inevitably took part in the rebodying programme of the post-1945 period gaining a new ECW body in 1949. This early venture into metal-framed body construction by Leyland was by no means trouble-free and it had done well to survive so long.

The typical Crosville single-decker of the late 'thirties was to this style, of which 138 had been delivered between 1937 and the outbreak of war in September 1939. The chassis was the oil-engined version of the Leyland Tiger of type TS7 or TS8 and the 32-seat body produced by ECW to a design peculiar to Crosville though based on a combination of features also found in other ECW bodies of the time. This one was the first of the final pre-war batch, dating from June 1939 – a final twelve arrived in 1940. There were some variations in design – early examples had wide window bays and the side indicator first appeared in 1939.

Jones' Motor Services of Flint and Harold Roberts of Connah's Quay ran services to Sandycroft, Mancot, Courtaulds' Flint Works and both sold out their services in the summer of 1936. They were followed in January 1937 by E Richards who traded as Crowther & Co. in the same district. This left only Harold Stanley of Buckley with Buckley-Shotton and Mold-Llay Main services and he sold out with one Leyland LT7, in March 1939.

New Networks

When substantial numbers of the small operators had been taken over, the way was left clear for rationalisation schemes which generally gave the travelling public superior facilities without the waste which had survived from the days of unregulated competition and without protection for certain operators. Where the independents still had a substantial presence, Crosville was reluctant to give ground and the Traffic Commissioners were often obliged to exert some pressure in order to secure the same objectives. A case in point was Wrexham. Despite its size, Western Transport had not been the most efficient of operators. The Traffic Commissioners in several cases granted licences on condition that fares and times were co-ordinated on routes served wholly or partially by more than one operator. Crosville undertook a major rescheduling exercise aimed at eliminating waste by rationalising services wherever possible and agreements were made with some local operators, many of whom were still suspicious of the big company's motives. Summer and winter time tables were worked out for routes with a seasonal fluctuation in demand.

A revision of services in the Wrexham area took effect on Monday, 19th March 1934, involving Crosville, John Phillips and Sons of Rhostyllen, Owen Brothers of Coedpoeth, Thomas Williams of Ponciau, E. Wright and

Son of Penycae, Meredith and Jesson of Cefn Mawr, F. W. Strange of Penybryn, George Sugg and W. T. Keeler, both of Garden Village. On the major Wrexham-Rhostyllen-Johnstown-Rhos corridor, Crosville provided a through service on a basic 10-15 minutes headway, augmented by Phillips, Williams and Wright (on his Penycae route) between Wrexham and Rhos and by Owen between Wrexham and Rhostyllen. Crosville was the sole operator on Sunday when many Welsh operators took the day off on religious grounds.

Crosville shared the Wrexham-Penycae route more or less equally with Wright, except that Wright was not allowed to carry local passengers between Johnstown and Wrexham. There was no Sunday service on this route. On the Wrexham-Chirk-Oswestry route, Crosville operated the through journeys, with Meredith and Jesson working between Wrexham and Rhosymedre, each operating approximately hourly during the week. On Sunday Crosville operated the complete service apart from one hospital journey.

The Wrexham-Acton-Garden Village local service was served by four operators: Crosville (20%), Keeler (20%), Strange (40%) and Sugg (20%). A headway of 3-6 minutes was maintained on weekdays, Keeler and Sugg using 6- and 7-seat 'cab buses' respectively. Only Crosville and Strange operated on Sundays, commencing at 2.0pm. The times of all the co-ordinated operators appeared in the local Crosville time table.

In the winter of 1936-37, the company's scheduling resources were devoted to rationalising the Flintshire services following the acquisition of three operators and in readiness for the opening of a new depot at Flint. More through Chester-Rhyl facilities were provided by joining up trips at Flint and thousands of dead miles were saved by transferring trips formerly worked from Chester, Mold and Rhyl depots to Flint.

Further deliveries of Shelvoke and Drury Low Freighter-based toastracks maintained the Brookes Bros tradition. Number U10 (FM 9065) was a 1935 delivery with a rather more enclosed body by Simpson and Slater while No. U12 (CFM 340) reverted to the open format with an ECW body. It is seen here in later livery. These pictures convey a little of the way rides in such vehicles were part of the seaside holiday atmosphere of Rhyl. Note how the conductor of U10 is using his ticket rack to signal the departure from the right-hand kerb.

The 1930s saw a revolution in the bus services in North Wales and some of the individualistic features of the acquired operators were retained including the SD Freighter toast-racks and open-top double-deckers at Rhyl, though the latter, being in some cases an illegal 8ft wide, soon had to go. Some of the SOS buses in Llandudno retained the blue livery for a considerable time. But the heterogeneous assortment of small buses was soon replaced by new Leyland Cubs or, in some cases, bigger buses where the traffic expanded under the impetus of better facilities.

Two physical obstacles prevented greater progress being made. The Menai Suspension bridge was restricted to vehicles weighing 4 tons 5 cwt. Crosville's answer was the 'O' class of forward-control Leyland Cub, seating 30 passengers of which there were 22, including two coaches. These were used for the more important services to and from Bangor, augmented by the more familiar forward-control Cubs, seating 20-26. But the weight restriction prevented the Anglesey services being integrated with the mainland routes and all, except the Caernarfon-

Newborough service, ran only to and from Bangor where passengers for destinations further afield had to change.

Telford's Conwy Suspension bridge was single track and had a low arch at the Conwy end. There was no restriction on normal weight single-deck vehicles but the arch prevented the use of double-deck buses, the two Caernarfon-based buses having to make the journey back to Chester for overhaul via the Llanberis Pass and the A5, where overhanging trees were a hazard. The bridge caused severe delays in summer and again, the full development of an integrated network was inhibited as it was prudent to isolate the services concerned as much as possible to avoid passing delays on to other sections of route. The Caernarfon-Llandudno service was frequently duplicated for its full length in summer and it would have been an ideal case for double-deck buses from the points of view both of capacity and scenic appeal.

7 EXPRESS SERVICES

The transition of long distance services from the status of excursions to regular services was somewhat blurred at a time when the law made no distinction between them. In many cases, the turning point was when single fares started to be issued and the service was advertised to run whether there were any pre-booked passengers or not. Most long distance services were started by independent proprietors as many large area bus companies saw no affinity between running bus services and operating charabancs or coaches. It was only when the popularity of long distance travel by road was seen to be no nine day wonder that most large companies started to take an interest.

Liverpool-London

The first Liverpool-London service was started by E J Jones who traded as Imperial Motor Services from Upper Parliament Street, Liverpool. His first southbound journey left Liverpool on 2nd May 1928, using a canvas-topped

Studebaker and he charged 17/6d (87½p) single, £1-10-0d (£1.50) return. His route took in Stratford-on-Avon and Oxford as he had already realised that, as road travel over such distances could not compete with rail on speed, it must do so on fares and scenic appeal. His service upstaged the ebullient C F Rymer, a Wallasey councillor who had planned to be the pioneer operator on the route, announcing his intentions so well and so far in advance that Jones had no difficulty in getting in first. Rymer started running to London on 14th May 1928, also via Stratford and Oxford, though other parts of the route were different from Jones'.

A different and unique service started on 14th August 1928 – the Albatross sleeping cars – 12-berth vans on Daimler CF6 chassis which ran on alternate nights, leaving Liverpool at 11.0pm, but soon advanced to 10.15pm and rerouted via Manchester in an attempt to attract extra traffic. This service lasted for just over a year, its failure being attributed to high laundry bills.

Gladwyn Parlour Cars of Nottingham started their service on 25th August 1928 but failed before the end of

Prior to the commencement of long distance services, Crosville was engaged in much private hire work and many charabanc type vehicles were retained for the purpose. Typifying the type of vehicle is this 27-seat United-bodied Leyland Lioness 6 LTB1 of 1929. The roof folded back completely allowing the driver to share the sunshine and fresh air on suitable occasions.

Imperial Motor Services (E J Jones) was the first operator of a Liverpool-London service and this well known view shows a Leyland Tiger of that company which passed to Pearsons, three months before they were acquired by Crosville.

Crosville would have drawn its coaches for London services from its newest vehicles, a practice which was to continue until the end of its scheduled coaching commitment to the capital in 1980. The year 1931 saw a batch of coaches based on Leyland Tiger TS3 chassis bearing United bodies. Number 618 (FM 6456) had only 27 seats in its 'sun saloon' style body. The interior was well appointed with comfortable seats and restrained decorative features. Although Crosville had bought some earlier United bodies, this was the beginning of the association with the Lowestoft 'coach factory' as a fellow-member of the TBAT group, a link that was to last until 1985.

the year, their goodwill being seized upon by MacShanes Motors Ltd. of 5 Commutation Row, Liverpool who had acted as their terminal agents at both ends. MacShanes had been planning their own service before Gladwyn ceased running and two routes were in operation by the summer of 1929, one via Stratford and Oxford and the other via Lichfield and the A5.

In late summer 1928, Crosville decided to make some experimental sorties of their own in the form of weekend excursions the first of which ran from Birkenhead (Woodside) on Fridays 24th and 31st August, returning on the following Mondays. A second series ran on Fridays 14th and 21st September with three return trips on Mondays 17th, 24th September and 1st October. It was therefore possible to stay in London for a weekend, 10 days or 17 days. The success of these experiments led to the introduction of the company's first regular daily London service on 28th March 1929, the same day on which James Pearson and Sons' Happy Days Motorways started yet another competitive service. Pearson's business dated back to coachbuilding in the 1870s and was destined to be

very successful. Initially Crosville did not serve Liverpool, their service starting at Birkenhead Park Station (which was only 10 minutes away from the city centre by underground electric railway) and proceeding via West Kirby, Chester, Crewe, Newcastle, Lichfield, Warwick, Stratford and Oxford. A second service running from Liverpool Pier Head via Widnes, Warrington, Northwich, Sandbach, Crewe, Newcastle, Lichfield, Coventry and the A5, started on 16th May 1929. The journey times were about 11 hours. Fares on both routes were 15/- (75p) single, £1-7-6d (£1.37½) return. Four Leyland Tiger 'buses-de-luxe' (175-8) were assigned to these routes, two based at Liverpool and two at West Kirby. They had standard Leyland bus bodies but were fitted with 25 luxury seats.

Meanwhile Samuelson Saloon Coaches Ltd., a London-based operator, had started on the route about November 1928. This firm had premises in Birmingham city centre and was the only operator on the route licensed to go right in, others picking up on the north-eastern outskirts, at Chester Road, Erdington, just outside the city boundary. John Pike's Claremont Luxury Coaches, a former London independent bus operator, also started a service in March 1929, bringing the number of Liverpool-London operators up to seven.

In an effort to increase receipts, Imperial who were running six Leyland Tigers with Hoyal canvas-topped bodies, started a night service on 12th July 1929; this soon forsook the Oxford route for the A5 as there was nothing to see at night. There was a further development in August when Claremont sold their service to the Merseyside Touring Co Ltd who changed the route to serve Warrington, Newcastle, Lichfield, Coventry, Northampton and Newport Pagnell; no other operator served the last two places. In April 1929, Claremont, Rymer, Pearson's and Samuelsons had agreed to charge fares of 17/6d (87½p) single and 30/- (£1.50) return but Crosville did not join in and the return fare came down to £1-7-6d (£1.37½) again. Some operators had suspended their services for the winter of 1928-29 but from mid-October 1929, Pearson's reduced their fares to 12/6d (62½p) single and £1 return, MacShanes soon following suit. This followed a trend on other services between the north west and London. Rymer and Imperial withdrew their services rather than run at these ruinous rates but, from 6th November, Crosville withdrew the Liverpool service but retained the Birkenhead one at fares of 12/- (60p) single and £1 return. Some of the other operators served Wallasey and/or Birkenhead, crossing on the goods ferries.

The Merseyside Touring Co. was purchased by Ribble Motor Services on 1st February 1930 though the deal was kept quiet for a time and nothing changed outwardly. Imperial was formed into a limited company, E J Jones (Liverpool-London) Ltd in March.

Meanwhile a new company, All-British Travels Ltd was formed on 24th February 1930 by Alfred Harding of Birkenhead (precursor of the present-day Hardings (Wirral) Ltd) George Taylor of Chester (both well-established coach operators) and J W Scott of Edinburgh who traded under the name of Azure Blue. A further member was Evan R Davies, Town Clerk of Pwllheli. Scott ran a couple of two-day services between Edinburgh and London, one with a stop-over at Chester and the other at York. Neither Taylor nor Harding had run express services though, early in 1929, Taylor had been granted licences in Chester for routes to London, Bournemouth, Cardiff, Edinburgh, Southport and Manchester. The latter was objected to by Crosville and North Western who were planning to extend the Chester-Northwich service to Manchester. None of these services had been started, probably due to a lack of capital resources. Chester, with its relatively small population, was not an ideal centre for a network of the kind. All-British Travels was not an operator but opened a travel agency near Russell Square, London. The intention seems to have been to develop a network using the member operators' coaches. Taylor was to run between Llandudno and London and Harding between Liverpool and London and both owners had some coaches lettered 'All British Line'. These services started on 14th April 1930, the times between Chester and London being identical so that only one coach need run through. The Merseyside Company's service was resumed on the same day.

The All-British Line coach started at Mount Pleasant, crossed the river by the Seacombe boat, called at Harding's Liscard and Birkenhead offices and, proceeded via Chester, Whitchurch, Brownhills, Erdington, Stratford and Oxford. The North Wales leg underwent various changes which are dealt with later. Harding soon dropped out, leaving operations to George Taylor.

For the 1930 season, Crosville's direct service from Liverpool was extended to start from Edge Lane garage and designated route 2. A new route 3 also started there, crossed by the Woodside ferry and called at New Ferry and Ellesmere Port en route to Chester where it met route 1 from Park Station. The Merseyside service restarted on 14th April and the influence of Ribble, the new owner, was seen from 18th July from which date there were two departures daily, at 7.45am and 10.0am and the London terminus was moved from Aldwych to London Coastal Coaches Lupus Street station. Return services left London at 8.30am and 2.0pm, the latter giving connections from many South Coast resorts with a midnight arrival in Liverpool. A Ribble bus connection from Southport was also advertised for the 10.0am departure. A southbound Friday night service commenced on 1st August. Pearson's also offered a night service on the A5 route but also serving Wolverhampton and Birmingham in 1930 though this was withdrawn for the winter.

Crosville suspended routes 2 and 3 from the end of September 1930 but extended route 1 to start from Liverpool. Under the territorial agreements between Tilling and BAT companies, Ribble could not retain the Liverpool-London service and it was handed over to Crosville, as route 4, on 9th November 1931. During the 1930-31 winter, the company offered to refund the bus fare from between all the places served by the suspended routes 2 and 3 and the nearest pick-up point on routes 1 or 4.

During the same winter, Rymer, who was in financial difficulties, arranged with Imperial to take over his services though, because of the imminence of the new licensing procedure, this was announced as an amalgamation. Imperial announced both day and night services for 1931 but dropped the route via Stratford and Oxford at some time, making the day and night routes identical, running via Coventry and A5. As Rymer's route via Stratford was not regularly run, a road service licence was eventually refused. MacShane abandoned the A5 route in October 1930.

The railways' right to oppose applications for road service licences was a new dimension which took effect in 1931-32. Long distance services were especially targeted, particularly those to and from London where the railway companies could claim superior services on all counts except cost. The North Western Traffic Commissioners instructed operators to submit co-ordination schemes at a sitting on 25th September 1931 and promised severe limitations on the number of vehicles which would be allowed to run. This was more easily said than done and the only real evidence of a co-ordination attempt was a joint timetable issued in 1932 by Crosville and All-British Line. In 1931, Crosville route 1 was rerouted via Seacombe ferry, to compete with All-British Line. Route 2 became the early service from Liverpool and the late return, in order to improve south coast connections. Routes 1 and 3 retained the terminus in Cartwright Gardens until 1934 as

During 1934 a batch of coaches was delivered from Duple bearing illuminated side panels advertising the London services. This was a practice which was to be revived nearly 30 years later with the first deliveries of Bristol RELH6G coaches with ECW bodywork. Number 965 (FM 8170) was posed prior to delivery by the coachbuilder – there were five similar vehicles, on Leyland Tiger TS6 chassis, but this was one of two with 24-seat capacity instead of 32, as illustrated below.

it was more competitive with the other operators, being convenient to the Bloomsbury hotel district; routes 2 and 4 went into Lupus Street until Victoria Coach Station replaced it on 10th March 1932.

Crosville applied for five licences between Liverpool and London and was granted three, the Commissioners refusing an extension to Southport and the diversion via Ellesmere Port. In 1932, routes 1, 2 and 4 were designated A, B and D; in 1933, the return fare was reduced from £1.7.6d (£1.37½) to £1.5.0d (£1.25). The Commissioners had previously outlawed the winter fares.

In September 1931, Samuelson's service was sold to Red & White Services Ltd. of Chepstow though the name was retained and in January 1933, All-British Travels Ltd was purchased together with an option for Red and White to purchase George Taylor's All-British Line service. Taylor was eventually paid £850 for the goodwill and the service ceased on 26th September 1933. In March 1933, MacShanes also fell under Red and White influence, their name being dropped on the service via Stratford and Oxford which was virtually the same as Samuelson's.

The railways opposed the renewal of all Liverpool-London licences in October 1933 and, after an appeal, the Minister of Transport restricted the capacity to the service coach and three duplicates. Red and White now wished to dispose of their Liverpool interests which also included Keswick, Glasgow and Torquay services and an excursion licence. Pearson's were prepared to pay for the suppression of the Liverpool-London licences but weightier matters were afoot as Red and White wanted admission to the Associated Motorways network which was to be set up in 1934. The deal involved London Coastal Coaches, Midland Red, Ribble and Crosville and the latter two each paid £2,500 to Red and White for the surrender of all their Liverpool licences. The London services were to be handed over on 10th January 1934 but the last Red and White coach departed Liverpool on the night of 7th January. There may have been some Crosville trips on hire to Red and White after this date to clear advance bookings but this is by no means certain.

In 1934, Crosville cut out the detour via Hoylake and Heswall on route A, saving over half an hour. Route B thus

EXPRESS COACH SERVICES DAILY
Between Liverpool and London

FIRST CLASS COMFORT
FARES LESS THAN A PENNY A MILE

CROSVILLE MOTOR SERVICES

HEAD OFFICE
CRANE WHARF
CHESTER

DETAILS FROM
ANY LEADING
TOURIST AGENCY

The Company was by this time becoming more sophisticated in its marketing and 965 was used as the basis of this publicity postcard used frequently at this time for minor communications. This was another practice to be revived in the 'sixties.

became identical with A except for the stops in Wallasey. Route D via the A5 ran only in July, August and September following which it was permanently withdrawn as the company decided it was better to concentrate the duplication on one route. Of the independents, only Pearson's and Imperial remained. Imperial was in dire straits having had its AEC Regals repossessed. Ribble had been trying to purchase the business but nothing came of it. Ribble and Crosville had been talking to Pearson's, undoubtedly the premier line on the London route, who had won an extension of the London service to Southport in summer 1933, a facility previously refused to Crosville; they also had a valuable Liverpool-Blackpool service. These negotiations were mysteriously suspended in September 1934. However, during the next few months Pearson's acquired not only Imperial but also two other Liverpool-Blackpool services which Ribble had been unable to buy and a Birkenhead excursion business, W B Horn. It seems possible that it was a put up job by the two big companies who correctly divined that the operators concerned would sell to Pearson's but not to a 'combine' company. The Imperial fleet was later sold by Ribble for only £625. Pearson's was taken over jointly from 25th May 1935, the fleet being divided between the two companies. Crosville's share comprised a Lancia (which was immediately scrapped), four Leyland Tigers, three AEC Regals, one AEC Q and two Bedford WTBs. Ribble took eight Tigers and two new ones not yet delivered; one cannot help feeling that it got the better of the deal.

Crosville now had a monopoly of the Liverpool-London services which were reorganised from 1st June as route A via Wallasey, Birkenhead, Chester, Crewe, Newcastle, Lichfield, Stratford and Oxford; route B commencing from Southport via Liverpool, Birkenhead, Chester, Whitchurch, Cannock, Erdington, Stratford and Oxford and route C, Liverpool-London night service via the same route as B. Route A was withdrawn for the winter, leaving Wallasey and Crewe unserved.

The competitive days were over but they had given a tremendous stimulus to the development of the luxury coach. Within seven years, the canvas-topped vehicle, not far removed from the earlier charabanc, had given place to

luxurious, heated vehicles with carpets, curtains, mirrors and travelling rugs. The services settled down into a routine, enlivened only by the extra traffic for the coronation of King George VI and Queen Elizabeth in 1937.

MERSEYSIDE-NORTH WALES EXPRESS SERVICES

The establishment of services between Merseyside and North Wales was one of Crosville's prime commercial objectives. Not only was there a strong demand for Merseysiders to visit the beauty spots and resorts but a century of Welsh immigration had established strong community links. Lack of access to Woodside ferry was a stumbling block and, from 1924, seasonal services were started from Singleton Avenue, Birkenhead and from Wallasey Village (Liscard from 1925) to Mold, and Ruthin, the two connecting at Heswall to enable loads to be combined. They were extended to Denbigh in 1925 and frequent bus services between New Ferry and Loggerheads became popular. From 1926, a Liverpool-Loggerheads service (via the Runcorn Transporter bridge) also connected for Denbigh though a through winter service was a failure. From 1928, Crosville started to develop Birkenhead Park station as an express terminal with a service to Llandudno via Mold and the Vale of Clwyd, followed, in 1929, by a Llanrwst service via Chester, Llangollen and Betws-y-coed. The Agreement with Birkenhead Corporation pledged the latter to support the introduction of long distance services and the Denbigh and Llanrwst services were run from Woodside in 1930, though the Llandudno service started at Seacombe.

Maxways & Wirral Motor Transport

Two Birkenhead coach operators laid the foundation of the important daily services between Liverpool, Birkenhead and Caernarfon. These were Macdonald & Co and the Wirral Motor Transport Co, both with offices near Woodside ferry. Macdonalds was by far the larger concern, having originated in horse-waggonette days. The motor

By the time it was acquired by Crosville, the ten coach fleet of Macdonald & Co (Maxways), of Birkenhead consisted entirely of AEC Regals all of which ran for Crosville until 1952-53 after rebodying. There were two batches, four being new in 1931, as typified by BG 208 *Caernarvon Castle*, with Duple 30-seat bodywork, seen here. Taken over on 1st December 1934, they became T6-15 in the 1935 series and never carried plain numbers.

coach business was set up after the 1914-18 war, with capital subscribed by two Liverpool business men, W M and A G Herd. There was also a garage business in Lark Lane, Aigburth which was later to figure prominently in the coach business. In 1920, the fleet comprised three Lancias, a Garford, a Rolls-Royce and a Daimler seating between 10 and 18 passengers.

Macdonalds were already advertising daily services between Birkenhead and the coastal resorts as far as Llandudno by 1925 but one wonders how accurate this description was. Although the later limitation of this kind of operation to day returns did not apply before 1931, it was common for operators to pool their passengers when there were few bookings or to cancel the trip altogether. Hire cars could, of course, be used when bookings were very low and the commodious touring cars of the time gave a high standard of comfort. A photograph of the Chester Street office published in March 1927 showed a permanently painted advertisement for a guaranteed service daily to Rhyl, Colwyn Bay and Llandudno. Single and period returns were being offered later in the 1927 season. However in 1928, the Llandudno service which recommenced on 13th April was not run on Tuesdays and Fridays though full daily operation started on 1st May. Fares were based on 2d per mile single, 1½-times single for day returns and double for period returns. The fares to Rhyl and Llandudno were thus:-

Rhyl	5/- single	7/6d day return	10/- period return
Llandudno	7/6d single	11/- day return	15/- period return

The year of commencement of the express service as distinct from the day excursion can therefore be fixed as 1927. Single and period return fares were also offered on a Saturday excursion to Corwen (10/- [50p] day return), Bala (12/- [60p]), Dolgellau (15/- [75p]) and Barmouth (16/- [80p]).

By June 1929, the Llandudno service had been extended to Bangor and, whilst facilities were also advertised to Caernarfon, it is reasonably certain that these were not being run regularly. Arrangements may have been made with a local operator and this was certainly the case in the

early part of the 1930 season when connections at Bangor for Caernarfon etc. were advertised. Licences to ply for hire in Caernarfon were granted, possibly on the evidence of the passengers transferred to connecting services and a through service from Birkenhead to Caernarfon started on 24th May 1930, about two weeks before the commencement of the Crosville service. The Caernarfon service left Woodside at 9.30am and was additional to the Bangor service which continued to leave at 10.30am via the coast route.

By April 1930 the fleet name Maxways had been adopted and Leyland Tiger coaches were in use. By July 1930, the Caernarfon service was running twice daily at 9.30am and approximately 5.0pm from each end and the Bangor journeys had been cut back to Llandudno. All the Caernarfon trips followed the inland route via Holywell and St. Asaph deviating from the A55 to serve Llandudno. The Caernarfon service continued to run throughout the winter months in order to establish a pattern on which to base the application for a road service licence under the new Road Traffic Act. There seems to have been a period when the service ran through to Pwllheli at a return fare of 12/6d [72½p] and this was advertised between March and June 1931. Doubtless the extension was found not to be worth while and was soon abandoned. Pearson's application for a similar service may have been prompted by Macdonald's withdrawal.

The Wirral Motor Transport Co Ltd was registered on 27th April 1922 to carry on business as a haulage contractor. Daily coach services to Llandudno were advertised in 1925. The pattern was similar to Macdonald's and 1929 was the watershed between excursion and regular service.

Latterly, the haulage and passenger businesses seem to have been separated as the latter was carried on without the 'Limited' in the title by H M Robinson. The Llandudno route followed the coast road through Flint, Prestatyn and Rhyl and was extended to Bangor in April 1930.

Robinson seems to have been less ambitious than Macdonald but he built up a good regular clientele which enabled him to survive and prosper despite the severe competition which developed on the route in 1930-31. When the new road service licensing laws came into effect

The Wirral Motor Transport Co acquired one AEC Regal as a measure of keeping up with the Macdonalds. BG 605 was employed on a Birkenhead-Bangor service, taken over by Crosville in February 1934. A board in the nearside bulkhead reads 'BIRKENHEAD via RHYL' while 'Limited Stops' is permanently painted on the cab dash. It became 980 and then T5, surviving, like the Maxways fleet, until 1952. It was new in 1932 and had Duple bodywork, popular on this chassis.

in 1931, he was granted his Birkenhead-Bangor service to run between Easter and October, subject to co-ordination with Crosville, with the proviso that on journeys to Bangor, no passengers were to be set down before reaching Rhyl and vice versa.

All-British Line & Pearson's

Crosville started a Chester-Llandudno express service in 1929 and, in the same year, both Royal Blue of Llandudno and North Wales Silver Motors were licensed in Chester. It is not certain if these services were started. In 1930 Crosville's service was described as 'regular daily service by special motor coach' and left Lower Bridge Street at 10.0am. The company was also granted a Chester-Caernarfon service but eventually used this as the basis of the inland route described below. George Taylor's All-British Line Llandudno-Chester service, which started on 14th April 1930, was part of a London service already described. By January 1931, an attempt was made to break into the Liverpool-North Wales market by integrating a service with the London workings. The Chester-Llandudno service was extended to Caernarfon and there were through trips from Liverpool via Wallasey, Birkenhead and Chester at 5.0pm on Fridays, Saturdays and Sundays, returning from Caernarfon at 7.10am on Mondays, Saturdays and Sundays, connecting with the London coaches at Chester. Because of licensing problems, the service was terminated at Port Dinorwic for a time. From 20th April 1931, the London-North Wales service was advertised as a feeder from Chester and extended to Llanberis, departing there at 6.40am and arriving at 9.50pm. This extension was very short-lived as the summer service terminated at Caernarfon. There were many changes, including a night facility from London with a three-hour wait in Chester!

All-British Line's application for a Liverpool-Caernarfon service was refused by the Traffic Commissioners in September 1931, a Chester-Llandudno feeder to the Liverpool-London service being granted in May 1932 with severe restrictions. This seems to have died when the London service was purchased by Red and White in September 1933.

Late in 1930, Pearson's Happy Days Motorways turned their attention to the establishment of a Liverpool-North Wales service before the new licensing laws took effect. They obtained licences in Liverpool, Llandudno, Penmaenmawr and Llanfairfechan but were refused in Birkenhead, Prestatyn, Rhyl, Bangor and Caernarfon. Although a Bangor council committee had recommended the grant, a liaison committee of Bangor and Caernarfon councillors rejected it. Pearsons raised a petition through the *Liverpool Echo* and although the cut-off date was 9th February 1931, their twice-daily *Welsh Coaster* service seems not to have started until about 26th, only return ticket holders being permitted to board in the towns which had refused licences. Various appeals all failed. The vehicles crossed the Mersey by the Seacombe boat, picked up in Liscard and then ran direct to Bromborough. Pearsons believed that Harry Macdonald had blocked their Birkenhead licences and attacked Maxways at every opportunity.

Connections between London and North Wales were advertised in 1931 but other services were more convenient. Applications to the Traffic Commissioners for Liverpool-Caernarfon-Pwllheli and a separate Liverpool-Llandudno service were refused and operations finished on 7th October 1931.

Crosville Caernarfon Services

Little detail of the Caernarfon-Birkenhead service of U N U Motors has survived. It may have been intended to run twice daily in 1929 but licences were refused in Birkenhead, probably because of the influence of Harry Macdonald and is more likely to have been run at 8.45am from Caernarfon, returning at 6.0pm. The U N U route was said to have been run throughout the year but there is no evidence of it running during the winter of 1929-30. Another Welsh based service was acquired with the business of Bethesda Greys in 1932. It ran between Bethesda and Birkenhead on Mondays and Thursdays only. It was reduced to Thursday operation and not reintroduced in 1935.

The balance of six AEC Regal coaches in the Maxways fleet on takeover dated from 1932 and had Massey bodywork, somewhat favoured as a coach bodybuilder among Merseyside operators in those days. Seen here is BG 614, *Rhuddlan Castle*. Here again, illuminated side display panels were favoured. The name *Rhuddlan Castle* was revived in 1983 when a Daimler Fleetline Open-Topper for service at Rhyl was so adorned as a member of the *Castle* class of vehicles.

The Crosville Birkenhead-Caernarfon service was started on 4th June 1930 with two departures daily at 9.0am and 6.0pm from each end. Because of licence restrictions, there were initially no stops between New Ferry and Conwy but the acquisitions of 1930-31 eliminated these within a few months, St. Asaph becoming the first setting-down point. From the start Crosville advertised a wide range of connections to and from all parts of Caernarfonshire and Anglesey, using mainly their own local services, a facility the competitors could not match. A number of seasonal services were kept going throughout the winter of 1930-31 and the Caernarfon services were extended to Liverpool via Woodside ferry in December 1930. These included the new 'Caernarfon B' service via Chester, Llangollen, Corwen, Betws-y-Coed and Bethesda.

The 1931 season was a testing time for all the Birkenhead-North Wales operators. A well-organised Crosville service, Wirral Motor Transport's established Bangor service, All-British Line running via Chester, and Pearson's semi-pirate service were all vying to establish a locus. Maxways and Wirral Motor Transport had the advantage of regular patrons and good reputations for service and reliability. Business was especially good in 1931. On 6th October, Macdonalds announced that the full summer service would continue until 20th October and this was subsequently extended to 31st. This was possibly an attempt to take advantage of the withdrawal of Pearson's *Welsh Coaster* service after 7th October.

Macdonalds applied to the Traffic Commissioners for several modifications. Extra Saturday journeys at 1.30pm from both Birkenhead and Caernarfon were planned, to be extended to and from Liverpool when the Mersey Tunnel opened; the Birkenhead-Bangor service was to be extended at both ends to become Liverpool-Caernarfon via the coast road and the 7.30pm Birkenhead-Llandudno trip, introduced during 1931, was to be extended to Caernarfon to return at 8.0am on the following morning. This facility was planned to connect with the Queen Line London-Llandudno service and was a deliberate tilt at All-British Line and Pearsons, both of whom were trying to establish North Wales-London connections, the one via Chester and the other via Liverpool. The All-British departures from Caernarfonshire were inconveniently early in the morning whilst Pearsons offered only night travel so the Queen Line route was an attractive one. However, by 1934, their 8.30am departure from Llandudno was too early to permit a connection being made and it is suspected that the Caernarfon and Bangor traffic was too insignificant to justify special arrangements.

The Traffic Commissioners insisted that there must be co-ordination between operators on the Merseyside – North Wales routes and, on 5th August 1931, Macdonalds, Crosville and Wirral Motor Transport agreed to a pooling arrangement on their services. As already stated, Pearsons, as interlopers, were refused licences outright and All-British Line was cut down to a Chester-Llandudno feeder. Crosville, Maxways and Wirral Motor Transport applications were granted, subject to co-ordination and with restrictions on the carriage of passengers between certain points. On the Crosville and Maxways summer services to Caernarfon the first setting down point was Abergele and only passengers for Bangor and beyond

could be picked up at Holywell, St. Asaph, Prestatyn or Rhyl. In winter similar conditions applied except that passengers could also be carried between Merseyside and Prestatyn and Rhyl as there was no separate service to cater for them.

The co-ordination arrangements, originally announced for 4th May 1932, came into operation one week later. Maxways now had access to Liverpool where their Lark Lane garage was adopted as their terminus, coaches calling also at Crosville's Edge Lane depot, Ribble's 30 Islington office and the Pier Head. Two of Maxways' Caernarfon trips ran via Flint and Rhyl and three of the four Llandudno trips now ran via Holywell and St. Asaph. There were now 13 departures daily of which eight terminated at Caernarfon, one at Bangor and four at Llandudno. Of these, eight originated in Liverpool, travelling by the Woodside vehicular ferry, and five at Birkenhead. Birkenhead-Rhyl traffic was the sole preserve of Crosville and Wirral Motor Transport in the summer and there were no facilities for Liverpool-Rhyl traffic, a serious deficiency in the co-ordination arrangements. In winter, Crosville's Liverpool-Llandudno service was withdrawn to make room for Maxways.

The co-ordination agreement lasted for two summers and a winter. Crosville was eager to extend the degree of co-ordination so that duplication could be run on any timing by any company instead of each operator sticking rigidly to its timings but Maxways had other ideas. They terminated the agreement on 24th May 1933 but the Commissioners insisted on delaying altering the timetables until the end of the season. Maxways applied for a revised timetable with new picking-up and setting-down facilities which would have given them considerable advantages, including a Liverpool-Rhyl service. Macdonald said that the loss in winter was 3d per mile compared with the 1931-32 operations. At the hearing on 10th September 1933, the application was opposed by both Crosville and Wirral Motor Transport, the latter complaining that Maxways would extract traffic from their service and expressing satisfaction with the co-ordination agreement. Crosville's main objection was that Maxways had obtained entry to Liverpool only as a result of co-ordination. In his evidence, Claude Crosland Taylor said:-

"...if there are two operators on the route, we maintain that the only way of dealing with such services is to pool results and to divide it in proportion to mileage run. In the first place, we have been granted licences – both of us – on the assumption that services to the public were to be united. As operators we ran it on a 50-50 basis or as near as may be. When we came to look into the question of timetables we decided to work it as economically as possible. The result was that it did not matter at all which operator had the more favourable time. We claimed that where duplication had to be introduced, each operator should take turns and I was prepared to institute the machinery and organisation so that it could be done."

The Commissioners requested certified details of traffic carried in 1930-31. Maxways' application was granted except that they were no longer permitted to serve Liverpool and there was some relaxation of conditions, mainly academic. Maxways now had Birkenhead-Rhyl traffic in the summer. Co-ordination was now limited to

Above: Coach travel in the mid-'thirties is beautifully encapsulated in this scene as passengers begin to emerge with their belongings on arrival at Caernarfon. Crosville's pre-war coach livery of grey and green conveyed an air of high-class travel. Number 744 was a 1933 Leyland Tiger TS4 with Leyland coach body – very unfairly, perhaps because of the body make, it was dismissed by the Company in an official list of the time as a 'bus de luxe'. The cantrail panels and the draught deflectors are both used to advantage to advertise the route the vehicle was to ply; at night the illuminated lettering would have presented a modern appearance to passers-by. The restrictions on picking up etc. are denoted by the small sign under the cab canopy.

Below: Another vehicle which worked express services to North Wales was the 1936 Leyland Tiger TS7 ordered by Prichard of Llanrug, but delivered new to Crosville. Burlingham built the body which was to a high standard. The coach is seen passing through the Market Square in Chester. The shop to the right of the coach still sells shoes to this day and the tower which appears to sprout from the roof of the coach is part of the Odeon cinema then being built. The building with arched windows behind the public convenience is the car showroom of rival George Taylor - the coaches were kept at the rear of the building and in Nicholas Street Mews, about half a mile away, but still within the City Walls.

the 1.30pm Birkenhead to Caernarfon trip on Saturdays which was worked by Maxways or Crosville on alternate weeks, but the return trip at 6.0pm was exclusively Crosville. Maxways was dissatisfied with the grant of what it saw as more favourable picking up and setting down restrictions to Crosville, particularly on the Birkenhead-Holywell service which the limitations on the Caernarfon services were designed to protect, and appealed unsuccessfully to the Minister of Transport in 1934.

The revocation of the co-ordination agreement was a retrograde step but it probably hastened the elimination of competition on the route. Wirral Motor Transport sold out from 10th February 1934 and, at the end of that season, Crosville made an offer for Macdonald & Co's business which was eventually accepted. Maxways service ran for the last time on 30th November 1934. Like many other old-established operators, Harry Mac had, to some extent, found it difficult to adjust to the new licensing conditions. Crosville acquired a very respectable fleet of 10 AEC Regal coaches from Maxways and another from Wirral which became T5-15 in the fleet, all of which were eventually rebodied as dual-purpose vehicles.

For some time after the takeover, 'Harry Mac' was employed by Crosville at the Woodside office. His brother Roy worked as a driver at Rock Ferry depot for many years. He was a popular character who organised a musical group called the 'Busketeers' which entertained at staff concerts.

In 1935, the Maxways and Wirral timetables were run by Crosville unchanged but the whole service was revised from 25th May 1936 from which date there were eight journeys between Liverpool and Caernarfon, four via Holywell and St. Asaph and four via Flint, Rhyl and

Llandudno, with roughly half the service in winter. Despite concerted opposition from excursion operators, day return fares were approved. At the same time, the Birkenhead-Llanrwst service was withdrawn in favour of a morning departure from Liverpool on the 'B' service on which, following the acquisition of Western Transport, stops had been introduced at Wrexham and Ruabon. Another consequence of this takeover was the Wrexham-Birkenhead express which had been introduced in 1930 as a 'daily excursion'. It ran on Mondays to Fridays with one fare – 2/6d (12½p) single or return. It was always run by an ex-Western Transport Tilling-Stevens bus which arrived in Birkenhead at 11.15am and returned at 8.30pm.

There was now stability on the Merseyside-North Wales services and no major changes were made until the outbreak of war. These services were a major source of revenue which amply justified the concessions made to Birkenhead Corporation in 1930, without which, in the face of railway opposition, they would never have been developed to the same extent.

New in 1939 was a twice-daily Caernarfon-Aberystwyth seasonal service via Porthmadog, Dolgellau and Machynlleth. Except on Saturdays, timings allowed almost a four-hour stay for day trippers.

A Liverpool-Caernarfon service via Rhyl and Llandudno was permitted to operate during the early months of the war. In June 1940, there were two return journeys daily and an additional trip on Saturdays though the latter had been discontinued by September. There were through bookings to Holywell via Greenfield. The afternoon winter services were brought forward to 4.0pm from 7th October 1940 and the service was suspended, probably in March 1941.

Broads Travel in Erdington, Birmingham served the Company loyally for over 45 years as agent and suburban stop point on London services. Until Crosville ceased to exert influence over what became National Express services Broads was shown as a timing point. Clearly there was a strong demand for the product as the prominent and permanent display outside the shop at 429 Birmingham Road shows. Note the reference to Worthington Motor Tours above the Broad's name sign – this was a leading West Midlands independent concern later to join Crosville in the National Bus Company fold.

The Midlands

In 1929, a seasonal Birmingham-Welshpool-Aberystwyth service was taken over from the Midland Red company. This had originally been started in the early 1920s as a joint venture with Jones Bros., passengers being exchanged at Newtown. The reason for giving it to Crosville is obscure as, with a morning departure from Birmingham, a sleep-out duty was involved. By 1930, a Birmingham – Barmouth service had been added but this did not last long. Both these services ran at weekends in the 'shoulder-season' and daily in July, August and early September.

After its London services had become well-established, the company received enquiries in its booking offices for a service to the centre of Birmingham. The service was planned during the period of outright LMS ownership and one cannot help but think that the LMS planned this with a view to abstracting traffic from its rival, the GWR. The service commenced on 28th May 1930, running twice daily between Birkenhead (Woodside) and Birmingham (Digbeth) though the morning departure from Birkenhead actually started from West Kirby. The route was through Chester, Tattenhall, Whitchurch, Prees, Shrewsbury, Wellington, Wolverhampton and West Bromwich; from 2nd June it was routed also via Ellesmere Port. It was advertised to run throughout the winter but was suspended in October and announced as running from 17th June to 27th September 1931.

After a rather Gilbertian hearing before the Traffic Commissioners, the licence application was opposed by both the LMS and GW railways and there was some amusement when the Chairman remarked that one of the objectors was a principal shareholder in Crosville. The application was adjourned and company officials were summoned to a meeting at Paddington station at which it was agreed to withdraw the service which last ran on 12th September 1931.

The Potteries

For the 1930 season Crosville made a determined effort to put its Potteries outpost on the express map. All the Liverpool-London services made a call at Newcastle-under-Lyme but the route was very competitive as the town was also served by the routes from Manchester, Blackpool and East Lancashire.

A daily service to Birkenhead (Woodside) via Crewe and Chester, allowing a visit to New Brighton or, by crossing the river on the ferry a full six hours in Liverpool, started on 4th June. From 1st October, it was revised to run twice daily, the bus hardly standing still in a 13-hour day.

From 1st July, new daily summer seasonal services were started to Rhyl, Colwyn Bay and Llandudno, picking up at Crewe, Nantwich and Tarporley and to Blackpool, picking up at Crewe, Sandbach and Middlewich. In 1931, there were plans to extend the Blackpool service to run from Birmingham but these were abandoned as there were already several other companies on the route.

The latter two services became a permanent feature of the network but the Birkenhead service was withdrawn sometime during the winter of 1930-31 following railway opposition. It had not been very successful as there was little social affinity between the Potteries and Merseyside, North Staffordshire people looking more to Manchester and Birmingham. The company's BAT and railway associations did nothing towards gaining access to the Potteries heartland as the Potteries Motor Traction Co Ltd who covered Stoke, Hanley and the other towns, was directly controlled by BET and had no railway shareholding.

Other Express Services

In the autumn of 1928, a Ribble service between Liverpool and Manchester was withdrawn and Crosville, Lancashire United and North Western agreed to operate a joint service, both via Eccles and via Altrincham. On 13th March 1929, George Cardwell, general manager of North Western wrote to Claude Crosland Taylor to the effect that 'at last' licences had been granted by Manchester City Council. Crosville immediately replied that they had no objection to North Western and Lancashire United starting without them but Leyland Lion No. 61 (later B22) had already been inspected and was licensed on 21st March. The service was advertised in the 1929 summer timetable with Crosville buses running trips by both routes but no Crosville bus ever ran, for what reason is unknown. Crosville retained a paper interest until 17th November 1934 when the road service licences were surrendered.

A Warrington – Llandudno summer service was advertised to commence on 17th June 1931, serving Chester, Prestatyn and Rhyl but it was granted only as far as Rhyl. From 1937 it was diverted via the new A5117 (avoiding Chester), Mold, Loggerheads, Ruthin, Denbigh and St. Asaph, enabling the Warrington – Loggerheads bus service to be withdrawn.

In addition to those already mentioned, several seasonal services were acquired with various businesses and most were continued virtually unchanged except for revised terminal points. The takeover of Western Transport in 1933 had brought with it express services to Blackpool, Llandudno and a vocational convalescent home at Rhyl while J. Price had services from Rhos to Blackpool and to the same convalescent home. Company records proclaim that a Chester-Blackpool service started in 1927 but it is not certain that that was so as it was not listed in 1931.

EXCURSIONS & TOURS

From quite early days, Crosville recognised that the operation of purely pleasure trips was a legitimate offshoot of the business of running regular bus services and, before the Road Traffic Act, 1930 gave legal definitions to various activities, it was often difficult to decide just what was an excursion and what was an express service. From 1931, an excursion was a journey for which there was only a return fare and which could be operated in accordance with demand whereas a regular service had to be run in accordance with the timetable approved by the Traffic Commissioners whether there were passengers or not.

In the early days, these trips were run by charabancs but the rapid technological advances of the late 1920s soon made this type of vehicle uncompetitive though a few survived until the 1939-45 war by which time they had a

Private Hire and excursion traffic continued to figure prominently. Many of the earlier vehicles which were rebodied by ECOC/ECW in 1935/9 with dual-purpose bodies were admirably suited to the task. This group of happy women were presumably on an Annual Outing of some sort, probably the highlight of the year for many at that time. The leading vehicle is K25 (FM 5900),a rebodied 1930 Leyland Tiger TS2. K32 is behind. To judge by the newness of the paintwork, the absence of either destination blinds or the overpainting of the glass, this view was taken for the company archive shortly after rebodying in 1936/7, in this case by ECW.

novelty value. Some local councils who regarded charabancs as somewhat *infra dig* fixed the stands in unsuitable, out-of-the-way places and limited the numbers and times of operation. A good example was Hoylake who would not permit the stands to be used on Sundays, potentially the most profitable day. Four charabancs were licensed and when Crosville asked for this to be increased to six they agreed but stipulated that not more than four were to be used on any one day. Sunday limitations in Calvinistic Wales were quite common.

From 1930-31, excursions provided the greatest opportunity for competition and a great part of the Commissioners' time was devoted to hearing applications and objections to them. Each operator was granted a schedule of destinations and a vehicle allowance. Trips to destinations which competed with regular services were often restricted as to the number of times they could be operated and many destinations had individual restrictions such as number of vehicles to be run in any one day or seasonal restrictions.

Mature operators realised that the best way to get some harmony among competing excursion operators was to put them all on a level playing field and Crosville took the initiative in several towns, securing agreement on a common schedule of destinations and common fares. The Traffic Commissioners encouraged these moves which were particularly effective in places such as Birkenhead and Chester.

Running seaside excursions was a specialist business and the company benefited by the injection of this knowledge from people whose services were acquired with businesses such as White Rose and Royal Blue. The man who could work for a big company and think like a small operator was a great asset. Excursion operation, apart from being very lucrative if expertly run, could be a morale builder among the drivers who looked forward to a welcome change from repetitive service work.

In the winter, football matches and race meetings provided sporadic revenue and a lucky Cup draw could lead to the special licensing of coaches previously put in mothballs for the winter.

Private Hire

Private hire was recognised by Crosville as a valuable revenue source, capable of development, as early as 1922 when J M (Joey) Hudson was appointed to look after it after his Ellesmere Port-Chester service had been purchased. In the 1920s there were no restrictions but, from 1934, when the Ministry of Transport had realised to what extent illegal service journeys could be dressed up as private hire, several onerous restrictions were introduced. Above all, organisers could receive no reward and trips could not be advertised. The last was a difficult one as any scribbled notice displayed in a place accessible to the public was classified as an advertisement. There were many cases where organisers advertised spare seats and were rewarded by having the trip cancelled by the Commissioners on information laid by a competing operator with an axe to grind. Nevertheless, the activity thrived and some operators existed on nothing else.

Enormous works outings involving dozens of vehicles provided a wonderful publicity opportunity to a large operator, though little or no profit was made as coaches often had to be brought from distant depots to make up the number. The companies such as Crosville were prevented from participating in private hire in the peak summer months as they could not spare the coaches which were needed for their express services.

Extended Tours

The term 'extended tour' covers a journey lasting several days for which the operator makes the accommodation and meal arrangements for the passengers. Crosville started such tours in 1927 with seven-day tours to Devon and Scotland and gradually built up a regular clientele. Nowadays, such tours are worked on a large scale and by specialist coach operators as it has been recognised that it requires so much organisation and individual attention that, on a small scale, it is not profitable at all.

Hudson organised the programme, booked the hotels, all of which were visited during the winter. A driver and a courier were employed on each coach and about two-thirds of the fare was paid out for meals and accommodation.

In The *Sowing and the Harvest*, W J Crosland Taylor quotes statistics showing how this activity grew progressively throughout the 1930s, as prosperity returned, to 995 tour days in 1939. The most popular destination, by far, was Scotland, followed by Devon and Cornwall. European tours were considered but dropped as the threat of war loomed in 1938.

Successful tour operation required a very special type of driver who was prepared to invest some of his own time in acquiring knowledge of the special interest features of the places en route. A placid, courteous and patient manner coupled with great skill as a driver, could bring considerable personal rewards from grateful passengers. A different kind of driver could ruin a holiday and ensure that the passenger never booked again.

Significantly, Crosville never revived their extended tour programme after the 1939-45 war. Initially, this was doubtless because of their inability to devote any resources to it and when the post-war crises were over, it was difficult to justify the revival of what would be seen to be a licence unused for several years and judged, therefore, to be redundant.

A slightly later 'excursion' using K102 (FM 9985). The party is that of Crosville's senior management lead by James Crosland Taylor. He can be seen, pipe in mouth against the pillar at the step in the waistrail. The location is Thurston Road, Leyland then the Headquarters of Leyland Motors and, ironically, the final Headquarters of Leyland Bus at the end of its short period of independence in the 'eighties. The coach was one of a pair of TS7 with Harrington 25-seat bodies normally used on tours. The party would be well-received, Crosville being among Leyland's best and most loyal customers between 1922 and 1941.

One important early wartime traffic was the carriage of 'Evacuees', children who were sent away from vulnerable industrial areas. Number J12 (FM8982), a 1935 Leyland Lion with its original body, provides the transport for this apprehensive group of youngsters. The advert in the windows of another vehicle in the convoy is for the Whitsuntide holiday, probably therefore 1940/41. The vehicle itself survived the war, was rebodied and eventually became a mobile shop in the Ellesmere Port and Chester area from 1959-65. One wonders if it served any of its 1940 charges.

8   THE 1939-45 WAR

When war broke out on Sunday, 3rd September 1939, the management and staff of Crosville little thought that, over the next decade, the company would be transformed. The Traffic Commissioners had already briefed operators of the likely consequences, bearing in mind that, at that time, there was no local source for oil products or the raw materials for tyres. Cuts in fuel consumption of 40% were seen as necessary and whilst some could be achieved by the total suspension of the

The Company's own collection provides this lighter aspect of the dark years of 1939-45. Members of 'The Crosville Team' portray the diminutive stature of Mr Hitler and Il Duce, Mussolini. Quite who the seated figure is supposed to represent is less clear, though it could be Joseph Stalin, regarded as unfriendly early in the war. The van, No. 25a, is a Morris.

non-essential services such as tours, excursions, private hire and summer express services, it was obvious that many other cuts would also have to be made.

The Chairman of the Traffic Commissioners, William Chamberlain, was appointed Regional Transport Commissioner, with virtually absolute powers; James Crosland Taylor served on his Advisory Committee. North Wales affairs were delegated to a Deputy Commissioner, J R Williams. Fuel was rationed and the allocation to each bus company was related to the mileage which had been approved. Many 'luxury' services were suspended immediately but the full cuts came on 24th September. Express services and excursions and tours were immediately suspended, as were seasonal services and a number of market day buses. Many inter-urban and rural services were reduced in frequency by between a third and a half but most trunk services, such as Chester-Wrexham-Llangollen retained their basic services though some duplication was eliminated. Imposition of a black-out not only made night driving difficult and hazardous but reduced passenger demand particularly as, initially, all places of entertainment were closed. The early months of 1940 saw various adjustments, some suspended journeys being reinstated where real hardship was caused and evening services being further curtailed, a trend which continued until 1943 when last buses were run at about 9.0pm. Reduced capacity was to a small extent counteracted by an increase in the permitted number of standees from five to eight and later to 12. All buses of the 'E' and 'F'

The Royal Ordnance Factory at Wrexham saw many hired vehicles and a Leyland LT2 of Ribble Motor Services (D5, CK 4530) precedes an AEC Regent of Morecame and Heysham Corporation; an ex-Western Transport Tilling Stevens (R49) is on the right. The pale green Morecambe bus must have looked quite exotic – its Weymann body was of a modern style belying its March 1932 date, only five months newer than the Tilling Regent shown below. Few photographs of vehicles engaged on ROF work exist – the shortages of photographic materials and the obvious security implications restricting even official record.

classes not converted to ambulances were converted to perimeter seating for 30 seated and 30 standees.

Not surprisingly initially, the Welsh services suffered greater cuts than those in industrial areas. Workers' services had to be maintained and, before long, there were many new demands as industry adjusted to war needs and new factories were hastily established. North Wales was seen as a 'safe area' where war factories could be built with less risk of attack by enemy aircraft. Soon the hotels of Llandudno and Colwyn Bay were filled by civil servants evacuated from London. Evacuee school-children were everywhere and more, not less, mileage was being run in some parts of North Wales.

The Royal Ordnance Factory at Marchwiel, near Wrexham eventually needed 200 buses, Vickers Armstrongs at Broughton, 73 and Rolls-Royce, making

aero-engines and the LMS at Crewe, making tanks, required 45. The Shell oil refinery at Ellesmere Port was extended though the Birkenhead traffic was carried by rail, a special station being built adjoining the works; Crosville buses carried intermediate traffic, starting at Bromborough Pool Lane. ICI in Runcorn and a number of new industries on the Welsh coast added to the overall demand. The company also served 66 airfields, camps and military hospitals.

At Wrexham, a large field behind Mold Road depot was taken over as a bus park as 290 vehicles were now based there. Thousands of tons of stone were rolled in to provide hard standing and tar boilers were brought in to supply hot water for the radiators of buses stored outside, to aid starting. A tractor was also kept busy tow-starting the more reluctant machines.

New vehicles could not furnish all the Company's needs and second-hand vehicles appeared as well as many hirings. Indeed many of the so-called hirings were to turn into permanent acquisitions. Strangely, vehicles appeared to be renumbered if they were transferred from the notional 'Hired' status to 'Acquired', even if there was no gap in their service with the company! Number L90 was former Brighton and Hove 6242, an AEC Regent/Tilling of October 1931. Whilst on hire from October 1943 it was numbered L102; it became L90 as if to celebrate its acquisition in August 1945.

In 1940 Manchester Corporation provided their No. 213 (VR 6002), a 1930 TD1 with MCCW framed bodywork completed by Crossley. Coincidentally it became L213 and stayed until March 1946. It is seen standing with a native Cub; the Widd board gives Port Dinorwig and Caernarfon as the destination. Manchester had rebodied all its TD1 buses with this lowbridge version of its 'Standard' style in 1935/6, but reconstruction of bridges allowed the famous 53 route to use highbridge buses from 1939, so 33 of the 40 spent most of the war years with Crosville.

The prewar fleet of around 1,000 vehicles was ill-equipped to deal with these sudden demands. Only 15% were double-deckers and these were all working in areas where their capacity was needed more than ever. Another 15% comprised small-capacity vehicles for which there was a decreasing demand, many rural services needing greater capacity as more women were drawn to war work and new camps provided new traffic. Ten double-deck buses from Birkenhead Corporation and 17 from Yorkshire Woollen District were hired for the first phase at Marchwiel but Birkenhead soon wanted theirs back as their demands increased. Many elderly buses were purchased outright, others were hired and, of the 200 buses required for Wrexham ROF, 160 came from within the Crosville fleet the remainder being hired, Wallasey Corporation supplying a big contingent after some of them had worked for the company in Liverpool. In all, 193 buses were hired for varying periods, the peak at any one time being between 60 and 70 in 1941.

Over 1,000 Crosville employees joined the services, many being reservists. Women eventually formed 70% of the conducting staff, 827 being recruited. They also took over cleaning, clerical and other tasks.

In October 1939 at least 15 Leyland LT3 Lions in the 'E' class were converted for use as emergency ambulances. It is possible that a further nine were converted and later returned to use as buses; all had been restored as buses by January 1946. The army commandeered 38 petrol-engined buses, mostly of low capacity or with coach seats. The 1940 order for 12 Leyland TD5 Titan double-deckers and 19 TS8 single-deckers was met. The company also received 26 Leyland TD7 double-deck buses diverted from Southdown and East Kent. No new buses were received in 1941, hence the large number of hired vehicles, but the following year saw the introduction of 20 utility-bodied lowbridge Leyland TD7 'unfrozen' double-deckers, followed by 11 Guys in 1943.

In 1943-44, 93 petrol-engined Tigers and Titans (10% of the fleet) were earmarked for conversion to run on producer gas and 111 gas producer trailers were supplied by Bristol Tramways and Carriage Co. As with most companies, the target was not reached, only 20 single-deck and 11 double-deck buses being fully converted; they were used at Chester, Crewe, Rhyl and Wrexham. Another vehicle similarly converted was a staff car, 1933 Chrysler RE34 saloon number 1A, FM 8132, which, when new, had been Claude Crosland Taylor's car. The test chassis for gas operation was ex-Brookes Brothers Leyland TS2 Tiger number K37, DM 6231, which had donated its body to a new TS8 chassis in 1940. However, it was not used in service in adapted form.

Enemy Action

Between July 1940 and January 1942, Liverpool and Birkenhead suffered grievously from severe air attacks. Buses were dispersed to avoid a catastrophe if a depot was hit and both Liverpool and Rock Ferry depots sustained serious damage, narrowly escaping total destruction. Raids were also recorded in the 'safe' areas, often as a result of enemy aircraft getting lost or dumping their loads under gunfire. Crewe depot also sustained some damage. In the summer of 1941, buses could not reach Liverpool Pier Head for several weeks as the city centre was devastated and services terminated at the Adelphi Hotel. Two emergency teams were established at headquarters, one under the Chief Engineer which dealt with damaged vehicles, the other under the Architect for emergency repairs to buildings. Remarkably, no vehicle was totally lost.

The air raids caused population movements which gave the company serious problems. In Liverpool and Wirral, people moved out of the vulnerable inner areas to the country districts, creating extra peak hour traffic which the company lacked the resources to handle. There were staff problems, too, as although the company was scheduled under the Essential Work Order which theoretically prevented any staff from leaving, in practice there were many problems not the least of which was the

Northern Counties provided the body on this 1942 Leyland Titan TD7, M136 (FFM 186) seen at Wrexham. This was one of the 'unfrozen' chassis built from parts in stock, but the body was of utility outline. It had received modifications to the opening windows and a post-war Tilling destination box by the time this 1949 photograph had been taken. The heavily-slatted radiator then being carried had come from one of the buses diverted from East Kent.

The archetypal utility double-decker was based upon the Guy Arab chassis, Guy having been designated one of the two builders of such vehicles by the Ministry of Supply. Crosville had examples of both Mk I and II variants in this instance being fortunate enough to receive some with Gardner 6LW engines. Another make of body was introduced – Roe. Notice that the characteristic Roe waistrail was retained even on utilities. MG 157 (FFM 275) was a 6LW-powered bus and in largely original form when seen at Crewe railway station, usual home for the type.

superior working conditions enjoyed by municipal busmen. Crosville had to seek help from Birkenhead Corporation for commitments at Ellesmere Port and Clatterbridge.

Despite government appeals to the public not to travel unnecessarily, there was a great deal of pleasure traffic in the wartime summers. Because of the extra burden on the railways, some long distance services were allowed to continue; these included the Liverpool-London 'B' service and a limited service between Caernarfon and Liverpool but all these were suddenly withdrawn by 1941-42. Extra fuel was allowed for summer services in 1940 but not subsequently and, in 1943, the Commissioner ordered all companies to suspend some Sunday services and break up through facilities to discourage travel and save fuel. This measure also reduced the working hours of bus crews some of whom were working continuously without rest days.

Change of Financial Control

The companies with both Tilling and BET shareholdings were, for practical purposes, attached either to one group or the other. The two Groups had different management philosophies, Tillings favouring more centralised control while BAT gave its companies more local autonomy. This led to serious personality clashes between very senior people and, despite wartime difficulties, it was decided to assign each company to one group or the other. Since 1930, Crosville had been in the BET camp but, following the split of Tilling and British Automobile Traction, it found itself a subsidiary of Tilling Motor Services Ltd from 3rd December 1942. This had no immediate effect on the travelling public but, within three years, the results were all too apparent. Tilling Group buses had to be either red or green and Crosville chose the latter to the disgust of Chester

In 1945 there arrived the first of what was to be the Company's standard chassis marque for nearly forty years, the Bristol. The last of the delivery of K6A with AEC 7.7 litre oil engine was M187. At this stage the chassis still utilised the pre-1939 high radiator and was fitted with Strachan bodywork to relaxed utility pattern. The vehicle is standing at Liverpool's Pier Head, bound for Warrington. Although the Widd board denoting the route letter is held aloft, Tilling Group pressure has brought about use of the destination display proper.

Below: Not many buses were repainted to virtually peacetime standard in wartime, but M88, a Leyland TD5 with ECW body dating from 1939, glistens when about to depart from Bangor for a reason, the destination display 'Holyhead' being the clue. It had been chosen to inaugurate the operation of double-deckers across the Menai suspension bridge on 26th March 1945, as shown on the opposite page. This type of bus was Crosville's standard double-decker as placed in service in the 1938-40 period, combining what was virtually the standard ECW lowbridge body of the time with the TD5 chassis, of which 54 had been supplied, including six with detachable top covers for use on the Rhyl sea-front service. The white paint on the wing edges and dumb irons was intended to aid visibility during the blackout, which had permitted only minimal light to show externally during the hours of darkness. This vehicle had the military-style headlamps which were widely introduced on buses in the latter part of the war, originally with the masks that had been obligatory from the beginning, but these had been removed at this very late stage of the war when air-raid risks were thought minimal. Another wartime innovation can be seen hanging from the platform edge – the conductress. Many operators introduced female platform staff for the first time to replace men conscripted for military service.

Traffic using the Menai suspension bridge had been restricted to a severe weight limit, causing Crosville to be restricted to lightweight Leyland Cub forward-control models as mentioned in Chapter Six, and even then passengers were required to walk across. During the war, the bridge was strengthened and widened, primarily for military strategic reasons. When the work was completed in March 1945, Crosville could provide a through service from Bangor to Holyhead, eliminating the change previously needed at Llangefni. A lunch celebrating the event for local dignitaries was held in Bangor and M88, the TD5 shown on the opposite page, is seen above on the bridge – it was driven by Gwilym Wynne, who had been driving for Crosville since 1910. Also crossing the bridge is KA20, a 1937 Tiger TS7 bus with ECW body of the standard late pre-war type, which would also have been too heavy hitherto.

Corporation whose buses, until that time, had carried a somewhat paler version. They then chose a darker version of Crosville's old maroon, which persists to this day.

Green was seen for the first time on some of Crosville's 1945 Bristol utility double-deckers and thereafter there was a sharp change away from Leyland in favour of the Tilling-owned Bristol marque.

It was inevitable that service reliability worsened during the war years. There were greater demands on men and machines and old vehicles, which would normally have been withdrawn, had to be kept going; this included a large number of petrol-engined vehicles,

both single- and double-deck. There were three consecutive harsh winters and, in January 1940, even the River Dee was blocked by ice floes. Passengers' complaints inevitably rose and the company ran a press campaign illustrated by 'Punch' cartoonist, Douglas England, to highlight its problems in a humorous way.

The most notable achievement was the enormous increase in productivity brought about by the elimination of mileage seen as unnecessary and the increased traffic due to wartime conditions generally. This is best illustrated by the following table reproduced from *Crosville on Merseyside* by permission of the author.

Year Ending 31st March	Revenue		Passengers		Mileage		Pence (d) per bus mile
	£000s	Index	000s	Index	000s	Index	Index
1939	1,250	100	94,455	100	33,465	100	8.98	100
1940	1,395	116	100,527	106	30,419	91	11.00	122
1941	1,741	139	115,900	123	28,348	85	14.74	164
1942	2,084	167	134,549	142	29,807	89	16.78	187
1943	2,044	164	129,836	137	26,738	80	18.34	204
1944	2,263	181	141,346	150	28,000	84	19.40	216
1945	2,366	189	148,544	157	28,859	86	19.68	219
1946	2,353	188	149,420	158	30,161	90	18.75	209

CROSVILLE FLEET LIST FROM INCEPTION TO 1945

As is perhaps inevitable, many gaps exist in the details of the early vehicles, although this list is certainly more complete than those which appeared, with commendable initiative, in the Company's own Handbooks between 1952 and 1960. The publishers would welcome any additional information that can be positively supported for incorporation into a second edition of this volume.

Throughout the period up to 1935 any renumbered vehicles have the new number shown in parenthesis.

Vehicles purchased for the commencement of Bus Operations 1910-11

Fleet Nos	Reg Nos	Chassis	Chassis No	Body	Seats		Acq	Sold	Notes
	L517	Herald	-	Ch	-		1907	1911	Ex Pontedawe Mtr Co
	-	Germaine					1910	1910	Bought at Auction in Chester
	-	Albion		?	Ch		1911	1912?	Ex Lawton Liverpool
-	M2963	Lacre		Eaton	Ch18		1910	1911	Ex Lightfoot, Kelsall
2 (4)	FM 387	Dennis		Eaton	B23R		1911	1913?	'The Alma'
8 (18)	-	Dennis					1911	1918	'Deva'
-	-	Herald					1911	1917	'Ella'

These vehicles had very short lives in the fleet.

New and second hand vehicles acquired 1912-15

Crosville gave names to their early vehicles, perhaps as well for the numbering system became somewhat confused with widespread renumbering and other changes of which records may well be incomplete. Number 5 (DU 2007) was an ex-demonstrator Daimler CC chassis with a Hora body. Later on it was numbered 19: it was sold 1927.

Fleet Nos	Reg Nos	Chassis	Chassis No	Body	Seats		Acq	Sold	Notes
3	FM469	Lacre		Eaton	B—R		1912	1927?	'Royal George'
5 (22)	DU 2007	Daimler CC	384	Hora ?	B23R		1913	1927	Ex Daimler Demo 'The Flying Fox'
9?	FM 535	Lacre	-	-	Ch18		1913	1928?	'Grey Knight'
12 (25)	FM 603	Daimler CD	596	Eaton	B28R		1913	1927?	
6(23)	FM 641	Daimler CD	631	Eaton	B32R		1913	1927?	'Busy Bee'
7(24)	FM 703	Daimler CD	560	Eaton	B32R		1913	1927?	
10/11	FM 963/4	Daimler Y	4638/68	Hora	B28R		1915	by 1924	
1	M5371	T/Stevens TS3	230	T/S	O18/18R	?	1915	1918	Ex Ward Bros
2	LH 9432	T/Stevens	329	T/S	H18/18R	?	1915	1918	Ex Ward Bros
8	FM 805	Daimler CB	935		B23		1914	1928	

Vehicles numbered 6/7/8/12 and possibly 5 were rebodied by Leyland or by Vickers with bodies to Leyland design (B26R) and fitted with pneumatic tyres in 1924. Short lives were typical of bus operations in those days and also were a facet of fast advancing design standards.

Hora was Messrs E & A Hora, 36 & 38 Peckham Road, London SE, a company first registered 16th October 1896.

New and second hand vehicles acquired 1916 and 1919.

The Daimler CK was introduced into the fleet after 1918 and No. 29 (FM 224) with London Improved body was new in that year. Unusually, many of these vehicles were rebodied by Leyland in the 'twenties. Note that Crosville was still wedded to the open rear platform.

19 (37)	HF 145	Daimler CB			Davidson	Ch32	1914	1930	Ex New Brighton Motor Coach Co 1916
20	HF 147	Daimler CB	664		Davidson	Ch32	1914	1925	Ex New Brighton Motor Coach Co 1916
14 - 16	FM 1091/2 1103	Lacre	-		Eaton	B23R	1916	1919	Bodies to 14-6 in 1919 (?)
17 (21)	CU 308	Daimler B	-		Daimler	Ch28	1914	1931	
18	FM 1087	Daimler ?	-		-	B23	1917	1922	
21	?	Lacre	-			?	1917	1919	
23	?	Lacre	-			?	1917	1919	
24	?	Lacre	-			?	1918	1919	
25 (16)	DM 1295	Daimler CB	Daimler			Ch28	1915	1930	
26 - 28	FM 9/131/ 143	AEC YC	13734/654 /744		-	B27R	1919	1923	
14 (28)	FM 1091	Daimler CK	3236		Eaton	B23	1919	1928	Body ex 14 ?
15 (35)	FM 1092	Daimler CK	3841		Eaton	B32R	1919	1928	Body ex 15 ?
16 (36)	FM 1103	Daimler CK	3621		Eaton	B32R	1919	1928	Body ex 16 ?
24	DU 1560	Daimler CB	940		?	B25	1916	1922	Ex Daimler Demo 1919
9 (27)	FM 937	Daimler CK	3216		?	B23R	1919	1927	
21 (38)	FM 1224	Daimler CK	3237			B32	1919	1931?	Body Ex 21?
23(39)(45)	FM 1234	Daimler CK	3803			B32	1919	1931?	Body Ex 23?
49	FM 1348	AEC YC	14216		?	Ch32	1919	1923	
29-34	FM224/5/ 73/80/91/2	Daimler CK	2875/6/3051 /71/79/131		London Improved	B23R	1919	1927-31	

The vehicles originally numbered 9/14-16/19/21/23/25/29-34 are believed to have been fitted with pneumatic tyres and new Leyland-style B26R bodies in 1924.

20 *was rebodied with a B32 saloon body by 1921.*

26 -28 *are believed to have had reissued registration numbers. This was not uncommon at the time. A Crosville fleet summary of 1921 records FM 1087 as a Daimler CB Chassis number 823. A Lacre chassis was believed to have existed though whether it bore this number or was not accepted by the Company, with subsequent reisssue of the intended registration is not known. A previously unrecorded vehicle, registration CC 1096, was licensed to Crosville by Crewe Council on 1/10/19. It may have been a Lacre, possibly No. 24 above, but its origin is unknown. It was only licensed once at Crewe and it is not certain these were the 'same' vehicle.*

Vehicles acquired new and second hand 1920

49 **	T 7082	AEC Y?				Ch20	1919	1923	Ex Colwills 1920
1/2	FM 1436/7	Crossley X	12282/54		?	B14F	1919	by 1924	Ex Royal Flying Corps 1920
35 (45)	FM 1382	Daimler CK	3014		Bartle	B23R	1920	1931?	
36 (46)	FM 1383	Daimler CK	3090		Bartle	B23R	1920	1931?	
37 (47)	FM 1384	Daimler CK	3124		Bartle	B23R	1920	1931	
38 (21)	FM 1385	Daimler CK	3263		Bartle	B23R	1920	1931	
39 (23)	FM 1386	Daimler CK	3186		Bartle	B23R	1920	1931	
40	FM 1387	Daimler CK	3300		Bartle	B23R	1920	1931?	
41 (43)	FM 1445	Daimler CK	3396		Bartle	B23	1920	1931	
42 (20)	FM 1446	Daimler CK	3367		Bartle	B23	1920	1931	
43	FM 1447	Daimler CK	3231		Bartle	B23	1920	1929	
44	FM 1448	Daimler CK	3315		Bartle	B23	1920	1931	
45 (18)	FM 1460	Daimler CK	3393		Charlesworth	Ch28	1920	1931	

A youthful David Deacon took this view of No. 59 (FM 426), a Daimler CK, at Birkenhead Park Station in 1930, shortly before the withdrawal of the vehicle. It had been fitted with a Leyland body and pneumatic tyres by this stage and its dusty appearance suggests that it might have been taken out of storage, perhaps to cover the duties of a vehicle which had failed in service. This bus had begun life as No. 100 when new in 1920, at the time the only bus in the fleet with a number above 60; it had become No. 59 by 1923. Some 45 Leyland-style bodies were supplied for Daimler chassis in 1924, enough for almost all then in the fleet.

46 (19)	FM 1461	Daimler CK	3423	Charlesworth	Ch28	1920	1931	
47 (20)	FM1449	Daimler CK	3276	Bartle	Ch23	1920	1929	
48 (21)	FM 1450	Daimler CK	3238	Bartle	Ch23	1920	1929	
50/1	FM 1750/1	Daimler	3853-4	Bartle	B26D	1920	1931/29	
58/9	FM1812/11	Daimler	3863/2	Bartle	B26D	1920	1928/22	
3	FM1872	Crossley X	10087		B14	1917	1925	Ex Colwills 1920
52-7	FM 1881-5	Daimler CK	3834/64/5 77/8/92	Bartle	B26D	1920	1931	
100(59)	FM 426	Daimler CK	3851	Bartle	B26R	1920	1931	

The vehicles originally numbered **29-34/38-48/50-8/90** *are believed to have been fitted with pneumatic tyres and new Leyland B26R bodies in 1924. On final withdrawal from the bus fleet the Leyland-style bodies were stripped from* **48/58** *and the chassis retained for use as lorries. Whether the lorry bodies were fitted is not known.*

**The vehicle registered T7082 is shown with fleet number 49; this would also appear to have been issued to another bus registered FM 1348, new to Crosville in 1919, at the same time. Contemporary records seem confused, though it has been suggested that it was numbered 33.

Charlesworth Bodies Limited were based at Much Park Street, Coventry and were established 28th February 1907 – they became well-known in the 'thirties for elegant bodywork on Alvis cars.

Vehicle design was advancing quite rapidly and although in 1921 vehicle intake fell to just three, the first of many new Leylands arrived. Number 61 (FM 2093) was the first with a Leyland body. It is noteworthy that destination equipment was fitted to both the front and the rear, something which is none too common today. The particular vehicle was rebodied and fitted with pneumatic tyres in 1924.

Vehicles acquired new 1921

60	FM 2044	Daimler CK	4035	Bartle	B26F	1921	1931
61/2	FM2093/4	Leyland 36GH7	12274/116	Leyland	B32R	1921	1928

60 *is believed to have been fitted with pneumatic tyres and a new Leyland-style B26R body in 1924.*

Vehicles acquired new and second hand 1922

59 ?	FM 2166	Crossley X	?		B14	1918	1924	Ex Royal Flying Corps 1922
4	FM 2183	Crossley J	?		B14	1918	1924	Ex Royal Flying Corps 1922
?	FM 2184	Crossley ?	?		B14	?	1924	Ex Royal Flying Corps 1922
18	FM 2185	Crossley X	11015	?	Ch14	1918	1924	Ex Royal Flying Corps 1922
24	FM 2186	Crossley X	11350	?	Ch14	1918	1924	Ex Royal Flying Corps 1922
?	FM 2187	Crossley				1918	1924	Ex Royal Flying Corps 1922
?/?	FM 2209/10	Crossley ?		?		1918	1924	Ex Royal Flying Corps 1922
63-71	FM 2173-81	Leyland 36GH7	12349-57	Leyland	B32	1922	1928	
72	FM 2182	Leyland 45GH7	12358	Leyland	B32	1922	1929	
83/4	FM 2242/3	Leyland 36GH6B	12388/9	Leyland	B32	1922	1929	
75	FM 2250	Leyland 36GH6B	12393	Leyland	B32	1922	1929	
76-78	FM 2251 /7/8	Leyland 36GH7	12421	Leyland	B32	1922	1928	
79	FM 2364	Leyland 45GH7	12416	Leyland	B32	1922	1929	
81/2 (99/100)	FM 2366/5	Leyland 36GH7LW	12407/8	Leyland	B40	1922	1931	
80	CC 1024	Leyland 45GH6B	12330	Leyland	B32	1922	1929	Ex W.H.Roberts Llanrwst

84 *was new to the associated Colwills concern but was transferred to Crosville as shown.*

80 *was acquired with the business of Roberts.*

The Crosleys were used as 'chasers' on routes pirated by competitors.

Vehicles acquired new and second hand 1923

1922 saw the delivery of this Leyland 30A9, No. 112 (FM 2617). Here it is seen at the Bowring Park tram terminus on the Prescot route via Huyton Quarry in 1924. Contemporary notes, again by David Deacon, suggest that by 1926 the vehicle was working out of Newtown on the route to Montgomery and later from Llanidloes to Rhayader. The most significant part of these notes is that the bus was one-man operated.

85-8 (101-4)	FM 2458-61	Leyland 30A7	10333-6	Leyland	B20R	1923	1931	
73/4	FM 2474/5	Leyland 36GH7	12495/6	Leyland	B32	1923	1928	
89/90 (10/11)	FM 2476/7	Leyland 30C1	19382/3	Leyland	Ch26	1923	1929	
91-100	FM 2478-87	Leyland 36GH7	12485-94	Leyland	B32R	1923	1928-9	
101-3 (106-8)	FM 2488-90	Leyland 36GH7LW	12502-4	Leyland	FB40	1923	1931	
104-8	FM 2609-13	Leyland 36GH7	12497-501	Leyland	B32D	1923	1929	
109-12	FM 2614-7	Leyland 30A9	12495-8 ?	Leyland	B20R	1923	1932	
1/2 (8/9)	FM 2622/3	Leyland 30C1	19201/2	Leyland	Ch20	1923	1929	
-	MB 452	Crossley Tender			B14	1917	1923	Ex Gibson 1923
-	MB 3628	AEC Y			B26	1919	1923	Ex Gibson 1923
-	MB 207	Daimler CK			B26	1920	1923	Ex Gibson 1923
-	MA 9430	Leyland 36GH7			B32	1922	1923	Ex Gibson 1923

*The Leyland chassis numbers 12497/8 are claimed by both **104/111** and **105/112** respectively according to contemporary records. The vehicles acquired with the business of Gibson were not operated despite being quite similar to the Company's contemporary stock.*

*Fleet numbers **1** and **2** were reissues.*

Vehicles acquired with the business of John Pye, Heswall, 1st January 1924

1P	CM 2107	Straker Squire	6002	?	B30	1920	1924
2P	CM 2127	Straker Squire	6056	?	B30	1920	1924
3P	CM 2135	Straker Squire	6094	?	B30	1921	1924
4P	CM 2136	Straker Squire	6097	?	B30	1922	1924
5P	MA 9642	Straker Squire	CO1027	?	B30	1922	1924
6P	MA 7077	Albion	978E	?	B20	1919	1924
7P	NB 9535	Albion	19911	?	B20	1922	1924
8P	MA 8259	Albion	30091	?	B20	1919	1924
9P	MA 6592	Albion N20	20061	?	B32	1923	1924
10P (178)	MA 2435	Albion	3039H	?	B32	1923	1925?
11P	MA 4067	Pagefield	8024	?	B32	1922	1925?
12P (177)	MA 9927	Pagefield FP	F6017	?	Ch30	1922	1925?
13P	MB 1037	Fiat	52B52245	?	B14	1919	1924?
14P	FY 3510	Bristol 4Ton	1175	?	Ch28	1919	1924
15P (?176)	MB 66	Tilling Stevens	1861	?	Ch32	1922	1924
16P (180)	MA 9220	Ford ? Tonner	64930360	?	Ch14	1921	1926
17P (179)	MB 1816	Ford ? Tonner	R12776	?	Ch14	1921	1926
19P	MB 3060	Dodge	891156		B14	1920	1924?
20P	MB 3061	GMC	F29811	?	B20	1923	1924?
18P	EK 2110	Albion	1960F	?	Lorry	1920	1924?

14P *was the first Bristol vehicle to enter Crosville ownership: there is a query over its registration which is also quoted as FY 2510.*

181	DD 2728	Ford	?	?	?	1923	1925

The vehicle registered DD 2728 has been attributed to Pye but it seems certain that it did not in fact comprise part of his fleet. Its origin is unknown. Other vehicles have been attributed to Pye but these are the ones commonly believed to have passed to Crosville.

Sale of Pye's business was apparently agreed on 7th November 1923; Crosville took over on 22nd January 1924 but the sale was backdated to 1st January.

New vehicles acquired 1924

113	FM 2624	Leyland 36GH7	12762	Leyland	B32F	1924	1932
114/5	FM 2818/9	Leyland 36GH7	12763/4	Leyland	B32F	1924	1932
121-7	FM 2834-40	Leyland 36GH7LW	12786-92	Leyland	B40D	1924	1931-2
1-7 (397-9)	FM 2841-7	Leyland 36GH7LW	12797-803	Leyland	B32F	1924	1932
12-4#	FM 2848-51	Leyland 36GH7LW	12793-6	Leyland	Ch32	1924	1928
15							
116-8	FM 2852-4	Leyland 30A7	19723-5	Leyland	B20R	1924	1932
119	FM 2855	Leyland 30A7	OM19726	Leyland	B20	1924	1932
120	FM 2856	Leyland 22Z5OM	25055	Leyland	B20F	1924	1932
89/90	FM 2857/8	Leyland 45GH6B	12804/5	Leyland	B32R	1924	1929
128-36	FM 3001-9	Leyland 36GH7	12897-905	Leyland	B32D	1924	1932
175 (105)	FM 3010	Leyland 36GH7	12865	Leyland	B32R	1924	1932
137-148	FM3193-204	Leyland 36SG9	13091/2//167/9/ 70/68/93-98	Leyland	B40D	1924	1931-2

120 *was delivered with pneumatic tyres and a jack-knife door. Many or perhaps all other 1924 vehicles were fitted with pneumatic tyres during their lives, although no definitive record is to hand of precisely which.* **148** *was the last new single decker to be delivered to the company with solid tyres.*

*The new vehicle delivered after number* **12** *and before number* **14** *was allocated the 'number'* **AC**. *Claude Taylor is believed to have been superstitious and the* **AC** *was based on the first and third letters of the alphabet.*

New vehicles acquired 1925

149-58	FM3205-15	Leyland 36SG9	13099-108	Leyland	B40D	1925	1932
159/60	FM 3215/6	Leyland 40SG9	13083/4	Leyland	B40D	1925	1932
161/2	FM 3217/8	Leyland 36SG9	13089/90	Leyland	B40D	1925	1932
163-5	FM 3219-21	Leyland 36C7R	35113-5	Leyland	B32R	1925	1932
166-70	FM 3222-6	Leyland 30A13	35116-20	Leyland	B26R	1925	1931
171-4	FM 3227-30	Leyland 36GH5	39085-8	Leyland	Ch32	1925	1928-29
182-6	FM 3320-4	Leyland 30A13	35394-98	Leyland	B26F	1925	1931
187-91	FM 3325-9	Leyland 36A9	35399-403	Leyland	B26F	1925	1931
192-4	FM 3590-2	Leyland 36SG11	13313-5	Leyland	B26F	1925	1932

All single deckers delivered from **149** *onwards were fitted with pneumatic tyres from new.*

The Leyland 36SG9 was thus called by virtue of its 36hp engine and side driver's position or half cab as was to become the common description. A typical bus of this type cost £1679 new at this time. Number 161 was registered FM 3217.

Vehicles acquired with businesses taken over 1925

From Gauterin Bros. Farndon 24th October 1925

195	MA 9729	Daimler CK	4135	?	B26F	1922	1931
196	ET 796	Daimler BB	3140	Brush	O??RO	8/14	1931

196 *is shown in certain records as ET 786 with 26 seat single deck body. It is as above in the Rotherham Borough Council records.*

From Richards, Busy Bee, Caernarfon 7th November 1925

Acquisitions continued to figure strongly in the fleet for many years. This 1925 Strachan & Brown bodied AEC 505 was to enter the fleet in 1925 with the business of Richards Busy Bee of Caernarfon. It was to last until 1931. CC 5214 became No. 198. The 505, with close affinity to the Y-type as built in 1914-18, was quite an old-fashioned bus for 1925.

197	CC 5011	AEC 503	503069	?	B36	1924	1928
198	CC 5214	AEC 505	505012	Strachan & Brown	B32R	1925	1931
199	CC 4860	Lancia	532	?	B26	1924	1926
200	CC 4958	Pentaiota	?	?	B26	1926	1926

197 *was converted to a lorry by Crosville in 1928 and ran thus until 1933.*

New Vehicles acquired 1926

The Leyland Leviathan appeared in 1926. Number 211 (FM 3782) was Crosville's first and posed for the Leyland photographer. The Leviathan LG1 was fitted with an 8-litre, four-cylinder, side valve petrol engine. These were Crosville's first double-deckers purchased new.

201-10	FM 3710/73-81	Leyland 29LSC1	45018-27	Leyland	B32F	1926	1935-42
211-22	FM3782-93	Leyland LG1	50014-26	Leyland	H52RO	1926	1931
223-34	FM3794-805	Leyland 36SG11	13548-59	Leyland	B40R	1926	1932
235-7(179-81)	FM4131-3	Leyland 36SG11	13590-2	Leyland	B40R	1926	1932

211-222 *were reseated to H56RO in January 1927.* **223-237** *were reseated to B36R in 1930.*

203 and 206 *later became lorries 35A and 43A respectively.*

210 *was in the short-lived bright red livery adopted between 1927/8 and 1929.*

New vehicles acquired 1927

The short-lived body on this Leyland 29PLSC1 chassis was by Queens Park. Although new in 1927 it was replaced with an ECOC bus body in 1933, no doubt because by that date such a design had become unacceptably dated for coach duties. Number 268 (FM 4304) is seen when new.

235-42	FM4271-8	Leyland 36SG11	13684-91	Leyland	B40D	1927	1932
243/4	FM4279/80	Leyland 40SG11	13692/3	Leyland	B40D	1927	1932
245-63	FM4281-99	Leyland 29PLSC1	45389-407	Leyland	B32F	1927	1949
264	FM 4300	Leyland 29PLSC3	45408	Leyland	B35F	1927	1949
265-8	FM 4301-4	Leyland 29PLSC1	45409	Queens Park	C32D	1927	1938
199-200	FM4333-4	Leyland 29PLSC3	45413/780	Leyland	B35F	1927	1949
269/70	FM 4350/1	Leyland 29PLSC1	45792/3	Queens Park	C32D	1927	1938
271-3	FM4486-8	Leyland 29PLSC3	45962-4	Leyland	B35F	1927	1949
274/5	FM 4561/2	Leyland 29PLSC3	46010/1	Leyland	B35F	1927	1941/49

235-44 *were reseated to B36D in 1930.*

245-63 *were rebodied by Eastern Counties Omnibus Company (B30F) between March and April 1936. The new bodies were numbered 3922/ 20/28/21/29/26/36/34/30/37/23/25/38/27/39/32/33/35/24 in fleet number order.*

264 *was reseated to B34F in 1930 and rebodied by ECOC 3913 (B32F) in 1936.* **265-70** *were reseated C30D in 1930 and rebodied by ECOC (B30F) 2813/6/4/1/5/2 in fleet number order in January 1933.*

199/200/71-5 *were reseated B34F in 1930 and rebodied by ECOC (B32F) in 1936. Body numbers were 3847/59/68/65/907/856/81 again in fleet number order.*

Company records show that at the time of rebodying **254** *adopted the chassis number 45402 (that of* **258***) and* **258** *became 47946. This number was new to a 1929 29PLSC1 originally numbered* **69** *(FM 5234). This in turn completed the circle by adopting 45398. It would appear that the chassis frames were muddled during the course of the rebodying.*

The marked change in chassis life brought about by these rebodyings and also the second World War is notable.

New Vehicles acquired 1928

In the late 'twenties, Leyland sub-contracted out some bodybuilding work when its own bodyshops were very busy, and this seems to have been the background to United building the bodies on nine Leyland Lioness PLC1 chassis in 1928, using Leyland drawings. This rear view of No.39 (FM 4834) shows a distinct affinity to the body design of the 'next generation' Leyland Tiger by then in production. Although there were two doors on the nearside, the absence of any step for the rear one indicated that it was intended as an emergency exit. Note the appearance for the first time of the grey and green coach livery, to remain standard until 1940. When rebodied by Eastern Counties as buses in 1934, these vehicles were rebuilt as forward-control to Lion PLSC3 specification, which must have meant that little but the engine, gearbox and axles of the original chassis remained. These sub-contracts provided the basis of a long lived relationship between Chester and Lowestoft.

276	FM4751	ADC 423	423002	UAS	B35D	1928	1935
277-300	FM4791	Leyland 29PLSC3	46496- -4814-46520	Leyland	B32D	1928	1941/49
301/2	4815/6	Leyland 29PLSC3	46520/1	Leyland	B36R	1928	1949
22-27	FM 4817-22	Leyland 29PLSC3	46522-7	Leyland	B35F	1928	1949
303-8	FM4823-8	Leyland 29PLSC3	46353-8	Leyland	B36R	1928	1949
34-39	FM4829-34	Leyland 29PLC1	46528-33	UAS	C29D	1928	1938
40-2	FM4835-7	Leyland 29PLC1	47117-9	UAS	C24D	1928	1941/49
28-33	FM4845-50	Leyland 29PLSC3	46942-7	Leyland	B35F	1928	1941/49
309/10	FM5027/8	Leyland 29PLSC3	46739/40	Leyland	B36R	1928	1949
329/30	FM 5210/1	Leyland TD1	70302/3	Leyland	L24/24RO	1928	1952

276 *had the first body for the Company from the coachworks in Lowestoft which was successively owned by United Automobile Services Ltd, Eastern Counties Omnibus Company Ltd and then Eastern Coach Works Ltd; it was built for the 1927 Commercial Motor Show.*

24-33 *were reseated to B34F,* **34** *to C28F then C26F,* **35-9** *to C27F,* **40-2** *to C25F all in 1930.*

In 1928, there was no financial link between Crosville and United. This arose as a result of both becoming part of the TBAT group in 1929-30.

34-42 were rebuilt to forward control with lengthened wheelbases and rebodied by ECOC in 1934. The new body numbers were 3239-44 and 3318-20 in fleet number order.

28-33 were downseated to 34 in 1930 and rebodied by ECOC/ECW in 1935/6. The new body numbers were 3857/44/93/36/67/61/3911/5.

277-310 were rebodied by ECOC (B32F) in 1935/6. The new body numbers were in fleet number order: 3890/40/84/81/902/839/85/919/908/869/903/850/60/ 96/91/42/51/70/86/909/871/917/875/76/72/37/52/62/910/18/906/914.

303 was sold in 1941, bought back in 1945 and withdrawn again in 1949.

311/15. 22-33 were similarly treated with bodies numbered: 3866/48//53/ 43/87/97/57/44/93/36/67/61.

329/30 rebuilt with enclosed staircases by Massey Brothers during 1936 and both converted to run on producer gas during 1943-4.

In 1929 and 1930 the Company changed names: firstly on the 1st May 1929 to LMS (Crosville) and then on 1st May 1930 to Crosville Motor Services Ltd.

Left: The 1927-29 PLSC Lions were rebodied by ECOC in 1935-36. No. 31, by now renumbered B10, stands at Oulton for the ritual ECOC view. There was a marked change in outline from the original Leyland square-cut body, as shown on page 35. This bus remained in service until 1949.

Above: An interior view of the same body.

Vehicles delivered new to the Crosville Motor Company Limited 1929

| 175-8 | FM 5218-25 | Leyland TS2 | 60402-5 | Leyland | C25D | 1929 | 1951-54 |
| 61-76 | FM522641 | Leyland 29PLSC3 | 47938-53 | Leyland | B40F | 1929 | 1941-50 |

175-8 *were originally dedicated vehicles for the Liverpool-London service. They were reseated to DP32D in July 1933 and rebodied by ECW (DP32R) in 1936/7: body numbers were 4536/34/42/53.*

175/7/8 *were fitted with perimeter seating in 1943 (DP30R) to increase overall capacity. They reverted to standard sometime after 1945.*

177 *was fitted with a Gardner 5LW engine in 1949 and reclassified in the scheme of the day to KC19.*

61-76 *were reseated to B32F in 1930 and rebodied by ECW (B32F) in 1935/6. Body numbers in fleet number order were 3898/58/900/844/88/ 74/89/98/904/16/54/45/77/41/38/78. 69 (FM 5234) 'acquired' the chassis numbered 45398 which properly belonged to* **258** *(FM4304). See 1927.*

Vehicles transferred to LMS (Crosville) 1st May 1929

The numbers shown here are the original fleet numbers allocated at delivery or upon acquisition.

17 (CU 308), **25** (DM 1295), **23** (FM426), **32-4** (FM 280/90/1), **38/9** (FM 1385/6), **41/2/4-6/8/50-7/60** (FM 1445/6/8), **45-8/50-7/60** (FM 1460/1/ 49/50,1750/1/1881-6/2044), **80-93** (CC 1024,FM 2366/65/2242/3/58-61,2476-80), **97-103** (FM 248490), **109-115** (FM 2614-7/24/18/9), 89/90/ **116-9** (FM 2857/8/52-6), **121-7** (FM2834-40), **1-7** (FM 2841-7), **1/2** (FM 2622/3), **128-36** (FM 3001-9) **175** (FM 3010), **137-70** (FM 3193-26), **182-94** (FM 3320-29,3590-2), **199/200** (FM 4333/4), **201-302** (FM 3710/73 -805,4131-3,4271-304,50/1/86-8/61/2/751/91-816), **22-27** (FM 4817-22), **303-8** (FM 4823-28),3442 (FM 4829-37), **28-33** (FM4845-50), 329/30 (FM 5210/11), **171-8** (FM 5218-25), **61-76** (FM 5226-41).
[Total 295 vehicles]

Vehicles delivered new to LMS (Crosville) 1929/30

The Leyland Titan, in its original TD1 form with standard Leyland open-staircase body, had been introduced in late 1927, but Crosville's first dozen did not begin to appear until a year or so later. No. 328 is seen in the bright red livery. By 1936, the open staircase was considered too old-fashioned to remain acceptable and all twelve were sent to Massey Bros for it to be enclosed; however, they retained their petrol engines to the end. When they were new it would have been quite unpredictable that ten of these buses, including this one (by then renumbered L39), would remain in service until 1952. One had been a victim of the Rhyl depot fire and the other was withdrawn in 1950.

This Leyland Lioness 6, No. 16 (FM 5246), is seen in the Sychnant Pass in North Wales showing the benefits of the soft-topped United body. The Lioness 6, model LTB1, used a chassis similar to the Lion LT1 but with normal-control and having the six-cylinder engine as used in the Titan and Tiger.

171-4	FM 5218-21	Leyland TS2	60440-3	Leyland	B32R	1929	1952
325-8	FM 5206-9	Leyland TD1	70002-4	Leyland	L27/24RO	1929	1945-52
331-6	FM 5212-7	Leyland TD1	70540-5	Leyland	L27/24RO	1929	1952-53
12/AC/14-5	FM 5242-5	Leyland Lioness 6	50270-3	UAS	C27D	1929	1936
16/7	FM 5246/7	Leyland Lioness 6	50268/9	UAS	C24D	1929	1936
337-42	FM 5526-31	Leyland LT1	50362-7	Leyland	B35F	1929	1936

Right: There was widespread interest in emergency exit provision on double-deckers in 1929-30, leading to the Conditions of Fitness provisions introduced in 1931 and the general use of the rear upper-deck window. Leyland built several experimental versions, amongst which was Crosville 367 (FM 5749), seen on the right which was exhibited at the 1929 Commercial Motor Show – 359 (FM 5887) of spring 1930 is known to have been similar. The idea of providing a kind of ladder from the upper deck was ingenious but had obvious dangers of its own. The normal driver's door was replaced by one at the offside front of the lower saloon, with cutaway front bulkhead to give access to the cab. This and the apertures in the body side must have weakened the structure considerably. Whether they, and perhaps others entered service in this form is not known but are thought to have been standard in later years, lasting to 1952/3.

Left: The Leyland Lion LT1 had a four-cylinder version of the Tiger/Titan engine but a different chassis having affinities to the Badger goods range. Crosville took 25 with Leyland bodies, including 347 (FM 5718) seen here, plus two acquired later. They had shorter lives than other types, being withdrawn in 1936.

311-24	FM 5704-17	Leyland LT1	50542-5 50551-4	Leyland	B40F	1929	1936
343-6	FM 5787-90	Leyland LT1	50517-20	Leyland	B40F	1929	1936
347	FM 5718	Leyland LT1	50556	Leyland	B40F	1929	1936
367	FM 5749	Leyland TD1	70816	Leyland	L24/26R	1929	1952
355	FM 5883	Leyland TD1	70841	Leyland	L24/26R	1930	1953

FM 5243 was the second vehicle to carry **AC** *instead of* **13**.

325-8/31-36 *had their staircases enclosed by Massey Brothers in 1936.*

The original Leyland body of **326** *(FM 5207) was transferred to* **L56** *in 1944,* **326** *gaining a 1931 Leyland body ex* **L14** *at the same time. This body was transferred to* **M39** *in 1950.*

171-8 *were rebodied by ECW (DP32R) in 1936/7. The new body numbers were 4541/58/48/9/36/34/42/53):*

171-3 *were converted to producer gas in 1943/4 and* **171/2/5/7/8** *were fitted with perimeter seating 1943-6.*

Titan number **367** *was exhibited at the 1929 Commercial Vehicle show.*

355 *was fitted with an oil engine in 1948.*

Vehicles acquired by LMS (Crosville) 1929/30

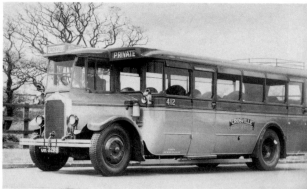

After the advent of railway control in 1929, four coaches of the LMS Road Motor Department, with headquarters at Watford (hence the Hertfordshire registration numbers) were transferred to Crosville. Three were Albion, much favoured by the LMS, and this pair, new in 1930, was unusual in being one each of the normal and forward-control versions of the same Viking 6 model – the front bumpers were non-standard for the type. Note the use of oil sidelamps, reflecting the railway distrust of electricity for the equivalent function on its locomotives. Two-door coach bodywork was quite common at that date, but the lines of the Watson body on UR 6298, still in railway colours, were significantly more modern than those of the London Lorries body on UR 6299. The latter is seen in Crosville standard coach livery and though recorded as having 26 seats, had legal lettering for only 19 in this view, suggesting use for touring work.

UR 6300 was another of the ex-LMS vehicles, originally having a Harrington body. In 1939 it gained this ECW body, loosely described as 'dual-purpose' although in coach livery with comfortable seats. The new body served a full twelve years in the fleet. Other acquired AEC Regals were similarly treated, the body design being as used to rebody early Leyland Tigers.

From LMS Railway Company

197	UR 3902	Albion PR28	7048B	Cowieson	C30R(F-?)	1929	1937
411	UR 6298	Albion Viking	5090F	Watson	C26D	1930	1937
412	AlbionViking	UR 6299	70511	Ldn Lorries	C26D	1930	1937
413	UR 6300	AEC Regal	662.015	Harrington	C21R	1930	1951

413 *was rebodied by ECW (DP32R) in 1939. The body number was 6091*

Vehicles acquired from Holyhead Motors (Mona Maroon) 4th November 1929

1	EY 3133	Albion PK26	5042G	Albion	B26F	1927	1935
2	EY 3301	Albion SPLB24	4282L	Albion	B20F	1928	1936
3	EY 3541	Albion SPLB24	4326K	Waveney	B20F	1929	1936
4	EY 3538	Albion	4326E	Waveney	B20F	1929	1936
5	EY 3537	Albion	4326F	Waveney	B20F	1929	1936
6	EY 3449	Albion	4282L	Waveney	B20F	1929	1936
7/8	EY 3539/40	Albion	4326J/G	Waveney	B20F	1929	1936
9/10	EY 3406/7	Dennis G24	70341/2	United Bodies	B20F	1928	1934
11	EY 3370	Chevrolet T20	20666	?	?	1928	1932
-	EY 3109	Chevrolet LM	17031	?	?	1927	1930
-	EY 3372	Chevrolet	T20	C23.4	?	1928	1930
-	EY 3371	Chevrolet	T220	?	?	1928	1930
-	EY 2166	GMC	K16RM ?	?	?	1924	1931
-	ND 6085	Albion (?)	4019L	?	?	1923	1930
-	EY 2204	Chevrolet 9B	23368	?	?	1924	1930
-	EY 1916	Chevrolet	17498	?	?	1923	1930
-	EY 3408	Chevrolet	?	?		1928	1928?

The vehicles without fleet numbers are believed not to have operated for LMS (Crosville) with the exception of ND 6085 which became lorry 37A for a short period.

EY 1916,2204,3109,3371/2, were sold by LMS (Crosville) prior to 1st May 1930.

EY 3408 was sold by LMS (Crosville).

Mona Maroon of Llangefni came under the Company's control in 1929. Inevitably few photographs exist but this view of Albion SPLB No. 7 (EY 3539) amply illustrates both the type of vehicle in this fleet and the fate of a considerable number of Crosville vehicles of this era when finally sold. It is seen standing at Talacre in 1954 as an immobile, if complete caravan. Had the preservation movement existed at this time, how many such gems would be around today ?

77	EK 6285	Leyland 29PLSC3	46281	Leyland	B40R	1928	1938
78	FR 8419	Leyland 29PLSC3	45879	Layland	B35R	1927	1938
79/80	EK 6286/7	Leyland 29PLC1	46216/269	Leyland	C28F	1928	1938
81/2	CC 8166/7	Leyland 29PLSC3	47289/90	Leyland	C28F	1928	1949
83	CC 8060	ADC 416	416.857	Leyland ?	C32F	1928	1934
84	CC 7967	ADC	416.613	Leyland	?	1928	1934
85/6	CC 8516/7	AEC 426	426.155/50	NCME	C32F	1929	1935
87/8	EY 3502/3	Thornycroft A6	18274/6	?	B26F	1929	1932
89-92	EY 3584-7	Vulcan Duke	3X547/5/4/6	?	B20F	1929	1930-31
93-5	EY 3648-50	Vulcan	3X549-51	?	B20F	1929	1931
96/7	EY 3652/1	Vulcan Duchess	D24/3	?	B26F	1929	1931
98	EY 3642	Vulcan Duke	3X548	?	B20F	1929	1931

*It is possible that **77/78** were charabancs or coaches.*

77/8/81/2 *were rebodied by ECOC in 1933/5 (B35F). The new body numbers were 2817/8/3864/99 respectively*

79/80 *were rebuilt from Lioness 4 (29PLC1) to Lion 29PLSC3 specification in 1933 and fitted with new ECOC bodies (B35F) numbered 2819/20 respectively.*

89/90: *There is some doubt that these vehicles passed to Crosville Motor Services Ltd.*

UNU was acquired in 1930 and comprised a quite modern fleet comparable with native Crosville machines. FR 8419 was a 1927 Lion 29PLSC3 with Leyland body. Perhaps inevitably, they fitted into the Company's rebuild programme and the product of this can be seen here. Only the registration mark conveys the true identity of the vehicle which lasted until 1938.

Vehicles transferred to Crosville Motor Services Limited 1st May 1930.

The following groups of vehicles were transferred:

1. Those vehicles shown above as transferred from the Crosville Motor Company to LMS Crosville in 1929 with the exception of the following which were sold in the period of LMS ownership:

   25 (DM1295), **51** (FM 1751), **83/4** (FM 2242/3), **89-93** (FM 2476-80), **97-100** (FM 2484-7), **1/2** (FM 2622/3), **4-6** (FM 284446), **89/90** (FM 2857/8), **220-22** (FM 3791-3).

2. All those vehicles shown as delivered new/or acquired during the period of LMS ownership.

Vehicles delivered new to Crosville Motor Services Limited in 1930

354	FM 5882	Leyland TD1	70840	Leyland	L24/24R	1930	1953
356-66/8	FM 5884-95	Leyland TD1	70842-53	Leyland	L24/24R	1930	1945/53
348-49	FM 5896-7	Leyland TS2	60964/5	Watson	B32	1930	1951
350-51	FM 5898-9	Leyland TS2	60966/7	Watson	C22D	1930	1951/56
352-3	FM 5900-1	Leyland TS2	60968/9	Harrington	C21D	1930	1952/53
369-74	FM 5902-7	Leyland TS2	60768-73	Leyland	DP25D	1930	1951-2
375-96	FM 5908-29	Leyland LT2	50960-77 51029-32	Leyland	B35F	1930	1938-52
401-6	FM 6014-19	Albion LC24	4347G/L 4348A-D	Albion	B20F	1930	1936

Lions continued to be delivered and this rear view of No. 376 (FM 5909) shows the roof rack and the precarious access arrangement on the nearside corner as well as the door in the rear wall. The driver's door was hinged to the rear as was typical of the period. Little confidence existed in the tyres of the day and a spare is seen stowed under the bus. Single-deck lives were not comparable with contemporary double-deckers and this vehicle was sold (as D4) in 1938. Only a few of the LT2, with its affinity to the TS3, had this 'square' type of body.

407-10	FM6020-23	Albion PJ24	4348K/L 4349A/B	Albion	C22F	1930	1936
211-22	FM6264-75	Leyland TD1	71538-49	Leyland	L27/24R	1930	1945/53
18	FM 6391	Leyland TD1	71550	Leyland	L27/24R	1930	1953

354/6-68 *were fitted with oil engines between 1945 and 1948.*

The body of **362** *was transferred to* **L14** *in 1944 receiving that of* **L37** *in exchange.*

The bodies of **365/368** *were transferred to* **M14** *and* **M12** *respectively in 1954.*

348-53/69-74 *were rebodied by ECW (DP32R) in 1936/7: the new body numbers were 4535/52/56/43/38/54/46/45/55/37/39/44.*

Some of **375-96** *were equipped with roof racks.*

390/3 *were reseated to B33F in 1950.*

With the exception of **217** *and* **222** *which were destroyed in the Rhyl depot fire of 1945, the second batch of Titans was fitted with oil engines in 1945-8.*

218/9/354 *were equipped to run on producer gas 1943-4.*

18 *was fitted with an oil engine in 1945.*

The Albions may have been an aftermath of LMS influence – Leyland had no small model at the time.

Vehicles acquired by Crosville Motor Services Limited in 1930

All the following vehicles were acquired with the businesses of their former owners.

From W. Edwards, Denbigh (Red Dragon Motor Services) 31st July 1930

604	UN 1712	Chevrolet R	16646	?	B14F	1928	1932
601	UN 2732	GMCT42	422487D	?	B26F	1929	1932
602	MP 6816	GMC	T14	?	B26F	1928	1932?
603	UN 1325	GMC T20C	206669	?	B20F	1928	1932?

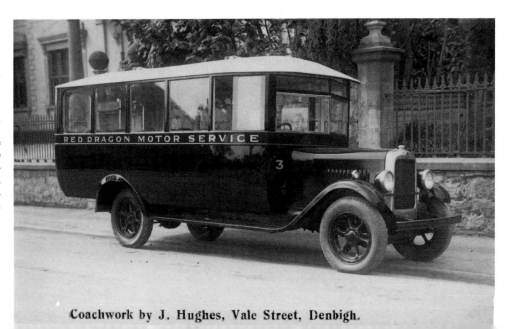

Another 1930 acquisition was Red Dragon of Denbigh. This GMC was typical of Edwards' fleet, used on rural services in the Denbigh area. The bodywork was by J. Hughes, Vale Street, Denbigh, one of numerous local builders of those days. The single rear tyres and size suggest this would be no more than a 20-seater and might have been UN 1325.

Coachwork by J. Hughes, Vale Street, Denbigh.

597	UN 2547	Crossley 2	90026	Hickman	B32F	1929	1932?
598	DT 1521	Merc Benz	?	?	B20F	1928	1932?
599?	FM 3183	Bean 25/30 cwt	?	?	B14F	1926	1930
599?	CA 9491	Dennis 30 cwt	50744	?	B14F	1926	1932?
-	UN 338	Chevrolet R	16646	?	B14F	1927	1930
-	CA 8597	Chevrolet R	16618	?	B14F	1927	1930
-	CC 6657	Chevrolet X	10012	?	B14F	1926	1930
-	CA 6927	GMC T34	342211	?	B14F	1924	1930?

599 *appears to have been duplicated but FM 3183 was known to have been sold by the Company in 1930 and may therefore not have actually borne the number or indeed entered service. The unnumbered vehicles were not used by Crosville Motor Services.*

From C. Burton, (Tarporley Motor Company) Tarporley, 31st July 1930

595	LG 2322	Karrier JKL	?	?	B32R	1929	1931?
596	TU 8783	Karrier OL4	?	?	B26R	1928	1931?
600	TU 4887	Dodge LB	?	?	B20F	1927	1931?

From Llangoed Red Motors, 30th September 1930

605	EY 839	Renault	?	?	B20F	1928	1931?

From Brookes Brothers, White Rose Motor Services, Rhyl 1st May 1930

468	DM 591	Leyland 36M	10611	Simpson/Slater	C26D	1920 [9]	1931
466	DM 1796	Leyland 36C	11233	Leyland	B30R	1920[46]	1931
467	DM 1799	Leyland 36M	10672	Massey	B32R	1920[30]	1931
473	DM 1797	Leyland 36O	10682	Simpson/Str	C26D	1920[11]	1931
470/1	DM 1800/1	Leyland 36M	10688/76	Leyland	Ch32	1920[12/1]	1931
469	DM 643	Leyland 36M	10610	Leyland	Ch26	1920[16]	1931
484	DM 1331	Lancia Z	5772	London Lorries	Ch14	1920[21]	1931
482	DM 2174	Lancia Pentaiota	61	Short	Ch20	1922[19]	1931
481/3	DM 2175/6	Lancia Pentaiota	63/4	Short	Ch20	1922[15/20]	1931
464	DM 1317	Leyland 36S4	3323	Leyland	OH53RO	1916[22]	1931
474	DM 2051	Leyland 36O	10954	Leyland	B36R	1920[24]	1931
495	DM 488	Fiat M2FDKG	173353	?	B8	1920[?]	1931
496	DM 2128	Fiat M2FDKG	174115	?	B8R	1921[?]	1931
449	DM 2123	Leyland 40G6	12373	Leyland	B36R	1921[26]	1931
475	DM 2127	Leyland 36 G8?	22519	Leyland	O52RO	1921[25]	1933
440/1	DM 2583/4	Leyland SG7	12535/6	Leyland	B44D	1923[27/8]	1931
450	DM 2526	Leyland GH6	12537	Leyland	B36R	1923[29]	1931
445/6	DM 3642	Leyland SG7	12822/3	Leyland	OH64D	1924[34/5]	1931
443	DM 2913	Leyland SG7	12662	Leyland	B44D	1923[32]	1931
444	DM 3518	Leyland SG7	12821	Leyland	B44D	1924[33]	1931
447/8	DM 3643/4	Leyland SG7	12824/5 ?	Leyland	OH64D	1924[39]	1931
476	DM 3640	Leyland Z5	25072	Leyland	B24F	1926[37]	1931
485/6	DM 3799/800	Lancia Pen	525/31	?	B24F	1924[41/40]	1931
487	DM 3883	Lancia Pen	524	?	B24F	1924[42]	1931
488	CM 5744	Lancia Pen	614	?	B25R	1925[43]	1931
460-2	DM 4015-7	Leyland C7	35283/69/70	Leyland	B36R	1925[44/7/8]	1932
457-9	DM 4117-9	Leyland C7	35506/499/503	London Lorries	C26D	1925[17/8/4]	1934
453	DM 4019	Leyland SG9	13297	Leyland	B44D	1925	1932
451/2	DM 4014/8	Leyland SG9	13080/296	Leyland	B44D	1924[38/49]	1931
456	DM 4120	Leyland SG11	13380	Leyland	B40R	1925[49]	1931
437	DM 4832	Leyland Lev LG1	50044	Leyland	OH56RO	1926[55]	1934
477-9	DM 3847-9	AEC 505	505006-8	?	B32R	1923[59-61]	1931
454/5	DM 4115/6	Leyland SG9	13298/412	Leyland	B44D	1925[51/2]	1932
480	DM 3850	AEC 503	593966	?	OH56RO	1923[62]	1933
438/9	DM 5256/7	Leyland Lev. LSP1	50059/60	Leyland	OH56RO	1927[56/7]	1934
422	DM 5258	Leyland 29PLSC3	45608	Leyland	B36R	1927[65]	1949
442	DM 2842	Leyland SG7	?	Leyland	B44D	1923[31]	1931
423-7	DM 5259-63	Leyland 29PLSC3	45684-6/45814/5	Leyland	B36R	1927[66-78]	1949
420/1	DM 5977/8	Leyland 29PLSC3	46909/8	Leyland	B36R	1928[94/5]	1949
489	MK 7807	Chevrolet T20	11057	?	B14F	1928 [?]	1931
463	EH 6445	Leyland C7	35391	Leyland	B36R	1925[63]	1931
428	DM 5267	Leyland 29PLSC3	47727	Leyland	B36R	1928[58]	1950
429/30	DM 5842/3	Leyland 29PLSC3	47728/9	Leyland	B36R	1928 [92/3]	1949
415-7	DM 5844-6	Leyland TS2	60450-2	Leyland	B32R	1929[96-8]	1951-3
418/9	DM 6230/1	Leyland TS2	60453/6	Leyland	B32R	1929[99/100]	1952
414	DM 6232	Leyland TD1	70555	Leyland	L27/24RO	1929[101]	1952
431-6	DM 6224-9	Leyland Lioness 6	50257/9/8 60-2	Burlingham	C26D	1929 [2-5/7/8]	1936
465	DM 720	Leyland 36S4	3243	Leyland	OH52RO	1916[23?]	1931

The original Brookes Bros 'White Rose' fleet of Leylands, photographed in 1914. From left to right are DM 721, with hood up; similar DM 722, with hood down; double-deckers DM 719 and 720, and on the right, DM 563 and DM 541. None of these vehicles survived into Crosville ownership, though some registrations of this period were transferred to vehicles that did.

Here DM 719 is seen again, possibly with a private hire party, with passengers from the nearside upper deck seats standing so that they are included in the picture. Two young ladies sit with the driver in the manner which was apt to draw criticism from oficialdom. The body from this vehicle was transferred to a later Leyland chassis. The white livery must have been very difficult to keep clean on such a bus. Note that the company's tour vehicles were described as motor coaches even though that term later tended to imply closed bodywork.

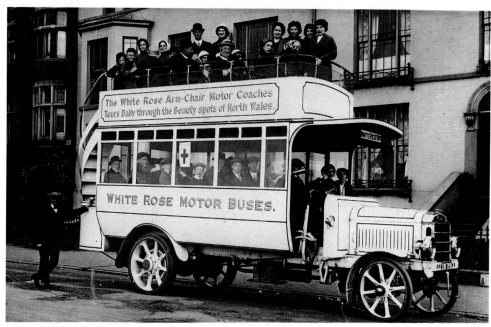

472	DM 1392	Leyland 36O	10182	Leyland	OH?RO	1919[6]	1931
498	DK 1487	Daimler TM30	16899	?	C8	1926	1931
500	LX 7911	Fiat	29086	?	C8F	1919	1931
499	DM 1647	Vauxhall E	2524	?	C8F	1920[?]	1931
497	DM 4834	Buick 26/500	108517	?	B8R	1926[?]	1933
493	DM 4833	S&D Low Ftr	83689	Simpson/Str	B32T	1926 [54?]	1932
494	DM 5266	S&D Low Ftr	67275	Simpson/Str		1928[64]	1952
490-2	DM 6233-5	S&D Low Ftr	99853/2/4	Simpson/Str		1929[71-3]	1938

The numbers in square brackets are the Brookes Bros fleet numbers. Where none is shown the vehicle may not have entered Crosville service.

The following were reseated at various times:

466- *B26R*, **467** -*B29R*, **470/1**- *Ch28*, **481-3** -*Ch18*, **464**- *OH44RO*, **4603/72/4** - *B30R*, **465/75**- *OH46RO*, **440/1/4/7-8/51-5** -*B40D*, **450** -*B32R*, **476**- *B20F*, **480** -*OH54RO*, **431-6** -*C30D*. **420-30** *were rebodied by ECOC (B32F) in 1935/6: Body numbers were, in fleet number order 3863/46/905/1/879//94/82/902/883/95/92.*

415-9 *were rebodied by ECW (DP32R) in 1936/7: The new body numbers were 4551/33/62/50/7. 415/6/9 were further rebodied by Burlingham (UB34F) in 1943. The ECW bodies displaced were transferred to KA 169-71 respectively.*

414 *had its staircase enclosed by Massey Brothers in 1936.* **417/8** *towed producer gas trailers 1943-5.*

Inevitably the Brookes fleet was absorbed into mainstream Crosville activities. Although new in 1929 as No. 101 with open staircase, DM 6232 is seen in Hoylake in May 1949 as L63. It still had a further three years' service to give at this stage and apart from the enclosure of the staircase by Massey Bros. in 1936, is remarkably unaltered, though the half-drop opening windows replacing the Leyland TD1 standard full-drop type implies a body rebuild.

648 VAUXHALL BRIDGE ROAD,
S.W.1.

LMS CROSVILLE MOTOR SERVICES

BY THE
Famous "TIGER" Saloon Coach Service

LONDON to BIRKENHEAD DAILY

Via OXFORD — STRATFORD-ON-AVON — CREWE — CHESTER

12/-
SINGLE

AT
EXCEPTIONALLY LOW
WINTER FARES

20/-
RETURN

Guaranteed Seats. —— Well Lighted Coaches.
Warm Rugs Provided for each Passenger.
A Journey with the Interest of a Tour through
the Heart of Historic England.

BOOK with L M S CROSVILLE and enjoy
the Finest Facilities the Road offers.

A handbill produced in 1929/30 after the LMS takeover, showing the oval logo and promoting the benefits of travelling with LMS Crosville. It is noteworthy that the Leyland Tiger coach fleet is given pride of place at the 'top of the bill' and again lower down — lest anyone missed the point. Advance booking facilities and information were available from the Central London Road Transport Station, Crescent Place, Cartwright Gardens, London WC1.

DM 5844 was a Leyland Tiger TS2 delivered to Brookes as number 96. Renumbered by Crosville to 415 it gained the ubiquitous ECW body in 1936 but subsequently was fitted with this Burlingham utility body in 1943. It is seen here on home territory at Rhyl in 1950. Although Crosville had adopted the Tilling standard destination display with some enthusiasm in the post-1946 period, contriving to fit it to so many vehicles without regard to appearance, this contemporary example went to the other extreme, the displays were overpainted !

From North Wales Silver Motors Ltd, Llandudno 1st August 1930

113/4	CC 440/1	Dennis	12888/946	?	Ch18/22	1921	1930
109	CC 5275	Guy B	B1761	?	Ch22	1924	1930
110	CC 4725	Guy J	J4502	?	Ch14	1924	1930
99	VT 2653	T/Stevens B10B	5961	?	C26	1929	1948
115	CC 1807	Dennis	12850	?	B32	1921	1931
105	CC 2287	Daimler CK	3686	?	B24F	1920	1931
119	CY 4969	Dennis	?	?	Ch26	1925	1931
106	CC 4762	Guy B	B22166	?	B31F	1927	1932
108	E 7162	Guy O	?	?	B14	1922	1932
111	EH 6314	Karrier HH	9028	?	B30F	1925	1930
116	EH 2559	Dennis	12341	?	Ch26	1921	1930
107	EH6070	Guy B	B1618	?	B25F	1925	1930
125	EH 8987	Dennis 4 Ton	45464	?	B32F	1927	1931
104	CC 8611	T/Stevens B10A	6466	Dickson	B35F	1929	1936
100/1	CC 8607/8	T/Stevens B10A	6359/7	Buckingham	B34F/B32F	1929	1936
120	EH 9137	Dennis 4 Ton	45469	?	B32F	1927	1936
124	EH 8967	Dennis 4 Ton	45761	?	B32F	1927	1931
122	EH 8951	Dennis 4 Ton	45460	?	B32F	1926	1931
123	EH 9425	Dennis 4 Ton	45489	?	B32F	1927	1931
118	RF 1096	Dennis 2½Ton	?	?	?	1925	1931
112	EH 7094	Karrier KL	5529	?	?	1925	1931
117	ON 1184	Dennis 2½Ton	45161	?	B32	1925	1931
102/3	CC 8609/10	T/Stevens B10A	6366/5	Buckingham	B32F	1929	1936
121	RF 3265	Dennis E	17171	?	B32F	1927	1932

99 *was evidently rebuilt as forward-control and was rebodied by ECOC (B32F) 1936: The new body, numbered 3940, was transferred to* **KA 168** *in 1940.*

From H. C. Pascoe, Tarporley 31st January 1931

-	MA 8176	Fiat	?	?	B14	?	1931?

It is unlikely that this vehicle was operated by Crosville and no fleet number O known.

From Llandudno Coaching and Carriage Co Ltd (Royal Blue) 18th February 1931

511	HA 3512	SOS S	269	Brush	B32F	1926	1933
512-6	CC 6821-5	SOS Q	385/91/9/ 426/48	Brush	B37F	1927	1933
517-30	CC 7741-54	SOS QL	608/19/34/ 46/7/52-4/48/ 66/81/4/7/734	Brush	B35F	1928	1934
531/2	CC 8185/6	SOS QL	788/98	Ransomes	B37F	1928	1934
533-8	CC 8561-6	SOS M	963/9/76/ 90/2/1000	Ransomes	B34F	1929	1936
547	CA 8709	Leyland C7	35939	?	B26	1926	1931
548	CA 8863	Leyland C7	41653	?	B26	1926	1931

The business of Llandudno Blue was added to Crosville in 1931 and this Brush-bodied SOS QLC was added to stock as No. 587 (CC 9284) It was successively numbered Q12 and Q1 and it is as the latter that it is seen in 1949, its year of withdrawal. Its position here, parked alongside a Leyland Cub, almost gives the illusion of being rebuilt to forward-control, but it remained 'bonneted' to the end.

555	KC 6303	Dennis 2½Ton	25058	?	Ch19	1923	1931
556	CC 3872	Dennis 3 Ton	13463	?	B25F	1923	1931
557/8	CC 3967/8	Dennis	30789/90?	?	B29F	1923	1931
559	CC 4839	Dennis 2½Ton	30789?	?	B29F	1924	1931
501	CC 4537	SOS S	4014	Brush	B32F	1924	1933
502/3	CC 4538/9	SOS ODD	4024/7	UAS	B26F	1924	1933
574-7	HL 2032-5	Bristol O 2T	0214/2/5/8	?	B20F	1924	1931
578/9	EY 2741/2	Bristol O 2T	0257/8	?	B20F	1924	1931
560	CC 4840	Dennis 2½Ton	30790	?	B30F	1924	1931
504	CC 4816	SOS S	4030	Brush	B32F	1924	1933
505	CC 5076	SOS S	38 ?	Brush	B32F	1925	1933
506	CC 5077	SOS ODD	58	UAS	B26F	1925	1933
507/8	CC 6121/2	SOS ODD	216/47	UAS	B26F	1926	1933
509	CC 6123	SOS S	248	Ransomes	B31F	1926	1933
510	CC 6424	SOS ODD	271	UAS	B26F	1926	1933
561	CC 6617	SOS 30cwt	50867	?	B19F	1926	1931
562	KA 4533	SOS 30cwt	50851	?	B19F	1926	1931
563	KA 4602	SOS 30cwt	50895	?	B19F	1926	1931
564	CC 7114	SOS 30cwt	51626	?	B20F	1926	1931
565/6	CC 7115/6	SOS 30cwt E	17230/26	?	Ch26	1927	1931
580/1	CC 7412/3	Guy EW	22059/433	?	B24/6F	1927	1931
567-70	CC 7980-3	Dennis G	70080/90/144/7	Vickers	B20F	1928	1934
571-3	CC 8787-9	Dennis G	70514/20/2	Vickers	B20F	1929	1934
582	KB 8317	Daimler CK	22/331	?	B23	1920?	1931
583/4	CC 6920/1	SOS QC	359/60	London Lorries	Ch32	1927	1936
585/6	CC 7862/3	SOS QLC	707/8	Brush	Ch29	1928	1936
587/8	CC 9284/5	SOS QLC	1323/31	Brush	Ch29	1930	1949
589-91	CC 3706-8	Dennis 2½Ton	25062/7/70	Dennis	Ch20	1923	1931
592	CC 6162	Dennis 2½Ton	25193	London Lorries	Ch24	1925	1934
593	CC 9232	Renault MY	191212	?	Ch14	1926	1931
594	CC 7411	Unic '1927' ?	22550	?	Ch14	1927	1931

511 *had been built for BMMO but was diverted after registration but before use.*

502/3/6-8/10 *had all been rebuilt from SOS 'S' types in May 1930. The original bodies were by Brush 502/3/6/10, BMMO's own Carlyle works (507) or Ransomes (508).*

583-8/92 *carried 'Royal Blue' titles in Crosville service.*

From Z. Woodfin, Tarvin 2nd February 1931

632	TU 4675	Vulcan 3XB	25	?	B20F	1927	1932
633	MB 9425	Vulcan VWB	341	?	B30F	1925	1932
634	MB 3536	Vulvan VSD	611	?	B25	1923	1931

All subsequent new vehicles from 1st May 1930 until 1989 were delivered to Crosville Motor Services Limited.

New vehicles delivered 1931

Number 635 (FM 6851) was a Weymann-bodied Leyland KP2 Cub delivered in 1931. The 'K' in the vehicle designation signifies that it was built at Leyland's Kingston upon Thames factory. The model had a 4.4-litre side-valve petrol engine.

19/20/1	FM 6392-4	Leyland TD1	71550-2	Leyland	L24/24R	2/31	1945-51
43-60	FM 6395-412	Leyland TD1	71553-71	Leyland	L27/24R	2-5/31	1945/53
551-4	FM 6413-6	Leyland TD1	71746-9	Leyland	L27/24R	5/31	1953/55
195/6	FM 6417/8	Leyland LT2	51289/90	Leyland	B35F	-/31	1950
440-50	FM 6419-26	Leyland LT2	51291-8	Leyland	B35F	5/31	1949-52
464-79	FM 6427-38	Leyland LT2	51299-310	Leyland	B35F	5/31	1949-52
539-44	FM 6439-44	Leyland LT2	51313-8	Leyland	B35F	5/31	1949-51
607-10	FM 6445-48	Leyland TS3	61439-42	Leyland	DP31F	5/31	1951/52/55
611-6	FM 6449-54	Leyland TS3	61443-48	Leyland	DP25D	5/31	1951-53
617-20	FM 6455-58	Leyland TS3	61600/436/ 636/437	UAS	C27R	5/31	1951-52
621/2	FM 6470/1	Leyland TS3	61598/9	UAS	C27R	5/31	1951/52
623-5	FM 6480-2	Leyland TS3	61435/637/ 4378	UAS	C27R	5/31	1952-53
545/6	FM 6473/4	Leyland LT2	51419/20	Leyland	B35R	-/31	1950
549/50	FM 6475/6	Leyland LT2	51421/2	Leyland	B35R	-/31	1952
484	FM 6477	Leyland LT2	51411	Leyland	B35R	5/31	1950
500	FM 6478	Leyland LT2	51412	Leyland	B35R	-/31	1950
582	FM 6479	Leyland LT2	51423	Leyland	B35R	-/31	1934
629-31	FM 6486-88	GMC T30C	308362/443/5	?	B20F	-/31	1934
635	FM 6851	Leyland KP2	217	Weymann	B20F	-/31	1941
105-16	FM 6861-71	Leyland LT3	51692-702	Leyland	B32F	9-10/31	1949-50/57
626-8	FM 6459-61	S&D L/F	161252 191253 181254	S/S	B32T	-/31	1952-53
606	FM 6472	Daimler CH6	68000	UAS	B35F	5/31	1938

629-31 *had been ordered by Edwards (Red Dragon) Denbigh prior to takeover in 1930.*

20/21/43-60/551 *were fitted with oil engines in 1945.*

552-4 *were fitted with oil engines in 1935.*

52 *was rebodied with a 1930 Leyland body ex **L56** in 1944. Its own body was transferred to **L37**.*

553/4 *were rebodied by ECW in 1949 (L27/26R): The new bodies were numbered 3075/7 of series 2. The new body on* **553** *was removed in November 1950 and transferred to M503. The new body on* **554** *was transferred to MB161 in May 1956.*

442/9/71/549/50 *were reseated to B30 in 1950.*

607-25 *were rebodied by ECW (DP32R) between 1936 and 1939. The new bodies were numbered 4540/47/59/60/6069/70/3/4/1/6/67/78/68/ 66/75/71/80/72/79.*

611/6/8 *were converted for producer gas operation 1943-5.*

607/8/105-13/15-7 *were fitted with perimeter seats for 30 1943-5.*

606 *was fitted with a Leyland 5.7 litre oil engine in November 1934.*

112 *was converted to OB36F in 1951 as a member of the 'Boat' class.*

New Vehicles delivered 1932

The KP series Cub continued to be favoured for a number of years and 1932 saw the arrival of this slightly longer KP3. This Brush-bodied variant was fitted with 26 seats. Many of these vehicles had extremely long lives, lasting until 1949/50 in many instances. A few were even painted up to masquerade as coaches in the post-1945 effort to meet the pent-up demand for excursions etc, the well-rounded lines helping a little in this regard. Number 719, registered FM 7446 is seen ready for delivery, using Crosville trade plates. The trade plate 044 FM was to serve the company for many years – virtually until disolution.

118-36	FM 6873-91	Leyland LT3	51704-22	Leyland	B32F	1/32	1950/52/57
182-91	FM 6892-901	Leyland LT3	51723-32	Leyland	B32F	-/32	1949/52/57
481-3	FM 6902-4	Leyland LT3	51733-5	Leyland	B32F	5-6/32	1949-50
555-60	FM 6905-10	Leyland LT3	51736-41	Leyland	B32F	-/32	1949-50
650-64	FM 6981-95	Leyland LT3	51690/1 51749-62	Leyland	B32F	5-6/32	1949-50/57
680-9	FM 7008-12/ 33-37	Leyland LT3	252/3/348 /50/708-12	Leyland	B32F	5-6/32	1949-50/57
645	FM 6916	Leyland TD2	131	Leyland	L27/24R	4-5/32	1954
646-9	FM 6917-20	Leyland TD2	125-8	Leyland	L27/24R	4-5/32	1955-6
702/3	FM 7233/4	Leyland TD2	1390/1	Leyland	L27/24R	6/32	1954/56
733-40	FM 7460-7	Leyland TD2	2003-6,1870-3	Leyland	L27/24R	10-1/32	1954-56
636-9	FM 6852-5	Leyland KP2	218-21	Weymann	B20F	-/32	1941/50
665-74	FM 6996-7005	Leyland KP2	242-51	Weymann	B20F	-/32	1941-50
677-9	FM 7040-2	Leyland KP2	389-91	Weymann	B20F	-/32	1941-50
704	FM 7431	Leyland KP2	708	Brush	B20F	-/32	1941
708	FM 7435	Leyland KP2	974	Brush	B20F	-/32	1941
710-2	FM 7437-9	Leyland KP2	976-8	Brush	B20F	-/32	1950
718	FM 7445	Leyland KP2	984	Brush	B20F	-/32	1950
166-70	FM 6856-60	Leyland TS4	103-7	Leyland	B32F	5-6/32	1952-53
640-4	FM 6911-15	Leyland TS4	109/12/8/10/1	UAS	C26F	5-7/32	1941/53
699-701	FM 7230-2	Leyland LT5	1392-4	Weymann	B32F	-/32	1950
751	FM 7478	Leyland LT5	1949	ECOC	B32F	-/32	1950
719-23	FM 7446-50	Leyland KP3	906-10	Brush	B26F	-/32	1949-50
725-30	FM 7452-9	Leyland KP3	966-71	Brush	B26F	-/32	1949-50

The Lion had moved on to the LT3, similar to the LT2 but longer, and Crosville placed a total of 75 in service, later to become the E class, thought to be the largest of this type in the country. The style of Leyland single-deck body had altered during 1930 to this less angular pattern, with very characteristic curved tops to the windows, this combination being the most typical Crosville single-deck bus dating from the early 'thirties. Despite the 27ft 6in length, seating capacity had been reduced one more to 32 and, with much improved interior trim, these were quite 'civilised' buses. Most remained in service until 1949-50, but a few even longer and six, including 682 (FM 7010), later E68, dating from 1932 seen here, were converted to open-topped 'boats' for Rhyl sea-front service, lasting until 1957.

118/21/23/4/6/8-35/82/4/5/7/9/483/556/8-60 *were all converted to longtitudinal seating for 30 1942/3: Some reverted to standard later.*

660 *received the 1933 Leyland B30F body of* **F37** *in 1950.*

183/651/660 *were converted to OB36F in 1951 (Boat Class)*

189 *received the ECOC B32R body from FA2 in 1950*

646 *by then oil-engined as M23, completed a million miles in January 1949, an event celebrated by the company.*

636/8/9/66/7/71/3/4 *were painted in cream/green livery in June 1946 to relieve pressure on the coach fleet.*

166-70 *were rebodied ECW (DP28*/ 32R) in 1939. The new body numbers were 6061*/57/60*/62*/58 in order.*

The original body of **167** *was fitted to* **W2** *(BU 8787) in 10/38.*

640-4 *were rebodied by Burlingham (C32F) in 1940 and fitted with oil engines in 1950 (KA class).*

643 *passed to Wilts and Dorset in 1941 and back to Crosville in 1947. The original ECOC body had been upseated to 33 at some time.*

702 *received the 1929 Leyland L27/24R body of* **M579** *(EK 8115) in 6/53.*

699-701 *other sources quote Leyland bodywork.*

From J. Williams (Bethesda Greys), Rachub 1st January 1932

690	CC 7998	Vulcan VWBL	28	?	B30	1928	1932
691	TE 642	Vulcan VWB	411	?	B30	1927	1932
692	TD 9572	Vulcan VWB	12	?	B30	1927	1932
693	TD 7660	Vulcan VWB	16	?	B30	1926	1932
694	CC 7740	Vulcan VWB	19	?	B26	1927	1932
695	CC 6942	Vulcan VWB	373	?	B26	1927	1932?
696	EC 7714	Vulcan 3x	1336	?	B18	1927	1932
697	CC 8692	Vulcan Duke	37	?	C20	1929	1932
698	CC 6288	Vulcan VWB	3	?	C25	1926	1932
-	FY 8011	Vulcan ?	?		B26	1925	1932?
-	WU 7948	Vulcan VSD	1777	?	B20	1926	1932?
-	CC 7244	Chevrolet LM	16534	?	-14-	1927	1932?
-	CC 6457	Chevrolet X	8976	?	-14-	1926	1932?

The unnumbered vehicles were probably not operated.

Seen in 1948 is Leyland coach-bodied TS4 FM 7468, new as 741 in 1934. A few of the coach lines can still be seen although the crude application of bus livery does little for its appearance. By the time of this photograph, the vehicle was numbered K68 but upon fitment of an ECW body and diesel engine in 1949, it became KA 189. A sister vehicle is shown in pristine condition on page 73.

This Titan TD2 was new in 1933 as No. 791. Fitted with an oil engine in the post-1945 period, it was still remarkably unaltered in appearance, even after being righted after an overturning accident in Birkenhead in 1947. The severing of the roof pillars can be clearly seen although the overall deformation was not as great as might have been expected timber breaking rather than bending. The external design of the Titan had altered little since 1929, even though beefed-up mechanically.

New vehicles delivered 1933

707	FM 7434	Leyland KP2	711	Brush	B20F	-/33	1941
709	FM 7436	Leyland KP2	975	Brush	B20F	-/33	1941
713-7	FM 7440-4	Leyland KP2	979-83	Brush	B20F	-/33	1950/52
724	FM 7451	Leyland KP3	965	Brush	B26F	-/33	1947
731/2	FM 7458/9	Leyland KP3	972/3	Brush	B26F	-/33	1950/47
741-5	FM 7468-72	Leyland TS4	2051-5	Leyland	C32R	4/33	1958
746-50	FM 7473-7	Leyland TS4	2056-60	ECOC	C26/21R	5/33	1951-52
752-70	FM 7479-97	Leyland LT5	1950-68	ECOC	B32F	5/33	1945-55
771-90	FM 7498-517	Leyland LT5	1972-90	Leyland	B32F	-/33	1938/50-52
791-4	FM 7760-3	Leyland TD2	2389-91/2697	Leyland	L24/24R	5/33	1954/57
795	FM 7764	Leyland TD2c	2740	Leyland	L24/24R	5/33	1954
934-6	FM 6276-8	Leyland TD3	3223-5	ECOC	L26/26R	10/33	1955-6
937-49	FM 6279-91	Leyland KP3	2050-62	Brush	B26F	-/33	1937-50
950-55	FM 6292-7	Leyland KP2	2042-9	Tooth	B20F	-/33	1941/45/50
956/7	FM 6298/9	Leyland KP2	2038/9	Roberts	B20F	-/33	1950
958-61	FM 8015-8	Leyland KP2	2040-3	Roberts	B20F	-/33	1945/50
1000	AMD 256	AEC Q	761002	Metro Camm	H33/27F	-/33	1945

Another long-lived batch of vehicles comprised the 1933 Leyland/ Eastern Counties TS4 coaches. Seen here when new is No. 748 (FM 7474). The lack of destination box was logical in view of Crosville's attitude to this item, but gave an odd look to an otherwise well-proportioned coach.

Above and Upper Right: The AEC Q made an appearance in the Crosville fleet in 1933 and the sole representative of the double-deck version in the fleet had a remarkably long life, surviving until 1945. AMD 256 was given the highest fleet number ever to be found on a Crosville vehicle, 1000. These two views show the key features of the design, the easy entry step under the clear supervision of the driver made possible by the offside mounted engine. This was the first double-deck example, following the prototype of late 1932 – it was completed before the TD2 batch shown opposite, yet the obvious advance in appearance is immense. The vehicle had a six-cylinder petrol engine which was coupled to a Daimler-built preselective gearbox which was vacuum-operated. The short rear overhang was due to the use of single tyres on the rear axle.

The year 1933's selection of Cubs brought No. 955 (FM 6297) into the fleet. Recorded in the Company's records as being Brush-bodied this photograph strongly suggests Charles T. W. Tooth of Wrexham to have been its bodybuilder. Physical differences would certainly support the contention. Note that this and other late 1933 vehicles had registration numbers reserved in 1930, but not then used.

741-5 *were fitted with oil engines in 1939.* **747-50** *were reseated to C32R in 1948.*

755 *was rebodied ECW (B33R) in 1949. The new body was numbered 3122/2. The original body was fitted to* **E39**.

791/4 *were fitted with oil engines in 1935.*

795 *was fitted with a gearbox in lieu of the torque convertor 1935. It also had free wheel gear until 1935.*

935/6 *were fitted with Leyland bodies ex M167/M225 in 1954. That from M167 was L27/24R from 1931. That from M225 was L24/24R from 1930.*

The registered numbers FM 6276-99 had been reserved in 1930 – for Leyland TD1s.

From Western Transport Co Ltd, Wrexham 1st May 1933

801-6	FM 3533-8	Daimler CM	4502/4/6/8/10/2	Brush	B31F	1925	1933
807-12	CA 7842-7	Daimler CM	4514/6/8/20/2/4	Brush	B31F	1925	1933
813/4	CA 8537/8	Daimler CM	4594/5		B31F	1926	1933
817-9	FM 4504/3/1	Daimler CF6	7238/28/30	Brush	B32F	1929	1934
815	FM 4505	Daimler CF6	7260	Brush	B32F	1927	1934
828	FM 4502	Daimler CF6	7242	Brush	B32F	1927	1934
816	UN 188	Daimler CF6	7224	Brush	B32F	1927	1934
820-2	UN 186/90/1	Daimler CF6	7240/32/4	Brush	B32F	1927	1934
823-6	UN 209-12	Daimler CF6	7219/05/17/03	Brush	Ch27	1927	1933

827/9	UN 187/9	Daimler CF6	7226/36	Brush	B32F	1927	1934
832/0/1/3/4	FM 4753-7	ADC 423	423017-21	Brush	B32F	1928	1934
835-9	UN 952-6	ADC 423	423029-33	Brush	B32F	1928	1934/37
844-7	FM 5268/70 /69/71	T/Stevens B10A	6375/9/6/80	Alexander	B32F	1929	1938
848-51	FM5782-4/91	T/Stevens B10A	6702-5	Brush	B32F	1930	1938
852-7	FM 6523-8	T/Stevens B10A2	8528-33	Brush	B32F	1931	1938
879-88	FM 7057-66	T/Stevens	8065-74	Brush	B32F	1932	1949
840-3	UN 1914/6 /5/7	T/Stevens B10A	6377/81/78/82	Alexander	Ch31	1929	1938
858-67	UN 4479-88	T/Stevens B10A2	8534-43	Brush	B32F	1931	1938
868-78	UN5390-400	T/Stevens B10A2	8054-64	Brush	B32F	1932	1949
889-93	UN 2920-24	Chevrolet LQ	56047/464 382/474/025	Rainforth &Sons	B20F	1929	1934
894	UV 9415	Guy OND	9139	Duple	B20F	1929	1933
895	YF 5746	Guy FBB	22351	Vickers	B32R	1927	1933
896	YE 7312	Guy FBB	22259	Hall Lewis	B32R	1927	1933
897	UK 5814	Guy FBB	22954	Guy	B32R	1928	1933
898	YV 1125	Thornycroft	15761	Vickers	B18F	1928	1933
899	YX 1529	Thornycroft A1	15770	Vickers	B18F	1928	1933
900	UC 5510	Thornycroft A1	15759	GWR	B18F	1928	1933
901	YW 5970	Thornycroft A1	15767	GWR	B18F	1928	1933
902	UL 4052	Thornycroft A1	15768	?	B18F	1929	1933
903/4	UV 4079/82	Thornycroft A1	18815/22	Vickers	B26R	1929	1934
905-7	YH 3798/9/5	Maudslay ML3	4098/7/9	Buckingham	C32F	1927	1933
908/9	YV1118/7197	Maudslay ML3	4276/82	Vickers	B32R	1928	1933
910/2	YV 8573/2	Maudslay ML3	4283/78	Buckingham	C34F	1928	1933
911	UC 7508	Maudslay ML3	4268	Buckingham	B32R	1928	1933
913/5	UU 4818/9	Maudslay ML3B	4681/2	Vickers	B32R	1929	1934/33
914	UL 8384	Maudslay ML3B	4588	Vickers	B32R	1929	1933
916	UU 4812	Maudslay ML3B	4618	Vickers	B32R	1929	1933
917/20	GU 6355/6	Maudslay ML3B	4604/8	Vickers	B32R	1929	1933
918/9	UL8385/9	Maudslay ML3B	4589/93	Vickers	B32R	1929	1933
921-4	UU5014/3/2/0	Morris R	1828/7/6/15	Buckingham	B14F	1929	1935
925	UN 3186	Dodge	D216256	?	B24	1929	1933
926	UN 2338	Dodge	D200499	?	B14?	1929	1933
927	UN 1680	Dodge	D174130	?	B14?	1929	1933
928	UN 2302	Dodge	D194814	?	B14?	1929	1933
929	UN 2368	Dodge	D196850	?	B14?	1929	1933
930	UN 1679	Dodge	D172426	?	B14	1929	1933
931	UN 3834	Dodge	D222025	?	B26F	1930	1933
932	UN 3040	Dodge	D214639	?	B20	1929	1933
933	UN 1833	Dodge	D2B5586?	?	C20	1927	1933

From Jones Brothers, Aberystwyth 1933

Six vehicles were acquired from Jones Brothers. No record of their identity is known to the Author(s) and it can be assumed they were not operated by Crosville.

New vehicles delivered 1934.

900/1	FM 8133/4	Leyland LT5A	4278/9	Leyland	B34F	9/34	1961
902-14	FM 8135-47	Leyland LT5A	4265/4/ 6/8-77	ECOC	B32F	5/34	1959-61
915	FM 8148	Leyland LT5A	4267	Tooth	B34F	5/34	1961
916-23	FM 8149-56	Leyland TD3	4256-63	ECOC	L26/26R	5/34	1957
924-9	FM 8157-62	Leyland SKP3	2692/3/ 20-23	Brush	B30F	-/34	1950
930-3	FM 8163-6	Leyland TS6	4280/6-8	Harrington	C33F	3/34	1953
962-6	FM 8167-70 /8270	Leyland TS6	4281-5	Duple	C32R	5/34	1941/53
981-4	FM 8412-5	Leyland LT5A	4684-7	ECOC	B32F	7/34	1958-60
985-8	FM 8416-19	Leyland KP3	2833-6	Brush	B26F	-/34	1949-50
989-92	FM 8420-3	Leyland KP2	2828-31	Brush	B20F	-/34	1942/50
582	FM 8424	Leyland LT5A	4789	Tooth	B34F	7/34	1960

900 *was rebodied by Burlingham in 1943 (UB34F):This body was transferred to H10 in 1949.*

900-15/81-4 *were rebodied by Burlingham (B35F) in 1949 and converted to oil engines. The new body numbers were 3845-54/3829/30/20-7 in fleet number order.*

965-6 *originally C24R*

FM 8151 was a 1934 Titan TD3 with remarkably modern looking Eastern Counties bodywork. The transformation in appearance of this batch, and the similar buses of October 1933, from the TD2 with traditional-style Leyland body of earlier in 1933 was immense.

Some Duple bodied TS6 formed part of the 1934 delivery of coaches. Number 964 (FM 8169) had an interesting career being sold to Wilts and Dorset in 1941, yet being bought back in 1946. It is seen here as K84 in 1950 but it was not yet in its final guise as it subsequently became KA 199 with an oil engine and the 1936 Harrington body from K 107.

Deliveries of Leyland Cubs with Brush 26-seat body continued and this 1934 example 986 (FM 8417) is seen renumbered as N76. Clearly looking its years, it is seen at Birkenhead Woodside in 1950. Quite apart from the bald tyres clearly on view, the front seat passengers seem somewhat vulnerable to being hurled out of the bus due to the lack of a decency screen behind the entrance!

*The original bodies of **910/4** were tranferred to H3/8 respectively in 1949.*

916-20/22/3 *were rebodied post 1945 by ECW (see below).*

932/3/62/4 *were converted to oil engines in 1949 and 962/4 received the Harrington C32F bodies from K108/7 in 1952.* ***932-62-4*** *were sold to the army in 1941 and repurchased in 1946.*

Vehicles acquired with various businesses during 1934.

From James Rothwell, Holt 1st January 1934

977/8	UC 1816/7	Maudslay ML3	4030/29	Hall Lewis	B30R	1928	1934
979	CK 3751	Maudslay	3856	?	B26F	1927	1934
976	TE 7675	Crossley Eagle	90039	?	C30F	1929	1934
980	DK 1483	Reo	1989	?	DP20R	1926	1934

From John Evans (Seiont Motors), Caernarfon 1st January 1934

967	JC 1343	Leyland TS3	2963	Massey	C32R	7/33	1957
968	JC 200	Leyland TS1	61786	Leyland	B32F	6/31	1952
969	CC 9401	Leyland TS2	60704	Leyland	B32F	4/30	1952
970/1	CC 8531/2	Leyland LT1	50137/316	Leyland	B30F	1929	1936
972	CC 8021	Leyland 29PLSC3	46939	Leyland	B32F	1928	1949
973	CC 7449	Leyland 29PLSC3	45857	Leyland	B30F	1927	1949
974	CC 8879	Albion PR28	7046J	Leyland	C30D	1929	1935
975	CC 9592	Morris Y6	075	?	-20-	1930	1935

968/9 *were rebodied ECW (DP32R) in 1937/6 respectively. The new bodies were numbered 4561/32.*

972/3 *were rebodied ECOC (B32F/B30F) in 1935/6. The new bodies were numbered 3855 and 3931.*

967 *was involved in the post 1945 rebodying exercise – see below.*

From H.M. Robinson t/a Wirral Motor Transport Company 10th February 1934

980	BG 605	AEC Regal	6621175	Duple	C32R	1932	1952

980 *was rebodied by ECW (DP32R) in 1939. The new body was numbered 6082*

From Nevin Blue Motors 15th February 1934

87	MY 1415	AEC Reliance	660371	Short Bros	B30D	1929	1936
88	UL 7229	T/Stevens B10A	5846	Tooth (1934)	B32F	1930	1938
-	CC 9340	Chevrolet	1192877	?	-16-	1930	1934
-	CC 8141	Graham Dodge	G85119	?	-20-	1928	1934

It is unlikely that the unnumbered vehicles entered service with Crosville.

From D. J. Williams, Mynytho 15th February 1934

-	TE 2021	Maudslay	4152	?	B30	1927	1934
-	MW 6989	Lancia	?	?	?	1927	1934

It is likely that neither vehicle entered service with Crosville.

From the Tocia Motor Omnibus Co Ltd, Aberdaron 17th February 1934

89	GJ 8075	Commer 6TK	28055	Grose	B19F	1930	1934
90	JC 690	Commer Corinthian	28312	Grose	C24F	1932	1934
91	JC 691	Commer Invader 6TK	28302	Grose	B20F	1932	1934
92	CC 9415	GMC T60	921D	Strachan	B26F	1930	1934
93	CC 9578	Morris Y86	076	Grose	B20F	1930	1935
94	CC 8048	Chevrolet	CAP25	London Lorries	B14F	1928	1934
-	CC 5516	Thornycroft	11856	?	-18-	1925	1934
-	CC 5313	Thornycroft	11251	?	-20-	1925	1934
-	CC 9414	GMC	1709D	?	B26F	1930	1934
-	RP 9295	Chevrolet U	67439	?	?	1930 ?	1934
-	YW 6381	ADC 416	416934	?	Ch32	1928	1934
-	CC 5424	Bean	2345	?	-14-	1925	1934
-	CC 6522	AEC 414	414045	?	-26-	1926	1934
-	CC 6277	Karrier GL	35013	?	-29-	1928	1934

It is likely that the unnumbered vehicles did not enter service with Crosville.

Tocia was one of the oldest established bus businesses in North Wales having been established, with horses of course, in 1881.

From S. Jackson and Sons, Malbank Services, Crewe 26th June 1934

137	VR 8862	Crossley Condor	90428	Crossley	L48R	1930	1935
138/9	LG 2367/6	Crossley Six	90207/6	Crossley	B32F	1929	1935
140	LG 2690	Crossley Six	90256	Burlingham	B32F	1930	1935
141	LG 7194	Crossley Six	90286	Crossley	B32F	1931	1935
142	TY 5999	Daimler CF6	7161S	?	B26	1929	1935
143	LG 2610	Leyland TS2	60377	Burlingham	B28	10/29	1952

143 *was rebodied by ECW (DP32R) in 1937. The new body number was 4563.*

The business of Seoint Motors brought nine vehicles into Crosville's fleet including this Massey-bodied TS6 coach, No. 967 alias K87. It was rebodied in 1949 by ECW again changing its fleet number to KA194 to signify an oil engine.

From T. O. Maddocks, Tattenhall 1st July 1934

146	WM 3899	Vulcan VWBL	43	?	B32F	1929	1934
147	VM 7980	Vulcan		?	B32	1929	1934
148	LG 212	Vulcan		?	B31	1929	1934
149	WM 386	Vulcan	?	?	B30	1927	1934
150	LG 2558	Vulcan VWBL	41	?	B32	1929	1934
151	RF 4697	Vulcan	?	?	B35	1928	1934
152	VO 729	Dennis G	?	?	B30	1929	1934
153	KF 512	Gilford 166OT	?	?	B30	1930	1934

From H. Lowe & Son, Audlem 1st August 1934

144	LG 5003	Vulcan 3X6	52	?	B20F	1930	1934
145	WM 5621	Vulcan VWBDS	?	?	B30R	1930	1934

From R. Jenkinson, Buckley 19th September 1934

154	DM 5780	Dennis G	70000	Griffith	B20	1927	1934
155	DM 5791	Dennis F	52281	Short	B18	1927	1935
156	DM 6717	Dennis F	55008	Griffith	B17	1929	1935

From Macdonald & Company, (Maxways) Birkenhead 1st December 1934

T6-9	BG 207-10	AEC Regal	6621027-30	Duple	C30F	1931	1952
T10-5	BG 613-8	AEC Regal	6621179-84	Massey	C32R	1932	1952-53

These fleet numbers were from the 1935 scheme yet allocated to 1934 acquisitions: Whether any 1934 numbers were issued is not known.

T6-15 *were rebodied by ECW in 1939: The new body numbers were 6093/5/4/0/84/8/5/9/1/6 in fleet number order.*

1935 Renumbering Scheme

By 1935 the original numbering scheme had become badly fragmented, both in respect of acquired vehicles and, more strangely, for new vehicles. The 1935 scheme allocated a letter to each type and each class had its own number series starting from 1. Strangely, although every Lion model had a separate letter, all the Tigers were grouped as K.

The new prefix letter numbering system introduced in 1935 soon became familiar to Crosville staff and interested onlookers, so that, for example, K instantly implied a petrol-engined Leyland Tiger (even though the first six numbers were allocated to Lioness LTB1 models which had the same Leyland T-type six-cylinder engine). Rather surprisingly at that date, at first no provision was made for a series for Tiger models with oil engines, of which there were none then in the fleet, even though L signified Leyland Titans (and initially the single AEC Q double-decker) with petrol engines while M indicated the oil-engined variety, later stretched to other makes of oil-engined double-decker. Hence KA, for oil-engined Tigers, destined to be the largest pre-war single-deck class, did not appear until 1936. Seen here in post-war green and cream coach livery is Leyland Tiger TS4 coach K73, which had begun life in 1932 as 746. It remained thus until withdrawal in 1952, though others of the type received KA numbers on conversion. It had acquired a Titan-style radiator – exchanges of radiator type became common in wartime and after, if interchangeable.

Class

A   Leyland Lion PLSC1
B   Leyland Lion PLSC3 and Lioness PLC1
C   Leyland Lion LT1
D   Leyland Lion LT2
E   Leyland Lion LT3
F   Leyland Lion LT5 (petrol)
G   Leyland Lion LT5A (petrol)
H   Leyland Lion LT7 (petrol)
J   Daimler CH6, Leyland Lion LT5/, ADC 423 (all oil)
K   Leyland Lioness LTB and Tiger TS (petrol)

L   Leyland Titan and other Double Deckers (petrol)
M   Leyland Titan and other Double Deckers (oil)
N   Leyland Cub normal control (petrol)
O   Leyland Cub forward control (petrol)
P   Leyland Cub normal control (oil)
Q   BMMO SOS
R   Tilling Stevens
S   Albion
T   AEC single deckers (petrol)
U   Miscellaneous

Vehicles which carried no classification were the staff cars and taxis.

A complete list of the vehicles renumbered in 1935 appears as Appendix I.

Inevitably the scheme was extended as new types entered the fleet and the need arose to identify significant variants and rebuilds. With these changes, the system remained in use until 1958.

1936
KA Leyland Tiger (Oil)
W Dennis (petrol)

1938
S Bedford and Dodge
WA Dennis Lancet (oil)

1946
MG Gardner-engined double-deckers (initially Guys renumbered)
MB Bristol K6A/B.Existing Bristol K6As were renumbered
KB Bristol L6A, L6B

1947
FA Leyland Lion LT5 rebuilt with Albion oil engines

1948
TA AEC Regal (oil)

1949
GA Leyland Lion LT5 (oil)
JA Leyland Lion LT7 rebuilt with Leyland 8.6Li oil engines
JG Leyland Lion LT7 rebuilt with Gardner 5LW oil engines
KC Leyland Tigers with Gardner 5LW engines
KG Bristol Ls with Gardner 5LW engines

1949 (Continued)
KW Bristol Ls with Bristol AVW engines
MA AEC Regent with AEC 7.7-litre oil engine
MW Bristol Ks with Bristol AVW engines
OA Leyland Cub forward control (oil)
PC Leyland Beadle rebuilds of Leyland Cubs
SC Bedford Beadle
SL Bedford OB coach

1952
CA Crossley single deck
SG Guy Vixen
UG Bristol LS6G

1953
UW Bristol LS6B

1954
ML Bristol LD6B

1957
SC Bristol SC
SP Beadle Bedford ex SC class

As earlier buses were scrapped and others renumbered, the significance of the class letters altered in some cases. Thus the renumbering of Dennis petrol models to create a separate class as W and the disappearance of other miscellaneous types meant that U thereafter signified the Shelvoke & Drewry toastracks. At first, MG implied the utility Guy Arabs when retrospectively applied to them in 1946, when there were no other Gardner-engined double-deckers in the fleet, but later was applied to various double-deckers with Gardner engines, both Bristol and conversions from petrol.

The renumbered buses soon began to be a familiar sight. Here D38, formerly 471, one of the Leyland Lion LT2 buses dating from May 1931, conveys how readily the application of the fleet number to the cab front, a slightly later innovation, made it readable on an oncoming vehicle. The Leyland bodywork on this batch was of the improved style introduced the previous year and also found on the LT3 buses, now Crosville E-class, which had begun to appear later in 1931 – these latter were, in effect, a lengthened version of the LT2 – and Leyland continued the body design for the broadly similar-looking but slightly heavier-duty LT5 (Crosville F-class). Another example of this type of body is visible from the rear on the left of the picture, which was taken in Northgate Street, Chester.

Bound for Birkenhead is M21 (FM 9057). of the same type as running in the late 'forties looking much as built save for the seemingly inevitable painted radiator in 1945.

Double-deckers were being bought only in small numbers in the mid 'thirties, following the rapid expansion of services so operated in 1929-31. The 1935 order was for nine oil-engined Titans with Leyland bodywork, the latter of the vee-fronted metal-framed type which had proved none too sucessful generally, although all these vehicles ran in original form at least until 1949/50, when eight were rebodied by ECW, the exception soldiering on until 1954, when a 1930 Leyland body was fitted for its final year in service. The vehicle shown, M20, was one of three with Leyland's 'Gearless' torque converter transmission, and thus of type TD4c rather than TD4 like the rest, though standard gearboxes were fitted in 1945. With new body, it ran until 1959. The oval fleetname panel was used at first with the new-style numbers.

New Vehicles delivered 1935

J4-28	FM 8974-98	Leyland LT7	5890-2/ 6139-45/ 5903-7	ECOC	B32F*	6/35	1959-61
H1-15	FM 8999-9013	Leyland LT7	5883-5/ 5924-35	Leyland	B34F	6-7/35	1951-53
O7-20	FM 9014-27	Leyland 1SKP3	4201-8/24-9	Brush	B30F	6-7/35	1950
N83-7	FM 9028-32	Leyland 1KP2	4082-6	Brush	B20F	7/35	1942-50
N88-92	FM 9033-7	Leyland 1KP2	4128-32	Brush	B20F	1935	1946/49
N93-7	FM 9038-42	Leyland 1KP2	4162/3/5/77/64	Brush	B20F	7/35	1946
P1-6	FM 9043-8	Leyland 1KPO2	4178/81/ 3/79/99/4200	Tooth	B20F	-/35	1945-50
M13-8	FM 9049-54	Leyland TD4	5941-6	Leyland	L26/26R	6/35	1949-50
M19-21	FM 9055-7	Leyland TD4c	5947-9	Leyland	L26/26R	6/35	1956
K90-2	FM 9058-60	Leyland TS7	5936-8	Harrington	C32F	6/35	1956
O21-2	FM 9061/2	Leyland 1SKP3	4230/1	Harrington	C26R	-/35	1952
U18-21	FM 9063-6	S&D LF	591863 501862 511861 581864	S and S	B31T	-/35	1952/56
P7-12	FM 9162-7	Leyland 1KPO2	4180/2/4-7	Brush	B20F	-/35	1949-50

*Body numbers J4-28: 3679/80/71/5/2/6/3/7/87/2-5/67-70/8/4/81/6/8-91. J4-19 seated 32 the remainder 34.

H3/8/14 were fitted with second-hand 1934 ECOC (B32F) bodies from G12/16/21 respectively in 1949.

H10 was fitted with a second-hand 1943 Burlingham (UB34F) body from G2 in 1949, and H13 with a 1935 ECOC (B34F) from J22 in 1949

J5-9/13-5/8/21/3/4/6-8 were fitted with Leyland 8.6 litre oil engines in May 1949 and were reclassified JA whilst J4/10-2/6/7/9/20/2/5 were fitted with Gardner 5LW oil engines in September 1949 and were reclassified JG.

They were all rebodied with new ECW B35R bodies (see page 149).

O7-20 were for routes crossing the Menai Bridge on to Ynys Mon (Anglesey).

P1-12 were equipped for one man operation.

M14 was rebodied with a second-hand 1930 Leyland (L24/24R) body from M223 in 1954. M19-21 were fitted with conventional gearboxes in 1945.

Leyland carried out a redesign of the Lion which produced an even more compact front-end design than the equivalent Titan TD3 and TD4, or Tiger TS6 and TS7. This had first appeared on the Lion LT5A of 1934 (Crosville class G), and the LT7 was the version with vacuum-hydralic brakes introduced in 1935. Crosville took both oil- and petrol-engined versions which were to prove the final stage in the Company's association with succesive Lion models. The oil-engined version picked up the J series used for some existing oil-engine single-deck conversions, one of an earlier Lion. Above is seen J27, one of the 25 vehicles with Eastern Counties bodies. This view shows an intermediate style of fleetname using sans-serif lettering, not unlike that of the 'twenties. The whole class was re-engined and rebodied by ECW in 1949.

This view of H7 (FM 9005) shows the short bonnet and 'slimline' radiator of the Lion LT7. These fifteen vehicles were petrol-engined and had Leyland metal-framed bodies, again of a design not generally regarded as up to that firm's best standards. Some were partially rebuilt as seen here, using ECW's post-1947 standard sliding window assemblies for three bays on each side - the end result was tidier than might have been expected from such a mixture of styles. It ran in this form until withdrawal in 1951. Four vehicles of the class received secondhand bodies, mostly Eastern Counties from G-class LT5A buses.

The oil engine was generally confined to larger sizes of vehicle in the mid-'thirties, but Leyland had begun offering such a version of the Cub, using a six-cylinder engine of the same 4.4 litre size as the petrol model but with overhead valves and a scaled-down version of the direct-injection system used on Leyland's larger models. Ironically, Crosville chose P as the type letter for such buses, of which there were a dozen in the 1935 deliveries, P10 being one of six with Brush bodywork, seen here at Heswall in February 1950.

The bridge to Ynys Mon (Anglesey) demanded the use of light vehicles and the Leyland 1SKP3 with Brush body was selected. These had the advantage over the KP series of being forward control (ie half cab) rather than normal control with bonnet ahead of the driver allowing a 33-seat capacity within the 4 tons 5cwt weight limit of the bridge. Note the lower build by comparison with the rebodied PLSC in front. Number O9 (FM 9016) is seen in this 1950 view nearing withdrawal.

Two further Cub forward-control chassis received Harrington 26-seat coach bodywork, entering service in April 1935, for use on Anglesey tour duties, similarly restricted to small vehicles at that time. The body design was of rear-entrance layout and a style of slightly earlier origin than the contemporary Harrington body for full-sized coaches, but suited the model well. This view of O21 when new shows how the SKP3 had the look of a scaled-down Tiger of the TS4 generation.

Vehicles acquired second hand in 1935

From J. W. Garner (Weaverside Motor Services), Runcorn 1st January 1935

| - | LG 1426 | Lancia | 2593 | ? | B26 | 1929 | 1935 |
| - | TY 4982 | Vulcan VWBL | 40 | ? | B32 | 1928 | 1935 |

Neither was operated.

From F. Watson, Runcorn 1st January 1935

U24 (W11)	LG 6106	Dennis Arrow	110012	Jackson	B32F	1931	1937
U23 (W12)	LG 9466	Dennis Arrow	110023	Jackson	B32F	1932	1937
U22 (W16)	AMB 652	Dennis Lancet	170469	Duple	C32R	1933	1949

These vehicles were renumbered W16/2/1 in 1936.

From R. Roberts, Rhos Hirwaun, Pwllheli 11th February 1935

| U25 | CC 9402 | Willys Overland | 11579 | Waveney | B14 | 1930 | 1935 |

From Tudor Evans, Llithfaen 25th February 1935

| - | JC 76 | Gilford | 11670 | ? | -26- | 1931 | 1935 |
| U26 | JC 1288 | Gilford 168SD | 10871 | Vickers | B26F | 1933 | 1935 |

JC 76 *was not operated.*

From J. A. Richards, Towyn 11th March 1935

| U27 | RP 5574 | GMCT20C | 205963 | Grose | B20F | 1928 | 1935 |
| - | IJ 7993 | Vulcan | ? | ? | -20- | 1928 | 1935 |

From W. B. Jones, Oswestry 18th March 1935

U31(U14)	UJ 2727	Bedford WLB	109363	Tooth	B20F	1934	1936
U29	UX 6242	GMC T19	1915077	Grose	B20F	1930	1935
U30	UX 9410	Bedford WLB	108151	Dobson	B20F	1931	1935
U28	UX 6946	Chevrolet U	66633	?	B20F	1930	1935

From Owen (New Blue Motors), Llandudno Junction 11th April 1935

U41 (W2)	CC 7163	Dennis 2½ Ton	45497	Owens	B28F	1927	1936
U42 (W4)	CC 8249	Dennis E	17503	Jackson	B32F	1928	1935
U43 (W5)	CC 8091	Dennis F	80059	Owens	B32F	1928	1936
U44 (W6)	RF 4372	Dennis E	17339	Jackson	B32F	1928	1935
U45 (W7)	VM 6302	Dennis E	17502	Jackson	B32F	1928	1935
U46 (W9)	CC 9945	Dennis EV	17921	Jackson	B32F	1931	1937
U47 (W10)	JC 46	Dennis EV	17840	Jackson	B32F	1931	1945
U48 (W14)	JC 722	Dennis Lancet	170190	Duple	B36F	1932	1935

These vehicles were renumbered in 1936.

From J. Price, Wrexham 14th April 1935

U37 (W3)	HD 3508	Dennis E	17458	Brush	B20F	1929	1936
U35	UN 3304	Guy ONDF	9486	Guy	B20F	1930	1935
U36 (U19)	UN 4843	Reo FB	1605	?	B20F	1931	1936
U32	UN 5227	Bedford WLB	108014	Willmott	C20F	1931	1935
U33	UN 5381	Bedford WLB	108111	Willmott	C20F	1932	1935
U38 (W13)	UN 5745	Dennis Lancet	170046	Willmott	DP35R	1932	1937
U39 (W15)	UN 7069	Dennis Lancet	170192	Willmott	B32R	1933	1949
U34 (U15)	UN 7509	Bedford WLB	109374	Willmott	B20F	1934	1936
U40 (W17)	UN 7645	Dennis Lancet	170220	Willmott	C32R	1934	1945
-	UN 3113	Chevrolet	?	?	?	1925 ?	1935

U34/6-40 *were renumbered in 1936.*

W15 *was requisitioned by the RAF during the 1939-45 War.*

With part of the business of J.Pearson and Sons (Happy Days Motorways), Liverpool — 25th May 1935

It was doubtless because of the presence in Crosville's fleet of the AEC Q double-decker that Pearson's Q coach was part of the Company's share of that fleet. It was bodied by Duple to a high-floor design that was chosen by several operators for this model as it permitted forward-facing seats to be provided throughout, despite the side-engined layout. Crosville numbered it T19 in the series used for AEC Regal coaches. It remained in Crosville's fleet until 1946.

A 1949 view of former Pearson Tiger TS6 (AKB 849). A 1935 vehicle with Duple body it is seen here at Aberystwyth in 1949 in substantially unaltered form. Duple built a wide variety of body designs in those days but this was unusually angular in some of its details.

-	CM 6911	Lancia	1315	?	?	Ch26-	1926	1935
K93	KF 3756	Leyland TS1	61494	Burlingham	?	C28F	1931	1952
T16	KF 5728	AEC Regal	662826	Duple	2353	C28F	1931	1953
T17	KF 8983	AEC Regal	6621247	Duple	2747	C28F	1932	1953
T18	KF 9009	AEC Regal	6621248	Duple	2748	C28F	1932	1951
K94	KF 9515	Leyland TS4	828	Duple	2782	C28F	1933	1952
U49	LV 4640	Bedford WLB	109178	Duple	3701	C16F	1933	1936
K95	LV 6690	Leyland TS6	3592	Duple	4045	C28F	1934	1952
T19	LV 8319	AEC Q	762011	Duple	4233	C32F	1934	1946
U50	LV 8409	Bedford WLB	109528	Burlingham	?	C20F	1934	1936
K96	AKB 849	Leyland TS6	5629	Duple	4816	C29F	1935	1952

Other vehicles in the Pearson fleet passed to Ribble Motor Services as described in the text.

CM6911 was not operated and **U49/50** *were renumbered* **U12/3** *in 1936.*

K93/4 *were rebodied by ECW(DP31R) and* **T16-8** *also by ECW (DP32R) in 1939. The new bodies were numbered 6065/4/92/87/83*

With the business of Williams (Mechell Maroon), Anglesey – 5th June 1935

U53	UN 1794	GMC T20C	208131	Waveney	?	B20F	1928	1936
U52	WX 5001	Reo FB	1533	Eaton	?	B20F	1930	1936
U51	WD 1917	Commer 6TK	28231	Willowbrook	2496	B20F	1931	1936

U51-3 *were renumbered* **U18,20/1**

With the business of Iorwerth Evans, Llanrhaeadr-ym-Mochnant – 21st December 1935

| U 33 | RF 6241 | Chevrolet LP | 57567 | Willowbrook | 2239 | B14F | 1929 | 1936 |
| U34 | UX 5096 | Chevrolet LQ | 55761 | ? | ? | B14F | 1929 | 1936 |

New vehicles delivered – 1936

The KA class for the oil-engine version of the Leyland Tiger appeared for the first time in 1936. Number KA1 (FM 9965) was a TS7 with ECOC body. Although classed as buses these contemporary views by the coachbuilder from the Company's archive show the seating to have been of high quality. Those familiar with ECW interiors will see similarities to the coachbuilder's post-1945 body for the Tilling Group, the seating being much as used on the express version.

KA 1-15	FM 9965-79	Leyland TS7	8185-9	ECOC	4135-42/ 4/3/5-9	B32R	5/36	1959-60
K97-100	FM 9980-83	Leyland TS7	8180-3	Harrington	?	C32F	5-7/36	1952-57
K101-2	FM 9984-5	Leyland TS7	8184/9506	Harrington	?	C25F	6/36	1952
K103-4	FM 9986/7	Leyland TS7	9507/8	Harrington	?	C32F	5/36	1952/53
K105-8	FM 9988-91	Leyland TS7	9509-12	Harrington	?	C25F	7/36	1952/53
K109	AFM 216	Leyland TS7	8539	Burlingham	?	C32F	5/36	1952/53
N98-105	FM 9992-9	Leyland KP2A	4415-20/30/1	Brush	?	B20F	-/35	1941-50
M41-46	AFM 495-9/ 501	Leyland TD4	10143-8	ECW	4322-7	L26/26R	7/36	1955-58

K109 was ordered by Prichard Llanrug (acquired March 1936). It had a half canopy body, sliding door and roof mounted destination gear. The body was substantially rebuilt by Burlingham in 1949. It received a Leyland 8.6-litre oil engine and was renumbered **KA183**.

KA11 was rebodied with an Alexander body (B35F) of unknown origin in 12/43. It later received Tilling destination gear in common with many members of the fleet.

KA 1-10/12-5 were rebodied by SEAS (B35F) between 11/49 and 3/50.

The bodies of **K107/108** were fitted to **KA199/198** respectively on withdrawal.

These two views show the Harrington-bodied Tiger coaches of 1936. The first shows K102 as delivered in grey and green. The second view shows K100 fitted with an oil engine as KA 210. Apart from the obvious livery change, the hinged slam door has given place to a sliding arrangement. This was Crosville's standard type of coach in the 1936-38 period, all petrol-engined as built, there being 22 on TS7 and six on TS8 chassis.

The odd man out of the KA1-15 batch was fitted with an Alexander bus body in 1943. The origin of the body is not known, though it seems very likely to be one of those made surplus when various SMT group companies were converting TS7 models to TD4, with new double-deck bodywork, at that time. As a result of several bouts of rebuilding, it is difficult to discern much of the precise origin. It survived until 1955.

All but one of the KA 1-15 batch were rebodied by Saunders Engineering in 1949/50. Number KA1 is again seen on the front at Rhyl. These vehicles had ungainly destination boxes which were quite quickly over panelled to show but a small ultimate destination. In this July 1952 view the original display is fitted together with the smoked glass flap which was intended to mask unwanted displays. It also shows an effort at standard Tilling livery; hitherto the batch had cream window surrounds as the only relief.

K98-100/4/6 *were fitted with oil engines and renumbered* **KA 208-10/4/6** *after 1945.*

M44/6 *were fitted with Tilling destination gear at an unknown time.*

M41-3/5/6 *were rebodied by ECW in 1949. See Below.*

Vehicles acquired second hand – 1936.

With the business of John Hughes, Carmel – 25th January 1936

U24	TE 5171	Maudslay ML4B	4456	?	?	B26F	1928	1936
U23	TE 6142	Maudslay ML4B	4554	?	?	B24F	1929	1936
U25	AG 5175	Guy OND	9554	Cowieson	?	B20F	1930	1936

With the business of G. Roberts, Southsea, Wrexham – 28th January 1936

W8	HD 3509	Dennis E	17459	Brush	?	B30F	1929	1937
W1	UN 6477	Dennis E	GL 70832	Waveney	?	B20F	1933	1938
U16	UN 7443	Bedford WLB	109468	Waveney	?	C20F	1934	1938
W18	UN 7674	Dennis Lancet	160714	Dennis	?	B32F	1934	1946
W20	UN 8053	Dennis Mace	240018	Waveney	?	B26F	1935	1942
W19	UN 8054	Dennis Lancet	170944	Dennis	?	C32R	1935	1949

W19 *was fitted with a new Burlingham body (UB34F) in 1943.*

W20 *was later converted into lorry 51a*

With the business of G.A. Williams, Pentre Broughton – 3rd February 1936

| W21 | UN 7673 | Dennis Ace | 200108 | Willmott | ? | B20F | 1934 | 1949 |

Acquisitions brought many odd vehicles into the Crosville fleet and the events of 1939-45 served to keep them in it for much longer than might otherwise have been the case. This Dennis Ace with a 20-seat body, new in 1934, came with the business of Williams, Pentre Broughton in 1936; it stayed until 1949. Number W21 (UN 7673) had bodywork by Willmott.

W22	UN 5780	Dennis Lancet	170140	Duple	2901	B32F	1932	1938
W23	PL 8849	Dennis EV	17822	Dennis	?	B32R	1931	1937
W24	UN 1723	Dennis G	70304	Dennis	?	B20F	1928	1936

With the business of D.M.Prichard and Son (DM Motors), Llanrug – 1st March 1936

B98	WW 1778	Leyland PL SC3	45821	Leyland	?	B36R	1927	1936
K110	CC 7853	Leyland Lioness 4	46849	Leyland	?	C26F	1928	1936
K111	UO 7950	Leyland Lioness 4	47427	Hall Lewis	?	C25D	1928	1953
B99/100	CM 8060/1	Leyland PLSC3	47161/2	Leyland	?	B36R	1928	1936
C28	TF 1928	Leyland LT1	50538	Leyland	?	B34F	1930	1936
U22	MY 6835	GMC T20C	203312	?	?	B20F	1930	1936
K122	JC 606	Leyland TS4	1141	Leyland	?	B32F	1932	1953
K123	JC 1156	Leyland TS4	2532	Leyland	?	B32F	1933	1953
G22	JC 1926	Leyland LT5A	3969	Burlingham	?	B32F	1934	1941

TF 1928 *was originally numbered* **E76** *but was renumbered* **C28** *prior to entering service.*

K122/3 *were renumbered* **K42/3** *in 1937 and rebodied by ECW (DP28R) in 1939. The new bodies were numbered 6063/5*

K110/1 *were erroneous entries for the K class, since they were of the PLC type, with mechanical design similar to the PLSC and thus the B class would have been more correct – however, they remained in the fleet only briefly.*

With the business of W.D. Humphreys, Bethel – 1st March 1936

U17	JC 1198	Bedford WLB	108610	?	?	B20F	1933	1936

With the business of E. Jones, (Jones Motor Services), Flint – 15th June 1936

B103	VT 204	Leyland PLSC3	45960	Leyland	?	B31F	1927	1936
-	DM 6476	Graham Dodge	D204004	?	?	-26-	1929	1936
U28	DM 7538	AJS Pilot	5049	Hayward	?	B32F	1929	1936
U30	VX 9935	Morris HF6	037H	London Lorries	?	C31R	1929	1936
U29	MV 2458	Morris HF6	14025	?	?	C31R	1929	1936
U31	DM 9281	Dodge PLB	1010	Duple	4902	C20F	1929	1938

U31 *was renumbered* **U13** *in 1937 and again to* **S1** *in 1938.*

With the business of Harold Roberts, Connah's Quay – 6th July 1936

-	VA 7941	Leyland PLSC	?	?	?	?	1928	1936
U32	DM 6016	Dodge GB	5626	Strachan and Brown	?	B20F	1928	1936
B101	UO 7303	Leyland PLSC	346747	Hall Lewis	?	B32D	1928	1936
B102	WW 4635	Leyland PLSC	46096	Leyland	?	B31F	1928	1936
U26	LG 2389	Reo GE	62	Eaton	?	B20F	1929	1936
U27	GO 5538	Daimler CH6	9061	Park Royal	?	C31F	1931	1937
T20	VU 2742	AEC Regal	662668	Burlingham	?	C29F	1934	1937

VA 7941 was not operated and was also not listed in the Crosville Handbooks. It is however believed to have been purchased, possibly for spares.

U27 *was renumbered* **U12** *in 1937.*

New vehicles delivered – 1937

P13-24	BFM 101-12	Leyland KPZO1	16852-6/6930-6	Brush	?	B20F	-/37	1949
P25-34	BFM 113-22	Leyland KPZO2	6913-7/79-83	Brush	?	B26F	-/37	1949
K1-6	BFM 123-8	Leyland TS7	12331-6	Harrington	?	C32F	4/37	1957/8
K38-41	BFM 129-32	Leyland TS7	12337-40	Harrington	?	C32F	4-6/37	1952/3
KA16-40	BFM 133-57	Leyland TS7	12341-65	ECW	see below	B32F	3-4/37	1952-60
KA 41-65	BFM 158-82	Leyland TS7	12366-90	ECW	see below	B32F	3-4/37	1952-60
KA 66-87	BFM 183-204	Leyland TS7	12391-12412	ECW	see below	B32F	3-4/37	1952-60

Body numbers of **KA16-87** *were 4586/7/97/84/1/5/2/67/72-4/68/4-6/9-71/5-80/3/88-96/4606/4598-600/4/1/2/8/5/10/07/3/9/11/4/4612/3/5/6/9/7/20/18/21-5/7/9/30/26/8/32-4/1/5.*

P13-34 *were suitable for one man operation.*

K1-6,38-41 *were fitted with Leyland 8.6-litre oil engines in 1948 and were renumbered* **KA 173-82**.

KA 16/8/20-2/5/7/8/37/41/6/7/57/60/3/6/70/1/4/5/7/ 81/3-6 *were all rebuilt by Crosville during 1950. The bodies sides were replaced by new units to a pattern of construction similar to contemporary ECW bodies. There were two principal patterns with either large or small windows as shown in the illustrations on page 155.*

Small windows **KA16/8/21/2541/46/7/66/77/81/5** *: Large windows* **KA20/2/7/8/37/57/60/3/70/1/4/83/4/6**.

KA19 *was also rebuilt but to DP32R configuration. This body gained a sliding door and a high standard of seats. It had small windows and retained bus livery.*

KA47 *was further rebuilt in September 1956 for one man operation with full width canopy and jack knife doors.*

Vehicles acquired second hand – 1937

With the business of E.Richards t/a Crowther and Co Shotton – 12th January 1937

-	OF 6080	Guy Conquest FC	23517	Guy	?	B32F	1930	1937
U14-6	OF6084/7/8	Guy Conquest FC	23521/4/7	Guy	?	B32F	1930	1937

Crosville arrived at the basis of its final pre-war single-deck design with the 72 KA-class front-entrance Leyland Tiger TS7 buses with BFM registrations which appeared in 1937. The ECW bodies on these had more purely bus-type seating than the first fifteen KA of 1936, but even so they were 'civilised' vehicles in which all seats faced forward, with none perched over wheel arches, and had the roomy parcel racks then regarded as essential on a country bus. These vehicles had five bays behind the entrance, unlike the subsequent versions with six as shown on page 63, and, as delivered, the cream roof extended over the cab, now of half-canopy type, this latter feature perhaps influenced by the adoption of this style by neighbouring companies North Western and Ribble. At this date the fleetname lettering had almost reverted to the pre-LMS version. In later years, many of these vehicles were to be rebuilt in Crosville's own workshops in a variety of formats, from major reconstruction to the top-sliding windows fitted to an otherwise unaltered body on KA32. However, KA29 was among those not modified when it was withdrawn in 1951, passing via a Manchester dealer in 1953 to a contractor in Salford.

The years 1938-40 brought batches of these ECW bodies on Leyland Titan TD5 chassis. The 52-seat bodies looked quite attractive as built, enhanced by the short lived cream centre portion to the roof and three cream bands on the maroon livery. The body design was essentially the newly adopted ECW lowbridge standard style as built mainly for the Bristol K5G chassis from its introduction in 1937, but with different cab to suit the TD5's lower bonnet line. Eventually the fitment of Tilling destination equipment beset many Crosville vehicles and the smooth lines of the body were disrupted to say the least. Number M53 was registered as CFM 355. Including the 'convertibles' shown opposite, there were ultimately 54 buses of this type.

New vehicles delivered – 1938

U12-4	CFM 340-2	Shelvoke and Drury LF	702422/3/4	ECW	5426-8	B32T	-/38	1960
K110-5	CFM 343-8	Leyland TS8	16367-72	Harrington		C32R	5/38	1941-58
M47-70	CFM 349-72	Leyland TD5	16361-6/73-90	ECW	see below	L26/26R	1-5/38	1956-9
M71-6	CFM 373-8	Leyland TS8	17401-6	ECW	5656-61	COL26/26R	6/38	1958/9
M77-88	DFM 287-98	Leyland TS8	300951-62	ECW	see below	L26/26R	11/12-38	1956-9
WA1	DFM 127	Dennis Lancet 2	175610	Dennis	?	B39F	-/38	1949
KA 88-94	DFM 299-305	Leyland TS8	300891-7	ECW	see below	B32F	12/38	1954-6
KA 96-110	DFM 307-21	Leyland TS8	300899-913	ECW	see below	B32F	10-2/38	1954-8
KA 112-21	DFM 323-32	Leyland TS8	300915-24	ECW	see below	B32F	11/38	1955-60

Note: There is some conjecture about the 'dates new' for KA 88-92/6/7/100/1/8/9 and M77-80/3-8. However Company records show them as late as 30th December 1938, whereas conventional wisdom has been to class them as '1939'.

*Body numbers of **M47-80** were 5238/29/39-42/20/3/6/4/7/5/21/36/22/32-4/7/0/1/43. **M77-88** were 6100/99/97/101/096/8/105/6/2/3/7/4.*

KA88-94 *were 6017/28/18/9/20/02/21.* **KA96-110** *were 6022/3/5999/6003/24/5/7/12/6000/1/5997/8/6026/7/04.* **KA112-21** *were 6005/6/11/08-10/4/3/5/6/31-3.*

K110-2/5 *were renumbered **KA 184-7** upon the fitment of Leyland oil engines post 1945.*

M47-76 *introduced revised destination equipment to the fleet and also had heaters in the lower saloon: **M77** and subsequent Leyland TD5s had heaters in both saloons. Later many were fitted with Tilling destination equipment.*

M64 *was rebodied with the 1940 ECW (L26/26R) body (body No. 6546) from **M97** in 1956.*

WA1 *had been ordered by Lloyd, Bwlchgwyn prior to the acquisition of his business by Crosville.*

U12-4 *were originally equipped with four-cylinder petrol engines although Bedford 28hp six-cylinder petrol engines were fitted in 1955.*

KA101/14 *were converted to towing vehicles in 1958.*

The year 1938 brought about the first programmed deliveries for the Sea Front services at Rhyl. These operations had a chequered history over many years but they have survived so that today they generate a sizeable income for Crosville Cymru. Two sorts of vehicle were delivered, Shelvoke and Drury Low Freighter toastracks following in the Brookes Brothers mould and the first convertible open top double-deck vehicles based on Leyland Titan chassis. ECW provided the bodies for both batches. Number U13 (CFM 341) represents the Shelvokes whilst the Titans are demonstrated by M72/3 (CFM 374/5). The bodywork for the toastracks was a strange-looking marriage of contemporary ECW outlines and the very traditional true char-a-banc.

The six Titans with detachable tops reflected the revival of interest in the open-top double-decker in the mid-'thirties, particularly for sea-front service, and the realisation that, out of season, such vehicles were almost useless. The appearance with cover in place was virtually standard, apart from the lifting hooks to allow the top to be removed and the slightly deeper framing at upper-deck waist level, though the metal rain louvre over the upper-deck windows was omitted and there was only one opening window on each side upstairs. Within, the appearance was much as any other ECW lowbridge body of the period, with the single-skin roof incorporating anti-drumming swages and the rectangular light fittings - in the lower deck, there were the pillar-mounted lights as used in ECW single-deckers of the day. The unladen weight went up very slightly, as conveyed by the 6tons 14cwt 2qr quoted on M53 shown on the opposite page and 6tons 16cwt 3qr on M72.

Vehicles acquired second hand – 1938

With the business of J.R.Lloyd, Bwlchgwyn – 2nd May 1938

W1	DM 7821	Dennis Lancet	170026	Dennis	?	C32R	1932	1949
S2	UN7445	Bedford WLB	109447	Tooth	?	C20-	1934	1944
S3	UN 8263	Bedford WTL	873785	Duple	4988	DP26F	1935	1950
W2	BU 8787	Dennis Lancet	170969	Dennis	?	C32R	1935	1949
O23	UN 8862	Leyland SKP3	4392	Spicer	?	C26F	1935	1950
W3	UN 9181	Dennis Lancet	171019	Dennis	?	C32R	1937	1949

W2 *was rebodied with the Leyland B32R body from* **K9** *in 1938.*

S3 *was renumbered* **S1** *in 1948.*

New vehicles delivered—1939.

KA95	DFM 306	Leyland TS8	300898	ECW	6029	B32F	2/39	1956
KA111	DFM 322	Leyland TS8	300914	ECW	6030	B32F	2/39	1954
KA122-47	DFM 334-59	Leyland TS8	300925-50	ECW	see below	B32F	2/39	1954-60
KA148-53	DFM 519-524	Leyland TS8	302481-6	ECW	see below	B32F	6/39	1955-7

Body numbers of **KA122-53** *were 6031-6/44/37/40/38/41-3/5/7/55/46/48/52-4/49-51/41/2/5/3/6/44.*

KA128 *was converted to a towing vehicle in 1958*

KA148 *was fitted with a side destination indicator in the first bay as were all subsequent KAs.*

Vehicles acquired second hand – 1939

With the business of H. Stanley, Buckley – 1st March 1939

| H16 | DM 9282 | Leyland LT7 | 6846 | Duple | 5382 | C32F | 1935 | 1950 |

From Ribble Motor Services Limited

The onset of war led to the purchase of twelve Leyland Lion PLSC buses with Leyland bodywork of the 1927-29 period from the Ribble fleet, the first of many second-hand vehicles from various major operators' fleets to be taken into stock over the next few years. There seemed to be some confusion about appropriate fleet numbers, for six buses of the longer PLSC3 type were given numbers in the A series appropriate to the PLSC1, including CK 4016, seen here still in Ribble livery, with large Crosville fleetname and the number A40 it was given at first – it was corrected to B40 in 1940 – remarkably, it survived to 1950, complete with original body, then passing to the Forestry Commission for further use.

A31/2	TE 2899/2901	Leyland PLSC1	46411/3	Leyland	?	B30F	1927	1942/0
A33-6	CK 3914/87/ 4014/8	Leyland PLSC3	46454/47 -4/31/5	Leyland	?	B32F	1928	1940/50
A37	TE 4056	Leyland PLSC1	47053	Leyland	?	B31F	1928	1950
A38-40	CK 33978/ 4011/6	Leyland PLSC3	46995/ 7028/33	Leyland	?	B32F	1928	1950
B13/4	CK 4000/ TE 7221	Leyland PLSC3	47017/523	Leyland	?	B32/5F	1929	1950

In 1943, six of the ex-Ribble Lion PLSC buses were fitted with new Burlingham bodies to wartime utility specification – they were among the oldest in any fleet to receive such bodywork. B38 (CK 3978) is seen thus in August 1947 at Llandudno Junction. It is said that these rebodied buses had two-line destination displays at first, thus not strictly conforming to the utility specifications, but more latitude was often shown in such matters on rebodied buses, equipment sometimes being transferred from the original bodywork. In any case, only one aperture is visible in this view and even that not used, a Widd plate being preferred.

These vehicles were acquired to augment the wartime fleet rather than adjuncts of acquired businesses as had been the case throughout the 'thirties.

A33-6/8-40 *were renumbered* **B15-8/38-40** *during 1940*

A37/B13-5/7/38 *were rebodied by Burlingham (UB30F-A37 and UB34F-others) in 1943.*

A31 *later became lorry* **44A** *and* **A32** *mobile canteen* **42B**.

New vehicles delivered/allocated – 1940/1

KA154-65	EFM 577-88	Leyland TS8	304011-22	ECW		6550-61	B32F	1/40	1955-8

Further deliveries of Leyland Tigers with ECW bodies broadly similar to the BFM batch followed in 1938-40. The chassis type advanced to the TS8 and there were detail differences in the bodies, notably an extra bay in the structure and, in 1939, a nearside destination indicator. The latter feature seems to have been regarded as superfluous as Widd plates remained Crosville's preferred means of advising would-be passengers of the vehicle's intentions. Number KA 162 was EFM 585, seen in post-war days with metal louvre over the windows and, in typical Crosville style, painted radiator.

KA166-8	EFM 589-91	Leyland TS8	304023-5	Burlingham	?	C33F	1/40	1947-58
M89-100	EFM 598-609	Leyland TD5	304062-73	ECW	6538-49	L26/26R	1-2/40	1956-9
K116	EFM 642	Leyland TS8	303754	Burlingham	?	C33F	3/40	1957
KA169-71	EFM 938-40	Leyland TS8	306616-8	ECW	4551/33/57	DP32R	5-7/40	1959
M101-110	BFN 932-41	Leyland TD7	305780-9	Park Royal	see below	L27/26R	6/40	1957-9
M111-3	GCD 670/1/3	Leyland TD7	306774/5/7	Park Royal	see below	H26/26R	11/40	1957-9
M114-26	GCD 676-88	Leyland TD7	306780-92	Park Royal	see below	H26/26R	5/41	1957-9

These deliveries demonstrated the first effects of the world war in that vehicles ordered by coastal operators were diverted to those serving industrial and other needs. These moves were made under the aegis of the Regional Transport Commissioners.

The body numbers of **M101-10** were 6465-74, and **M111-26**, 6942-57: in each case the order is unknown.

M101-10 were diverted from East Kent Road Car Co Limited of Canterbury. **M111-26** were diverted from Southdown Motor Services Limited of Brighton. In both cases, they had been built to those companies' requirements.

KA169-71 were fitted with second hand bodies which had been removed from **K37/4/3**.

K116 was fitted with a Leyland 8.6-litre oil engine in 1948 and was renumbered **KA188**.

M93/4/6-1 – /2/4/13/4/6-22 were modified with Tilling destination gear in later years.

In 1952 **M116** was fitted with a five bay Crosville finished body on Pearson frames. Subsequently in 1952/3 **M101-10/4/5/7-20/2/3/5/6** received similar bodies to six bay pattern.

On withdrawal in 1956 the body of **M97** (1940 ECW L26/26R No. 6546) was fitted to **M64**.

The final delivery of to pre-war pattern double-deckers arrived in 1940. The EFM batch of Titan TD5s again had ECW bodies. This is a post-1945 view and clearly shows the effect of the penchant felt by the Company for grafting Tilling destination screens on to its buses; excellent clarity of display but a lack of sensitivity on appearance is the way it was done. M94 (EFM 603) is seen in a typical Liverpool setting.

Burlingham received the order for Crosville's coach bodywork for 1940, doubtless placed before the outbreak of war and possibly influenced by the good impression made by the Tiger TS7 with Burlingham body that had been ordered by D. M. Pritchard and added to the fleet in 1936. Four TS8 models were taken into stock in January 1940, three with oil engines, the first coaches so powered from new in the fleet, and one further example in March, the last new full-sized petrol vehicle purchased and the last new full 'luxury' coach until well into the post-war period. This view when new at Rock Ferry depot conveys the lines of the standard late pre-war Burlingham body. It received an 8.6-litre oil engine, as standard for this model when new, in 1948, being renumbered KA188 and then surviving until 1957.

Also photographed at Rock Ferry was KA170, one of three new TS8 chassis for which no bodies had been available as the supply position worsened. Accordingly, three of the ECW dual-purpose bodies dating from 1936/7 that had been built on ex-Brookes Bros Tiger TS2 chassis were transferred, the vehicles entering service in May to July 1940.

The East Kent batch of Leyland Titans were actually finished by Park Royal in their intended owner's livery, complete right down to Alfred Baynton's name as Secretary and General Manager. This photograph was taken at the bodybuilder's works at some date early in 1940, BFN 938 being complete apart from adding headlamp masks, often omitted when official portraits were being taken early in wartime. The 53-seat lowbridge design, rather plain in outline but finished to quite a high standard, with such features as glass rain louvres over the opening windows and quite a generously-sized destination display, was much as East Kent's earlier batches of Titan TD4 and TD5 buses bodied by either Park Royal or Brush in 1936 to 1939. However the ten vehicles diverted to Crosville were on the TD7 chassis Leyland had introduced in the autumn of 1939. This vehicle became M107, and was one of those rebodied in Crosville's own workshops in 1952-3, remaining in service until 1959.

Number M101 of the same batch (BFN 932) is seen post-1945 at Rhyl complete with Tilling destination screen and Widd plate.

Southdown was also the source of diverted Titan TD7 buses which had been bodied by Park Royal but to a different style in accordance with that operator's specification. Here again, many features were as on previous batches of Titan for that fleet, but the 1940 vehicles were to have introduced a curved profile to the Southdown fleet for the first time, a design feature then growing in popularity. Southdown used full-height buses with centre gangways on both decks as far as possible, and the sixteen TD7 buses received were of this layout, at the time the only ones in the Crosville fleet except for the solitary AEC Q. The first of the batch, M111 (GCD 670), is seen in substantially original form in this post-war picture, though the destination box was much smaller than Southdown's standard pattern. This bus was not rebodied and was withdrawn in 1956. They were used mainly in the Rhyl area, along with other highbridge types, reducing the possibility of accident under low bridges.

Vehicle acquired second hand – 1940

From Thames Valley Traction Co Limited, Reading

K117	GN 5150	Leyland TS3	61671	?	?	B31F	6/31	1953

K117 *was exchanged for* **N45**: *some doubt exists as to the date of actual acquisition-there is a suggestion that it was on loan until 1942. It was converted to run on producer gas in 1942/3. In 1948 it was fitted with a Leyland oil engine and the ECOC B32F (3940) body from* **R35**. *It was renumbered* **KA168** *at this time.*

Vehicles acquired second hand – 1941

With the business of Owen Roberts, Colwyn Bay, 1st February 1941.

-	UN 3695	Chevrolet ?	?	?	?	?	4/30	1941
-	UN 3863	Chevrolet U	66418	?	?	B14	6/30	1941
-	UN 8534	Bedford WLB	110035	Duple	?	?	7/35	1942
S1	UN 9741	Bedford WTB	110329	Spicer	?	C20F	7/36	1944

Only **S1** *was operated as a PSV and this and* **UN 8534** *were converted into van/lorry* **41A** *and* **38A** *respectively.*

New vehicles allocated – 1942-3

The first buses with bodywork to the utility specifcation adopted in wartime to economise on materials and skilled manpower that arrived in the Crosville fleet, in February 1942, were three Leyland Titan TD7 chassis with bodywork by Brush, including M128 (FFM 178) seen at Wrexham in largely original condition in April 1949. Although the utility specification enforced sparse standards, each bodybuilder had its own interpretation of design, the Brush one being among the better proportioned, though early examples had short skirt panels necessitating double lifeguard rails and hence giving an oddly old-fashioned side elevation. It remained in service until 1955, latterly with a post-war Tilling standard destination box, as applied to most of the type.

M127-29	FFM 177-9	Leyland TD7	307743/812/788	Brush	?	UL27/28R	2/42	1955-9
M130/1	FFM 180-1	Leyland TD7	307813/4	Roe	GO739/40	UL27/28R	3/42	1956
M132-5	FFM 182-5	Leyland TD7	307780/97/8/801	Willowbrook	3701-4	UL27/28R	6/42	1956-9
M136	FFM 186	Leyland TD7	307786	NCME	?	UL27/26R	5/42	1955
M137-39	FFM 214-6	Guy Arab I 5LW	FD25495/531/5	NCME	?	UL27/26R	10/42	1955
M140-3	FFM 217-20	Guy Arab I 5LW	FD25550/2/661/2	NCME	?	UL27/26R	10-12/42	1955
M144-6	FFM 221-3	Guy Arab I 5LW	FD25586/600/9	Brush	?	UL27/28R	11/42	1955
M147	FFM 250	Guy Arab I 6LW	FD25759	Roe	GO1255	UL27/28R	3/43	1955
M148	FFM 251	Guy Arab I 6LW	FD25765	NCME	?	UL27/26R	3/43	1955
M149/50	FFM 252/3	Guy Arab I 5LW	FD25777/840	NCME	?	UL27/26R	2/43	1955
M151/2	FFM 254/5	Guy Arab I 5LW	FD25927/9	Roe	GO1254/47	UL27/28R	3/43	1955
M153	FFM 271	Guy Arab II 6LW	FD25960	Roe	GO1263	UL27/28R	6/43	1955
M154-6	FFM 272-4	Guy Arab II 5LW	FD25981-3	NCME	?	UL27/26R	5-6/43	1955
M157	FFM 275	Guy Arab II 6LW	FD26054	Roe	?	UL27/28R	6/43	1955

M127-36 *had so called 'unfrozen' chassis assembled from Work in Progress at the Leyland plant. All of these vehicles had bodies to MoS Utility specification.* **M137-46** *were delivered in grey primer but repainted maroon before use. Detail specifications varied between vehicles.*

M133 *was rebodied with a Crosville six bay body in 1953. It has been suggested that this had Pearson frames but it seems unlikely.*

M137-57 *were reclassified as* **MG 137-57** *in 1946.*

One of the 1942 allocation was this Willowbrook-bodied Leyland Titan TD7. It is seen here in largely original condition at Heswall in 1951. Willowbrook's version of the utility body was one of the most box-like, having no inward taper at the front of the upper deck. M133 was rebodied in 1953.

Mixed body allocations were often a feature of the early utility period and Northern Counties supplied one body on a TD7 to Crosville, M136, arriving in May 1942 though, as it turned out, there were also to be eleven more generally similar bodies of this make on Guy chassis. Northern Counties had gone over to metal-framed construction pre-war, and persuaded the all-powerful Ministry of Supply to permit its utility bodies to be the same, despite the specification calling for wood-framed construction. They thus had window-pan glazing, with rounded corners, and this particular bus even had outswept skirt panels, evidently a sign of use of part of a structure intended for a body to peacetime standards. It is seen in largely original condition.

The Guy Arab is represented by another make of body even less seen on Crosville buses – Charles H. Roe of Leeds. Number M157 (FFM 275) was a 1943 Guy Arab II with 6LW Gardner engine, itself something fortunate. After these wartime allocations the next new Roe bodies for the Company were on two Leyland luxury coaches in 1985. Extra opening side windows had been added by the time this picture was taken, but the panelling over the hinged vents at the front of the upper deck must have made forward vision for passengers very poor.

Vehicles acquired second hand – June 1944

From Bolton Corporation

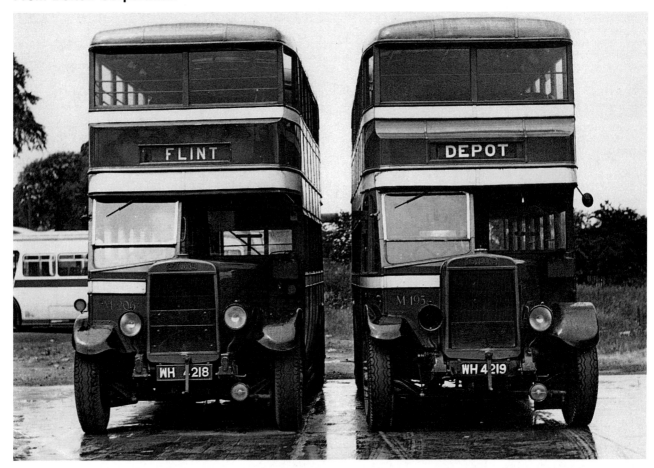

Bolton Corporation found itself with a surplus of buses due to delivery of a new fleet for tram replacement that was postponed due to the war, so many older buses were lent to other operators, including Crosville. Then, in 1944, three Leyland Titan TD2 buses that had been on loan since the previous year were purchased, together with four others of the same type. Like many municipalities, Bolton had given part of its body orders to a local firm, in this case Bromilow and Edwards, better known as manufacturers of tipping gear for lorries. The bodies on these buses were built to the standard Leyland lowbridge piano-front design of the time. Six were put into Crosville service as buses, being fitted with oil engines in 1946/7 and the bodies rebuilt by ECW in a manner widely used in the Tilling group, generally retaining original appearance except for a modified windscreen shape, as shown here. By the time this photograph was taken some time after 1950, M195 (WH 4219) on the right, had swapped bodies with an ex-Plymouth TD2, receiving one of Leyland's own make, similarly rebuilt by ECW, the picture underlining the close similarity, save that the B&E body has a deeper indicator panel (though even this was also sometimes found on Leyland versions). Also noteworthy is the fact that this bus, with Leyland chassis number 1650, has the rounded front dumb-irons adopted for later TD2 and related models (giving an effect not unlike the TD1, though heavier-looking) whereas M206 (WH 3218) on the left, with chassis 1649, has the square-cut type that had been used on the TD2 from its introduction in late 1931. General adoption of the rounded type came slightly later - the two versions were interchangeable despite their different appearance, and there could have been replacement due to an accident - but the comparison on consecutive chassis is intriguing.

L23/69/70	WH4218/3/5	Leyland TD2	1649/4/6	Bromilow and Edwards	?	L24/24R	02/33	1954
L76-8	WH 4214/6/9	Leyland TD2	1645/7/50	Bromilow and Edwards	?	L24/24R	12/32 02/33 03/33	1954
-	WH 4212	Leyland TD2	1643	Bromilow and Edwards	?	L24/24R	02/33	1954

These vehicles had been new to Bolton Corporation numbers 69/4/6/5/7/70/3. **L23/76/8** *had been on loan since 1943 as* **L369/5/170.**

L23/69/70/6-8 *were fitted with oil engines in 1946/7 and reclassified as* **M206/30/1/3//4/195.** *Their bodies were also rebuilt by ECW at this time except that L78 was fitted with the 1932 Leyland body from L45 (DR 9869) which had also been rebuilt by ECW.*

WH 4212 had its body removed and was used as a lorry **(20A)** *until about 1946 when it was used as a service vehicle (***55A***) without body possibly towing chassis between the shops at Crane Wharf and Sealand Road in Chester. It was then fitted with a 1933 Leyland body (ex* **M37**)*, renumbered* **L109**, *and put into PSV service.*

There is some conflict on the actual dates of acquisition of these vehicles. The Company records them as 1944 but other sources suggest that **L76-8** *were not formally acquired until February 1945.*

New vehicles delivered – 1945

Bristol, like most bus chassis makers, had been put on other work during much of the war but was allowed to resume production in 1944. The operating companies in the Tilling group, to which Crosville by then belonged, ceased ordering Guy buses after 1943, holding back until the 'own brand' Bristol became available. Under Ministry of Supply direction, it had the AEC 7.7-litre engine and, if lowbridge layout was required, Strachans bodywork. Although frustrated by group policy from buying its beloved Leylands (apart from limited exceptions), Crosville found the AEC engined Bristol acceptable, continuing to standardise on it for most of its post-war buses until 1949. On the other hand the Strachans body often suffered from poor timber quality and was, at first, among the most austere-looking of all the utilities, especially from the rear, as conveyed by this view of the first example, M171 (FFM 310) is seen here at the Liverpool, Pier Head, terminus in May 1951, by then running as MB171.

The relaxed specification for utility bodywork permitted rounded domes, with marked improvement to the rear end, even if less altered at the front, and Strachans began supplying Bristol K6A buses so fitted to Crosville from June 1945. Deliveries of this style continued until early 1946, and the vehicle shown arrived as M192 (FFM 382), the last of the utility series. By that stage the large Tilling destination display was being fitted from new.

M171-4	FFM 310-3	Bristol K6A	W1-055/6/78/9	Strachan	?	UL27/28R	4/45	1967
M175-7	FFM 314-6	Bristol K6A	W1-101/2/24	Strachan	?	UL27/28R	6/45	1967
M178-81	FFM 334-7	Bristol K6A	W2-072/5/6/9	Strachan	?	UL27/28R	11/45	1967
M183-4	FFM 339-40	Bristol K6A	W2-082/3	Strachan	?	UL27/28R	12/45	1967
M186-7	FFM 342-3	Bristol K6A	W2-085/6	Strachan	?	UL27/28R	12/45	1967

These deliveries were the first influences of the new Tilling ownership of the Company. However there was still fairly strict oversight by the Regional Transport Commissioner and the MoS both in the allocation and the specification of vehicles. The first 'Tilling Standards' were to come to the Company in 1946.

M171-81/3/4/6/7 were allocated MoS chassis numbers B055/6/78/9/101/2/24/2/5/6/9/32/3/5/6. The bodies represented a mixed selection of 'strict' and 'relaxed' (M174-88) specifications. M171 was the first vehicle to enter service new in Tilling Green livery.

M171-81/3/4/6/7 were renumbered MB171-81/3/4/6/7 in 1946 and again to DKA171-81/3/4/6/7 under the 1958 scheme described in volume two.

All were fitted with PV2 radiators and new ECW (L27/28R) bodies in 1953. The new bodies were numbered 6302-19/2. Some of the old bodies were fitted to acquired Bristol chassis for a short time pending the release of other post war ECW bodies which had been fitted to pre-war Leyland Titans.

The Crosville Handbooks published up to 1960 show M171-7 as new in 1944. The registration documents showed the above dates- it is unlikely that they would have been stored at this time so the above is believed to be correct.

Vehicles acquired second hand – 1945

During this year (and indeed subsequently) many vehicles were acquired from a wide variety of sources to cope with the extra traffic on offer. In many instances the vehicles had been nominally on loan during the 1939-45 period but they were almost invariably renumbered upon acquisition. Many of the vehicles were fitted with oil engines and had their bodies rebuilt by ECW. Generally, however, they were withdrawn by 1954/5 as the supply of new vehicles strengthened and the rapid contraction of demand set in.

From Leigh Corporation Transport.

L71	TE 9530	Leyland TD1	70819	Leyland	?	L24/24R	2/29	1945
M165	TE 9531	Leyland TD1	70820	Leyland	?	L24/24R	10/29	1953
L72	TE 9532	Leyland TD1	70821	Leyland	?	L24/24R	10/29	1952
L73-5	TF 6358-60	Leyland TD1	72306-8	Leyland	?	L27/24R	10/31	1945-53

These vehicles were acquired during January.

M165 *had been fitted with an oil engine by Leigh Corporation it was renumbered to* **M158** *2/45.*

L72/4/5 *were rebuilt by ECW during 1945.*

L74/5 *were re-engined with Leyland 8.6-litre oil units in 1945.*

L73-5 *had been on hire since 3/43,* **L71/2, M165** *since 2/44. They were numbered* **L130 /M231 L132/39-400** *respectively.*

From Plymouth Corporation Transport

DR9849 came from Plymouth Corporation in 1945 as part of a Tilling Group purchase. It had a Mumford body and when fitted with a Leyland oil engine became M236. It is seen at Crewe Garage in company with MG147 (FFM 250) a wartime Guy Arab II 6LW with Roe body. Mumford's body design was more modern-looking than the contemporary Leyland, but had been slightly re-styled in the course of an ECW rebuild. Note the Tilling destination box fitted in the Guy's body.

L79	DR 9635	Leyland TD2	282	Mumford	?	L 24/24R	3/32	1954/5
L80-1	DR 9849/50	Leyland TD2	1255/6	Mumford	?	L 24/24R	7/32	1954/5
L82	DR 9851	Leyland TD2	1254	Mumford	?	L 24/24R	8/32	1954/5
L83	DR 9853	Leyland TD2	1257	Mumford	?	L 24/24R	9/32	1954/5
L84	DR 9858	Leyland TD2	1262	Leyland	?	L 24/24R	5/32	1954/5
L85	DR 9860	Leyland TD2	1242	Leyland	?	L 24/24R	5/32	1954/5
L86	DR 9863	Leyland TD2	1267	Leyland	?	L 24/24R	5/32	1954/5

These vehicles were acquired during March.
In early 1945 Western National bought a number of Plymouth Corporation double-deckers on behalf of the Tilling Association. These were allocated to subsidiaries from Headquarters. Technically therefore these vehicles should be regarded as purchased from Western National Omnibus Company Limited.

L85 *was fitted with a Leyland oil engine and the body of* **L78** *which had been rebuilt by ECW. It was renumbered* **M197.**

L79-84/6 *had their bodies rebuilt by ECW between 11/45 and 6/46 and were also fitted with Leyland oil engines. They were renumbered* **M235-41** *at this time.*

From Exeter Corporation

L87	FJ 7832	Leyland TD1	72150	Brush	?	H28/20R	8/31	1953
-	FJ 7834	Leyland TD1	72152	Brush	?	H28/20R	8/31	1945
L88	FJ 7837	Leyland TD1	72155	Brush	?	H28/20R	8/31	1954

These vehicles had also been acquired by Western National Omnibus Company Limited and were subsequently transferred to Crosville during March.

L87/8 *were fitted with Leyland oil engines in 1946 and the body of* **L88** *was rebuilt by ECW.* **L87** *received a second hand Leyland body, also rebuilt by ECW – the source is unknown. The pair was renumbered* **M242/3** *5/46.*

From Brighton, Hove and District Omnibus Company Limited

L91	GH 6206	AEC Regent	6611520	Dodson	?	H27/25RO	4/31	1954
L89	GP 6231	AEC Regent	6611669	Tilling	?	H27/25RO	9/31	1954
L90	GP 6242	AEC Regent	6611680	Tilling	?	H27/25RO	10/31	1954
L92	GW 6288	AEC Regent	6611791	Tilling	?	H27/25RO	6/32	1954

These vehicles had been on hire to Crosville since 3/43 and were acquired during March. They were then numbered **L103/1/2/4.** *Company records suggest that a plan existed to rebody these and two later acquisitions with BRCW H30/24R bodies originally new to Birmingham Corporation: these bodies had been removed from Daimler COG5 chassis by Bird of Stratford upon Avon. It is not known why the scheme did not proceed but all four were rebuilt in 1948 on new longer-wheelbase frames, fitted with AEC 7.7-litre oil engines of a similar type to those fitted to contemporary Bristols and new ECW bodies.* *See page 148.*

From York-West Yorkshire Joint Committee, Harrogate

D3	VY 2223	Leyland LT2	51220	Roe	?	B32RP	10/30	1952
-	VY 2224	Leyland LT2	51221	Roe	?	B32RP	10/30	1945

These vehicles which were new to York Corporation had apparently been stored between 12/38 and purchase by Crosville in November 1945. This was somewhat unusual, to say the least. VY 2224 was used for spares and did not enter service. In 1949 the body of D3 was rebuilt by Bankfield Engineering incorporating an enclosed entrance and sliding door.

The foregoing covers all Crosville vehicle purchases up to the end of 1945. In subsequent years, many were rebodied or rebuilt. For example, in 1952, Crosville rebodied all of the ten Titan TD7 buses diverted from East Kent in 1940, ten of the sixteen from Southdown and one of the Willowbrook-bodied TD7 utilities of 1952 with this very angular highbridge style in its own workshops. By that date, highbridge bodies had become accepted for operation on suitable routes in the Rhyl area following the fortuitous breakthrough created by the ex-Southdown buses, but all of these had the typical lowbridge seating capacity of 53, with 27 on the top deck, though this represented an increase of one for the Southdowns. By that date six bays between bulkheads was very unusual for double-deckers, and although the standee windows followed a short-lived adoption of this idea by Northern Counties, the overall effect was of a barely-updated utility design. Withdrawals began in 1957 and all had gone by 1959. Other work of this kind is covered in Appendix IV.

APPENDIX I

New fleet numbers allocated in 1935

New class	Old number	Registration	Chassis type
A1-10	201-10	FM 3710/73-81	Leyland Lion PLSC1
A11- 29	245-63	FM 4281-99	Leyland Lion PLSC1
A30-35	265-70	FM 4301-4/50/1	Leyland Lion PLSC1
A36	973	CC 7449	Leyland Lion PLSC1
B1 - 21	22-42	FM 4817-22/45-50/29-37*	Leyland Lion PLSC3 (*conv from PLC1)
B22 - 43	61-82	FM 5226-41, EK 6285, FR 8419, EK 6286/7*, CC 8166/7	Leyland Lion PLSC3 (*conv from PLC1)
B44/5	199/200	FM 4333/4	Leyland Lion PLSC3
B46	264	FM 4300	Leyland Lion PLSC3
B47-85	271-310	FM 4486-8, 4561/2, 4791-4816/23-28 FM 5027/8,	Leyland Lion PLSC3
B86-96	420-30	DM 5977/8, 5258-63/7, 5842/3	Leyland Lion PLSC3
B97	972	CC 8021	Leyland Lion PLSC3
C1-14	311-24	FM 5704-14	Leyland Lion LT1
C15-25	337-47	FM 5526-31, 5787-90, 5718	Leyland Lion LT1
C26/7	970/1	CC 8531/2	Leyland Lion LT1
D1-24	195/6/375-99	FM 6417/8, 5908-29	Leyland Lion LT2
D25-44	440-50/64-79	FM 6419-38	Leyland Lion LT2
D45/6	484/500	FM 6477/8	Leyland Lion LT2
D47-56	539-50	FM 6439-44/73-6	Leyland Lion LT2
E1-41	105-36/82-91	FM 6861-6901	Leyland Lion LT3
E42-44	481-3	FM 6902-4	Leyland Lion LT3
E45-50	555-60	FM 6905-10	Leyland Lion LT3
E51-65	650-64	FM 6981-95	Leyland Lion LT3
E66-75	680-9	FM 7008-12, 33-7	Leyland Lion LT3
F1-3	699-701	FM 7230-32	Leyland Lion LT5
F4-24	751-71	FM 7478-98	Leyland Lion LT5
F25-42	773-90	FM 7500-17	Leyland Lion LT5
G1	582	FM 8424	Leyland Lion LT5A
G2-17	900-15	FM 8133-48	Leyland Lion LT5A
G18-21	981-4	FM 8412-5	Leyland Lion LT5A
J1-3	606/772/836	FM 6472/7499/UN 953	Daimler CH6/Ld Lion LT5/ADC 423 (see footnote)
K1-6	12-17	FM 5242-7	Leyland Lioness LTB1
K7-20	143/66-78	LG 2610, FM 6856-60, 5218-25	Leyland Tiger TS2, TS4, TS2
K21-32	348-53/69-74	FM 5896-907	Leyland Tiger TS2
K33-7	415-9	DM 5844-6, 6230/1	Leyland Tiger TS2
K38-43	431-6	DM 6224-9	Leyland Lioness LTB1
K44-62	607-25	FM 6445-58, 70/1, 80-2	Leyland Tiger TS3
K63-7	640-4	FM 6911-5	Leyland Tiger TS4
K68-77	741-50	FM 7468-77	Leyland Tiger TS4
K78-81	930-3	FM 8163-6	Leyland Tiger TS6
K82-9	962-9	FM 8167-70, 8270, JC 1343, 200*, CC 9401*	Leyland Tiger TS6 & TS1 or TS2*
L1-4	18-21	FM 6391-4	Leyland Titan TD1
L5-22	43-60	FM 6395-412	Leyland Titan TD1
L23	137	VR 8862	Crossley Condor DD
L24-35	211-222	FM 6264-75	Leyland Titan TD1
L36-47	325-336	FM 5206-17	Leyland Titan TD1
L48-62	354-68	FM 5882-94, 5749, 5895	Leyland Titan TD1
L63	414	DM 6232	Leyland Titan TD1
L64-71	551-4/645-8	FM 6413-6, 6916-9	Leyland Titan TD1 & TD2
L72-81	702/3, 733-40	FM 7233/4, 7460-7	Leyland Titan TD2
L82-6	791-5	FM 7760-4	Leyland Titan TD2
L87	1000	AMD 256	AEC Q DD
M1	649	FM 6920	Leyland Titan TD2 (oil engine)
M2-9	916-23	FM 8149-56	Leyland Titan TD3 (oil engine)
M10-12	934-6	FM 6276-8	Leyland Titan TD3 (oil engine)

APPENDIX I

New fleet numbers allocated in 1935

New class	Old number	Registration	Chassis type
N1-5	635-9	FM 6851-5	Leyland Cub KP2
N6-20	665-79	FM 6996-7005/38-42	Leyland Cub KP2
N21-49	704-32	FM 7431-59	Leyland Cub KP2 & KP3
N50-74	937-61	FM 6279-99, 8015-8	Leyland Cub KP2
N75-82	985-992	FM 8416-23	Leyland Cub KP2 and KP3
O1-6	924-9	FM 8157-62	Leyland Cub SKP3
Q1-6	533-8	CC 8561-6	SOS M
Q7-12	583-8	CC 6920/1, 7862/3, 9284/5	SOS QC & QLC
R1-7	88/99/100-4	UL 7229, VT 2653, CC8607-11	Tilling Stevens B10A & B10B
R8-11	840-3	UN 1914/6/5/7	Tilling Stevens B10A
R12-25	844-57	FM 5268/70/69/71, 5782-4/91, 6523-9	Tilling Stevens B10A & B10A2
R26-46	858-78	UN 4479-88, 5390-400	Tilling Stevens B10A2
R47-56	880-8	FM 7057-66	Tilling Stevens B10A2
S1-8	1-8	EY 3133, 3301, 3541/38/7, 3449, 3539/40	Albion PK26 & SP LB 24
S9	197	UR 3902	Albion PR28
S10-21	401-12	FM 6014-23, UR6298/9	Albion LC24, PJ24 & Viking 6
S22	974	CC 8879	Albion PR28
T1-3	85-7	CC8516/7, MY1415	AEC 426 & Reliance
T4	413	UR 6300	AEC Regal
T5	980	BG 605	AEC Regal
U1	93	CC 9578	Morris TB6
U2-5	138-41	LG 2637/6/90, 7194	Crossley Six
U6-9	490-500	DM 6233-6, 5266	S & D Low Freighter
U10-2	626-8	FM 6459-61	S & D Low Freighter
U13-6	896-99	UU 5014/3/2/0	Morris R

Although these changes brought some order to the often chaotic Crosville method of numbering up to this time, the unwary should take note of various subsequent renumberings particularly affecting classes Q and U. It was not until 1958 that a 'clean' system emerged.

At this stage, the only class of new oil-engined vehicles was the M series of Leyland Titan double-deckers, though the J class, then only comprising three vehicles, was of conversions using four-cylinder Leyland oil engines, though further new Leyland Lion LT7 buses with similar engines then on order were to follow. A list issued at the time also included J4-28 (the oil engine LT7 buses), H1-15 (petrol-engined LT7), O7-22 (Cub SKP3), P1-12 (oil-engined Cub), M13-21 (Titan, TD4 oil), K90-92 (Tiger TS7), and U18-21 (S & D) as well as a few acquired buses, some having old-style fleet numbers.

The 1935 renumbering had the effect of collecting up vehicles of the same type that had come from different fleets. This Leyland Tiger TS2, CC 9401, had been acquired with the business of Seiont Motors, Carnarfon, in 1934, becoming number 974 among a mixed bag of acquired makes and types at that time. It was renumbered K89, thus joining the other Tigers in the fleet. Even so, the resulting class was somewhat muddled in terms of age and type, and this 1930 chassis took the highest number then issued, coming after batches of later TS3, TS4 and TS6 models. It is seen here as running in post-war days, with ECW body dating from 1936, intended at that time for excursion and similar duty, but demoted to bus work in later years.

APPENDIX II

Producer gas and other wartime practices

This view of an ambulance conversion shows the way in which the standard Leyland body of an E-class Lion LT3 was converted to accept the tubular-framed stretchers, using wooden benches with removable tubular steel supports. Wooden planks across the windows were provided to prevent the casualties being thrown against the glass.

Among the early effects of the war, in some cases put in hand during the crisis days before the actual outbreak on 3rd September 1939, was conversion of some single-deck buses as ambulances, Crosville providing 24 examples, mainly in October 1939. The thought behind this was that the heavy bombing anticipated from the start was expected to produce numerous casualties and operators were directed to provide suitable vehicles. In practice, such ambulances were not very widely used, even when bombing of major cities began in earnest in late 1940, being found too inflexible for most such duties, and smaller vehicles, often adapted from large saloon cars, tended to be favoured. Accordingly the Ministry of Health returned many of them, though some were retained for the duration of the war to 1945.

The Government began encouraging experiments on alternative fuels for buses in the 1938-9 period, it being realised that oil, all imported in those days, might well be subject to submarine attack and become scarce. When war was declared in September 1939 rationing of diesel fuel and petrol was imposed almost immediately, and major cuts in services were necessary. A few operators experimented with operation on town gas, carried in balloon-like containers on the roof of single-deckers. Others tried producer gas, made by burning coke in what amounted to a miniature gas works, in a few cases carried on the vehicle, though the use of a small trailer became accepted as a more practical means, although a change in the law was needed to permit it.

All this was on a very small scale until 1942 when the shipping losses had become very serious. Frederick Heaton, Chairman of the Tilling group, had responded enthusiastically, and Crosville was studying its efforts when it was decreed that operators were to convert 10 per cent of their fleets, with the threat that even more might be needed. Mass production of producer gas trailers was put in hand, and Crosville was required by the Ministry of War Transport to buy 101, to provide the correct proportion for its fleet, allowing for spares, although delivery is not thought to have been completed.

By the time this was in hand, Crosville was itself in the Tilling group, and doubtless found itself under pressure to persevere. Spark ignition was generally used, so petrol vehicles were chosen for conversion, and as there was quite severe power loss, the more generously powered Leyland Tiger was the usual choice. Even so, conversion work was needed on the vehicles and, amid other wartime pressures, only sixteen vehicles are thought to have been converted before the scheme was dropped in September 1944 – twelve K-class Tigers and four L-class Titans, the latter being very limited in their capabilities. There was a sense of relief, as the system was very troublesome at a time when skilled staff were scarce. Even so, Heaton got a knighthood on the strength of his and the Tilling group's efforts with the scheme.

As timetables were pruned and many buses were needed to carry workers to war factories, notably in

This view of K23, a Leyland Tiger TS2 with chassis dating from 1930, complete with producer gas trailer, conveys the way in which such a vehicle, rebodied by ECW to a standard making it suitable for coach duties in 1936/7, had taken on a shabby air by the latter part of the war. This was quite apart from its enfeebled engine due to the change of fuel, though the frustrations of the latter doubtless kept staff busy enough simply keeping it running.

The lack of headlamp masks suggests this might date from 1945, and hence perhaps was a record photograph of one of these vehicles before being converted back to petrol. The seating capacity had been reduced to 30, the seats, evidently from another vehicle, being mounted in 'perimeter' fashion, so performance with the intended load of up to 60 must have been abysmal. Cast aluminium radiators tended to go black if not cleaned, and Crosville was one of several companies which began painting radiators as a quick way of 'improving' them, a habit that stuck. The snag was that when scratched, as here, doubtless as the bonnet side was repeatedly lifted off to coax the engine to perform (and seemingly discarded altogether), the effect was even worse. In later years, this vehicle received a Gardner 5LW oil engine, then becoming KC23, and thus having run on petrol, producer gas, petrol again and then derv.

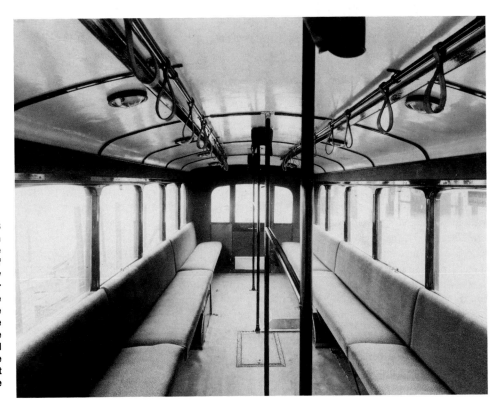

This view of the interior of E18 taken by the Company in November 1941 may have indicated it was something of an experiment. It clearly has new bench seating whilst other conversions merely had the normal seats repositioned. The stanchions for the use of the standees are evident and the ceiling lights have been fitted with cowls to ensure they shine downwards during the blackout – the other lights would not have been used.

Crosville's case the Royal Ordnance Factory at Wrexham, the remaining vehicles regularly became unable to carry all the passengers wishing to travel, even in off-peak times. To help in overcoming this problem, many operators, including Crosville, converted some of their single-deckers to longitudinal or 'perimeter' seating, the space in the centre of the vehicles being used to carry standing passengers, and they were often described as standee buses.

A fairly standard pattern was the provision of seats for 30 and standing space for 30, and such loads were frequently carried or even exceeded. The springs of such vehicles were usually strengthened. Crosville had an unusually large number, 127, mainly Lion LT3 or LT5 but also a number of K-type Tigers. Naturally, such vehicles were unpopular, not least for the unfortunate conductor who had to struggle round to collect fares,

but wartime travel was a matter of necessity and matters such as passenger comfort became very low on the list of priorities.

Another type of vehicle which began to become more common in wartime was the mobile canteen. It seems to have been recognised that providing the proverbial 'cuppa' would have even more of a morale-lifting effect in wartime. One of the ex-Ribble Leyland Lion PLSC1 buses that had been acquired in 1939, A32 (TE 2901), was converted into a canteen in 1940, and it proved useful when Liverpool suffered severe bomb damage in May 1941, destroying premises which Crosville crews had used. An advantage under such conditions when further bombing was to be expected, was that it was removed at night – in wartime, evening services stopped earlier than in peacetime – and reinstated early the following morning.

CONVERSIONS

Vehicles converted to Producer Gas operation.

K 13-5, 23,29-32/5/6 /48/55
L 31/2, 40/1   Total – 16

Vehicles converted to Ambulances

The majority of the conversions were undertaken in 10/39- the vehicles then left the ownership of the Company at the time of conversion, being transferred to the Ministry of Health, and Crosville was fortunate in that all appear to have returned for further use as buses between 1941 and 1946.

E 6/8/14/5/17/19/20/2/4-9/31/3/6/8/40-3/5/7   -   Total – 24.

Vehicles converted to Perimeter Seating/ Standee Layout

The majority of these conversions were carried out in the 1940-3 period: all had provision for thirty seated passengers in this format – standing capacity was nominally usually 30 but in practice tended to have been dependent upon the girth of the individual passengers presenting themselves for each journey and whether they were wearing the heavy overcoats then usual in winter. They were very unpopular and many vehicles reverted to normal layout during or just after the war. In some instances the seated capacity altered – possibly because either the original seats were not matched with the correct body – or some were diverted to other conversions.

E 1-13/6/18/9/21/23-31/4/5/7/9/44/6/8-75
F 1-42.
K 13/4/7/19-27/30/1/44/5.   Total – 127

It is noticeable that only K13 /4//23/30/1 were both producer gas powered and intended to carry large loadings! Also amongst these conversions are many early returns from those vehicles requisitioned for use as ambulances.

The Royal Ordnance Factory at Wrexham, newly completed in the early months of the war, required many of the hired buses to carry the workers., Those in this scene include a Leyland Titan TD3 and two TD4c 'Gearless' models with English Electric bodywork from the Wallasey Corporation fleet, dating from 1934 and 1936 but unusual for that date in being petrol-engined. Also visible are four AEC Regent ST-class buses of 1930-31 from London Transport. The latter were of the open-staircase type that had been acquired with the London bus operation of Thomas Tilling Ltd when the LPTB had been formed in 1933 – other buses of the same type, also registered in London, had been allocated to Tilling's Brighton branch, some being hired and later acquired by Crosville.
　　The numbering system for the hired vehicles used Crosville's class letter prefixes, in many cases combined with the owner's fleet numbers. The London buses simply retained theirs, but with the ST prefix replaced by L, but the Wallasey fleet numbers clashed with Crosville's own so, in effect, L400 was added, so 24 became L424, etc. On the left, a Leyland Lion LT2 from the Ribble fleet can just be seen – these, almost identical to Crosville's D-class, took numbers then blank in that series as a result of the sale of some of the type in 1938.

APPENDIX III

Wartime loans
and hirings

During wartime the Regional Traffic Commissioners had almost unlimited powers and many vehicles were directed to Crosville's use – a total of 222 are listed below. The normal PSV Licence carried by the vehicles was replaced by a Defence Permit – the sale of old vehicles was also controlled as well as applications for new ones, their allocation being controlled by the Ministry of War Transport and their manufacture and specification by the Ministry of Supply.

After 1942, the Tilling group's centralised vehicle policy, already well established in pre-war days, included Crosville within its remit. Wartime philosophy encouraged the extension of its thinking beyond the pressure to buy Bristol chassis and ECW bodywork that had been in force pre-war to encompass a completely standardised range of body as well as chassis designs. The highbridge and lowbridge Bristol K-type prototypes with ECW bodies evolved from that concern's wartime design being sent round the group from 1944. When suitable second-hand vehicles were hard to find, Tilling set up a centralised arrangement for their purchase and distribution within the group, early fruits of this being the ex-Plymouth Titan TD2 buses that found their way into several Tilling fleets.

From Birkenhead Corporation Transport

CMS No.	Reg	Make/type	Chassis No.	Body	Capacity	New	Loan from/to
L124-125	CM 9385-86	Leyland TD1	71291/2	Leyland	L24/24R	6/30	6/40-10/40
L132-138	CM 9756-62	Leyland TD1	71511-7	Leyland	L27/24R	8/30	6/40-10/40
L185	BG 1509	AEC Q	761007	MCCW	L31/28R	8/33	6/40-10/40

From Yorkshire Woollen District Transport Company Limited, Dewsbury

CMS No.	Reg	Make/type	Chassis No.	Body	Capacity	New	Loan from/to
F199-203	HD 4610-14	Leyland LT5	539-43	Leyland	B32F	3/32	10/40-1942
L214-225	HD 4625-36	Leyland TD2	503-14	Roe	H24/24C	4/32	6/40-1942/43
L206-7	HD 4617-8	Leyland TD2	521/2	Leyland	L27/24R	3/32	1942-10/42
L208	HD 4619	Leyland TD2	523	NCME	L27/24R	3/32	1942-10/42

From East Yorkshire Motor Services Limited, Hull

CMS No.	Reg	Make/type	Chassis No.	Body	Capacity	New	Loan from/to
B98	WF 1156	Leyland PLSC3	46784	Leyland	B32R	3/28	10/40-3/43
B99	WF 1158	Leyland PLSC3	46786	Leyland	B32R	3/28	10/40-3/43
B100	WF 1161	Leyland PLSC3	46789	Leyland	B32R	4/28	10/40-3/43
B101	WF 1163	Leyland PLSC3	46791	Leyland	B32R	4/28	10/40-3/43
B199	KH 7017	Leyland PLSC3	47120	Roe	B32F	7/28	10/40-3/43
B200	KH 7565	Leyland PLSC3	47072	Roe	B32F	10/28	10/40-3/43
C220	WF 2450	Leyland LT1	50210	Leyland	B32F	5/29	10/40-3/43
C218	WF 2497	Leyland LT1	50233	Leyland	B32F	6/29	10/40-3/43
C219	WF 2499	Leyland LT1	50232	Leyland	B32F	6/29	10/40-3/43
C167-8	WF 2532-3	Leyland LT1	50230/1	Leyland	B30F	6/29	10/40-3/43
K120	KH 7914	Leyland TS2	60364	Roe	B30R	4/29	10/40-3/43
K121	KH 7915	Leyland TS2	60365	Roe	B30R	3/29	10/40-3/43
K122#	KH 7916	Leyland TS2	60366	Roe	B30R	3/29	10/40-11/44
K123#	KH 7917	Leyland TS2	60367	Roe	B30R	4/29	10/40-3/45
K125#	KH 7919	Leyland TS2	60369	Roe	B30R	4/29	10/40-3/45
K128#	KH 7922	Leyland TS2	60372	Leyland	B30F	7/29	10/40-11/44
K221#	WF 2609	Leyland TS2	60438	Leyland	B30F	7/29	10/40-11/44
K222#	WF 3275	Leyland TS2	61012	Leyland	B30F	4/30	10/40-3/43
K223#	WF 3276	Leyland TS2	61013	Leyland	B30F	4/30	10/40-11/44
K185#	RH 4793	Leyland TS4	986	ECOC	B30R	5/32	10/40-4/45
K186#	RH 4794	Leyland TS4	987	ECOC	B30R	5/32	10/40-11/44
K188-189#	RH 4796-7	Leyland TS4	989/90	ECOC	B30R	5/32	10/40-11/44

Equipped for producer gas operation 1943-44.

From Manchester Corporation Transport Dept

CMS No.	Reg	Make/type	Chassis No.	Body	Capacity	New	Loan from/to
L226	VR 5469	Leyland TD1	71054	MCCW/Crossley	L26/26R	2/30	10/40-3/46
L228	VR 5471	Leyland TD1	71051	MCCW/Crossley	L26/26R	2/30	10/40-4/46
L229	VR 5749	Leyland TD1	71065	MCCW/Crossley	L26/26R	2/30	10/40-1945
L233$	VR 5753	Leyland TD1	71071	MCCW/Crossley	L26/26R	3/30	10/40-7/45
L234	VR 5754	Leyland TD1	71072	MCCW/Crossley	L26/26R	3/30	10/40-5/46
L241+	VR 5760	Leyland TD1	71061	MCCW/Crossley	L26/26R	3/30	10/40-11/43
L242	VR 5761	Leyland TD1	71063	MCCW/Crossley	L26/26R	3/30	10/40-5/46

Inevitably, the hired vehicles looked shabby after a long service in difficult conditions, with no more attention than was needed to keep them running, and none to paintwork beyond perfunctory cleaning. Manchester Corporation's 223 (VR 6019), one of the 37 Leyland Titan TD1 buses from this fleet, had been with Crosville since October 1940 when seen not long before return to its owners in November 1945. In fact, these vehicles, although having 1930 chassis, had 1936 bodywork based on durable Metro-Cammell framing, and were basically sound.

James Crosland Taylor, in his book, *The Sowing and the Harvest* hints at regret at not buying them, as was done with some buses initially operated on loan. Manchester might well have been quite willing to sell at least some, once post-war bus deliveries began, having no specific use for buses with the side-gangway lowbridge layout by that date – they tended to be used only as rush-hour extras during their final years in that city, this one being typical in being withdrawn in 1949. If oil engines had been fitted, and the bodies tidied up mildly and repainted, as was done with may other TD1 buses by Crosville, they might well have run successfully into the mid 'fifties.

L243	VR 5762	Leyland TD1	71066	MCCW/Crossley	L26/26R	3/30	10/40-3/46
L244	VR 5763	Leyland TD1	71075	MCCW/Crossley	L26/26R	3/30	10/40-12/45
L211	VR 5766	Leyland TD1	71067	MCCW/Crossley	L26/26R	3/30	10/40-2/46
L245	VR 5767	Leyland TD1	71074	MCCW/Crossley	L26/26R	3/30	10/40-2/46
L246	VR 5768	Leyland TD1	71076	MCCW/Crossley	L26/26R	3/30	10/40-2/46
L213	VR 6002	Leyland TD1	71056	MCCW/Crossley	L26/26R	3/30	10/40-3/46
L247	VR 6015	Leyland TD1	71077	MCCW/Crossley	L26/26R	3/30	10/40-12/45
L210 (L323)	VR 6019	Leyland TD1	71084	MCCW/Crossley	L26/26R	3/30	10/40-11/45
L212 (L324)	VR 6020	Leyland TD1	71085	MCCW/Crossley	L26/26R	3/30	10/40-12/45
L325	VR 5258	Leyland TD1	71053	MCCW/Crossley	L26/26R	2/30	10/41-12/45
L227	VR 5470	Leyland TD1	71059	MCCW/Crossley	L26/26R	2/30	10/41-1/46
L230	VR 5750	Leyland TD1	71046	MCCW/Crossley	L26/26R	3/30	10/41-1/46
L231	VR 5751	Leyland TD1	71068	MCCW/Crossley	L26/26R	3/30	10/41-1/46
L232	VR 5752	Leyland TD1	71069	MCCW/Crossley	L26/26R	3/30	10/41-12/45
L235	VR 5755	Leyland TD1	71070	MCCW/Crossley	L26/26R	3/30	10/41-12/45
L236	VR 5756	Leyland TD1	71073	MCCW/Crossley	L26/26R	2/30	10/41-12/45
L238	VR 5757	Leyland TD1	71058	MCCW/Crossley	L26/26R	3/30	10/41-4/46
L239	VR 5758	Leyland TD1	71049	MCCW/Crossley	L26/26R	3/30	10/41-2/46
L240	VR 5759	Leyland TD1	71060	MCCW/Crossley	L26/26R	3/30	10/41-4/46
L209-210	VR 5764-5	Leyland TD1	71050/7	MCCW/Crossley	L26/26R	3/30	10/41-5/46
L212	VR 6001	Leyland TD1	71055	MCCW/Crossley	L26/26R	3/30	10/41-5/46
L314	VR 6003	Leyland TD1	71048	MCCW/Crossley	L26/26R	3/30	10/41-6/46
L316	VR 6005	Leyland TD1	71064	MCCW/Crossley	L26/26R	3/30	10/41-12/45
L318	VR 6007	Leyland TD1	71080	MCCW/Crossley	L26/26R	3/30	10/41-1/46
L248	VR 6016	Leyland TD1	71081	MCCW/Crossley	L26/26R	3/30	10/41-12/45
L319	VR 6681	Leyland TD1	71078	MCCW/Crossley	L26/26R	3/30	10/41-1/46
L320	VR 6682	Leyland TD1	71079	MCCW/Crossley	L26/26R	3/30	10/41-4/46
L215	VR 6004	Leyland TD1	71062	MCCW/Crossley	L26/26R	3/30	2/43-12/45
L321	VR 6017	Leyland TD1	71083	MCCW/Crossley	L26/26R	3/30	1/43-7/45

$ Destroyed in Rhyl fire
+ Scrapped by Crosville following an accident.

From North Western Road Car Company Limited, Stockport

R292	DB 5192	T/Stevens B10A	6203	ECOC	B31R	11/28	10-11/40
R297-8	DB 5197-8	T/Stevens B10A	6207/8	ECOC	B31R	12/28	10/40-1944
R300	DB 5200	T/Stevens B10A	6210	ECOC	B31R	1/29	10/40-1944
R301	DB 5201	T/Stevens B10A	6211	ECOC	B31R	11/28	10/40-1941
R307	DB 5207	T/Stevens B10A	6217	ECOC	B31R	1/29	10-11/40
R308	DB 5208	T/Stevens B10A	6218	ECOC	B31R	1/29	10/40-1941
R319	DB 5219	T/Stevens B10A	6274	ECOC	B31R	2/29	10-11/40
R320	DB 5220	T/Stevens B10A	6275	ECOC	B31R	3/29	10-11/40
R321	BD 5221	T/Stevens B10A	6276	ECOC	B31R	2/29	10-11/40
R329	DB 5229	T/Stevens B10A	6284	ECOC	B31R	3/29	10/40-1941
R331	DB 5231	T/Stevens B10A	6286	ECOC	B31R	3/29	10/40-1944
R334	DB 5234	T/Stevens B10A	6289	ECOC	B31R	3/29	10-11/40
R338	DB 5238	T/Stevens B10A	6293	ECOC	B31R	3/29	10-11/40
R340-1	DB 5240-1	T/Stevens B10A	6295/6	ECOC	B31R	3/29	10-11/40

R345	DB 5245	T/Stevens B10A	6300	ECOC	B31R	3/29	10-11/40
R347	DB 5247	T/Stevens B10A	6302	ECOC	B31R	3/29	10-11/40
R350	DB 5250	T/Stevens B10A	6305	ECOC	B31R	3/29	10-11/40
R354	DB 5254	T/Stevens B10A	6309	ECOC	B31R	2/29	10/40-1944
R359	DB 5259	T/Stevens B10A	6314	ECOC	B31R	2/29	10/40-1944
R361	DB 5261	T/Stevens B10A	6316	ECOC	B31R	2/29	10/40-1944
R372	DB 5272	T/Stevens B10A	6327	ECOC	B31R	3/29	10/40-1944
R376	DB 5276	T/Stevens B10A	6331	ECOC	B31R	3/29	10/40-1944
R377	DB 5277	T/Stevens B10A	6332	ECOC	B31R	3/29	10-11/40
R379	DB 5279	T/Stevens B10A	6334	ECOC	B31R	3/29	10/40-1941
R382	DB 5282	T/Stevens B10A	6337	ECOC	B31R	3/29	10/40-1944
R383	DB 5283	T/Stevens B10A	6338	ECOC	B31R	3/29	10-11/40
R387	DB 5287	T/Stevens B10A	6342	ECOC	B31R	3/29	10/40-1944
R389	DB 5289	T/Stevens B10A	6344	ECOC	B31R	3/29	10/40-1944

From Bolton Corporation Transport

M216	WH 6858	Leyland TD4c	7765	Roberts	L26/26R	1/36	12/40-3/43
M218-220	WH 6860-2	Leyland TD4c	7759-61	Roberts	L26/26R	3/36	12/40-3/43
M223	WH 6865	Leyland TD4c	7757	Roberts	L26/26R	3/36	12/40-3/43
L170	WH 4219	Leyland TD2	1650	Bromilow & Edwards	L24/24R	3/33	10/42-2/45
L365	WH 4214	Leyland TD2	1645	Bromilow & Edwards	L24/24R	12/32	12/42-2/45
L369	WH 4218	Leyland TD2	1649	Bromilow & Edwards	L24/24R	2/33	12/42-6/46

From Yorkshire Traction Company Limited, Barnsley

L332	HE 5216	Leyland TD1	72046	Leyland	L27/24R	3/31	12/40-1941
L334-335	HE 5218-9	Leyland TD1	72048/9	Leyland	L27/24R	3/31	12/40-1941
W397-398	HE 6310-1	Dennis Lancet	170571/2	Roe	B32F	3/34	12/40-1941
W401-403	HE 6314-6	Dennis Lancet	170576-8	Roe	B32F	3/34	12/40-1941
W406	HE 6319	Dennis Lancet	170581	Roe	B32F	3/34	12/40-1941
W408	HE 6321	Dennis Lancet	170584	Roe	B32F	3/34	12/40-1941
W414	HE 6327	Dennis Lancet	170591	Roe	B32F	3/34	12/40-1941

From Wallasey Corporation Motors

L469	HF 7857	Leyland TD2	707	English Electric	H27/21D	3/32	7/41-11/46
L470	HF 7859	Leyland TD2	705	English Electric	H27/21D	3/32	7/41-11/46
L471	HF 7861	Leyland TD2	706	English Electric	H27/21D	3/32	7/41-9/46
L475	HF 8253	Leyland TD2	1783	English Electric	H27/21D	7/32	7/41-11/46
L476	HF 8255	Leyland TD2	1784	English Electric	H27/21D	7/32	7/41-12/46
L477	HF 8257	Leyland TD2	1785	English Electric	H27/21D	7/32	7-11/41
L478	HF 8259	Leyland TD2	2144	English Electric	H27/21D	3/33	7/41-10/46
L479	HF 8261	Leyland TD2	2145	English Electric	H27/21D	3/33	7/41-10/46
L480	HF 8263	Leyland TD2	2146	English Electric	H27/21D	3/33	7/41-10/46
L488	HF 9179	Leyland TD3	3597	English Electric	H27/21D	12/33	7/41-9/45
L489	HF 9181	Leyland TD3	3598	English Electric	H27/21D	1/34	7/41-4/45
L490	HF 9183	Leyland TD3	3599	English Electric	H27/21D	1/34	7/41-2/44
L491	HF 9185	Leyland TD3	3600	English Electric	H27/21D	1/34	7/41-10/43
L492	HF 9381	Leyland TD3c	4464	Roe	H29/23C	8/34	7/41-10/46
L493	HF 9383	AEC Regent	6612677	English Electric	H27/21D	3/34	7-8/41
L494	HF 9385	AEC Regent	6612678	English Electric	H27/21D	3/34	7-8/41
L495	HF 9387	AEC Regent	6612679	English Electric	H27/21D	3/34	7-8/41
L496	HF 9389	AEC Regent	6612680	English Electric	H27/21D	3/34	7-8/41
L497	HF 9391	AEC Regent	6612681	English Electric	H27/21D	3/34	7-8/41
L498	HF 9393	AEC Regent	6612682	English Electric	H27/21D	1/36	7-8/41
L422	HF 5240	Leyland TD4c	8208	English Electric	H27/21D	1/36	7/41-2/46
L423	HF 5242	Leyland TD4c	8209	English Electric	H27/21D	1/36	7/41-2/46
L424	HF 5244	Leyland TD4c	8210	English Electric	H27/21D	1/36	7/41-1/46
L425	HF 5246	Leyland TD4c	8211	English Electric	H27/21D	1/36	7/41-10/45
L426	HF 5248	Leyland TD4c	8212	English Electric	H27/21D	1/36	7/41-11/45
L427	HF 5250	Leyland TD4c	8213	English Electric	H27/21D	1/36	7/41-3/46
L428	HF 5252	Leyland TD4c	8214	English Electric	H27/21D	1/36	7-11/41
L429	HF 5254	Leyland TD4c	8215	English Electric	H27/21D	1/36	7/41-1/46
L430	HF 5256	Leyland TD4c	8216	English Electric	H27/21D	1/36	7/41-3/46
L431	HF 5258	Leyland TD4c	8217	English Electric	H27/21D	1/36	7/41-12/45

From Sheffield United Tours Limited, Sheffield

K142	WD 5055	Leyland TS2	60711	Burlingham	C32F	1/29	10/41-1942
K141	FV 1131	Leyland TS2	60707	Burlingham	C30F	6/30	10/41-1942
K146	WJ 6503	Leyland TS4	2152	Cravens	C31R	4/33	10/41-1942
K148	WJ 6505	Leyland TS4	2153	Cravens	C31R	4/33	10/41-1942
G56-58	WJ 9962-9964	Leyland LT5A	4162-4	Cravens	C32R	5/34	10/41-1942

G60	WJ 9970	Leyland LT5A	4165	Cravens	C32R	6/34	10/41-1942
G62-63	AWA 331-332	Leyland LT5A	4296/7	Duple	C35F	6/34	10/41-1942
K151	AWA 333	Leyland TS6	4720	Duple	C33F	6/34	10/41-1942
K150	AWA 334	Leyland TS6	4721	Duple	C33F	6/34	10/41-1942

From London Passenger Transport Board, London SW1

L846	GJ 2022	AEC Regent	661573	Dodson or Tilling	H27/25RO	7/30	1/42-1/46
L852	GJ 2028	AEC Regent	661580	Dodson or Tilling	H27/25RO	6/30	1/42-11/46
L858	GJ 2034	AEC Regent	661587	Dodson or Tilling	H27/25RO	7/30	1/42-10/46
L859	GJ 2035	AEC Regent	661583	Dodson or Tilling	H27/25RO	7/30	1/42-12/46
L863	GJ 2039	AEC Regent	661592	Dodson or Tilling	H27/25RO	8/30	1/42-3/46
L868	GJ 2044	AEC Regent	661600	Dodson or Tilling	H27/25RO	7/30	1/42-4/44
L875	GJ 2051	AEC Regent	661603	Dodson or Tilling	H27/25RO	7/30	1/42-11/46
L976	GK 6252	AEC Regent	6611046	Dodson or Tilling	H27/25RO	3/31	1/42-10/46
L1016	GK 6292	AEC Regent	6611083	Dodson or Tilling	H27/25RO	6/31	1/42-12/46
L88	GF 410	AEC Regent	6612296	LGOC	H28/20R	3/30	1/43-8/44
L304	GH 3880	AEC Regent	661802	LGOC	H28/20R	9/30	1/43-8/44
L733	GN 2153	AEC Regent	6611378	LGOC	H28/20R	2/31	1/43-8/44

From Southern National Omnibus Company Limited, Exeter

B204	TW 9357	Leyland PLSC3	45657	Mumford	B32R	5/27	3/43-1947
B202	VW 204	Leyland PLSC3	45897	Mumford	B32R	5/27	3/43-1947
B203	VW 4740	Leyland PLSC3	46832	Mumford	B32R	5/28	3/43-1947
B201	VW 5924	Leyland PLSC3	47323	Mumford	B32R	7/28	3/43-1947
B205	VW 5999	Leyland PLSC3	47327	Mumford	B32R	7/28	3/43-1947

From Western National Omnibus Company, Exeter

B209	TW 9355	Leyland PLSC3	45730	Mumford	B32R	5/27	3/43-1947
B210	VW 4576	Leyland PLSC3	46626	Mumford	B32R	5/28	3/43-1946
B206	YC 2852	Leyland PLSC3	46837	Mumford	B32R	5/28	3/43-1946
B207-8	VW 5609-10	Leyland PLSC3	47320/19	Mumford	B32R	7/28	3/43-1947

From Ribble Motor Services Limited, Preston

D12	CK 4517	Leyland LT2	51382	Leyland	B30F	3/31	3/43-1944
D5	CK 4530	Leyland LT2	51395	Leyland	B30F	3/31	3/43-1944
D3	CK 4533	Leyland LT2	51398	Leyland	B30F	3/31	3/43-1944
D4	CK 4547	Leyland LT2	51498	Leyland	B30F	3/31	3/43-1944
D6	CK 4549	Leyland LT2	51432	Leyland	B30F	3/31	3/43-1944

From Leigh Corporation Transport

L139-41 (L73-5)	TF 6358-60	Leyland TD1	72306-8	Leyland	L27/24R	10/31	3/43-1/45
L130 (L71)	TE 9530	Leyland TD1	70819	Leyland	L24/24R	9/29	2/44-1/45
M231 (M165)	TE 9531	Leyland TD1	70820	Leyland	L24/24R	10/29	2/44-1/45
L132 (L72	TE 9532	Leyland TD1	70821	Leyland	L24/24R	10/29	2/44-1/45

From Brighton Hove and District Omnibus Company Limited

L103 (L91)	GN 6206	AEC Regent	6611520	Dodson	H27/25RO	4/31	3/43-8/45
L101 (L89)	GP 6231	AEC Regent	6611669	Tilling	H27/25RO	9/31	3/43-8/45
L623 (L93)	GP 6238	AEC Regent	6611676	Tilling	H27/25RO	10/31	12/45-1946
L625 (L94)	GW 6255	AEC Regent	6611730	Tilling	H27/25RO	1/32	12/45-1946
L102 (L90)	GP 6242	AEC Regent	6611680	Tilling	H27/25RO	10/31	3/43-8/45
L104 (L92)	GP 6288	AEC Regent	6611791	Tilling	H27/27RO	6/32	3/43-8/45

From Morecambe and Heysham Corporation Transport

L133	TF 7469	AEC Regent	6611815	Weymann	H30/26R	3/32	3/43-1944
L135	TJ 2490	AEC Regent	6612245	Weymann	H30/26R	8/33	3/43-1944

From East Kent Road Car Co Ltd, Canterbury

L350	FN 9095	Leyland TS2	60076	Short	O30/26RO	8/28	12/40-4/44

*Hired vehicles **L101/2/4/623-5** and **M231** were subsequently purchased by Crosville and renumbered as shown.*

APPENDIX IV

Post War Recovery – refurbishing the fleet

In common with most other fleets in the land, Crosville's buses had been called upon to work harder and way beyond their projected life span during the 1939-45 war. Whilst they were not 'neglected' per se, the maintenance plan had called for minimum attention. This was the only policy that could be adopted when skilled manpower, materials and resources were all scarce and, particularly from 1940, when the threat of invasion led to a situation where all manpower was under strict control. Crosville, despite its obvious importance as the main provider of bus services in an area where there were many important factories serving the war effort, lost the use of some of its premises and parts of others. Oswestry depot and part of Bangor were requisitioned after the bombing of Coventry in November 1940, the latter to accommodate part of Daimler's activities. Even in Chester, two bays out of the seven of Sealand Road works were taken over by Vickers-Armstrongs to make aircraft parts, and in 1942, two more were wanted, but a deal was done under which two new ones were built.

In addition, Crosville found itself in charge of a motley collection of buses, mostly themselves old, from other fleets, notably for the munitions factory at Wrexham, where a large fleet had to be stored in the open – even getting them all started in bad weather could be a problem. So inevitably, standards dropped, notably in terms of appearance, and wartime neglect of painting helped to take its toll, as rain found its way through panel joints into the timber framing and rot accelerated.

Whilst new vehicles would continue to be scarce, Crosville still had one abiding problem. The expansionist policies pursued both by the Crosland Taylors and the LMS had generated a territory in North Wales which was dependent on the company for most of its public transport and yet which failed to create enough cash for proper reinvestment. This reliance upon the English routes was to dog the company to its dissolution in 1989, yet it played its part in creating one of the most interesting fleets in the country.

Throughout the 'thirties the Company had followed a policy of rebodying – because new vehicles could not be afforded – and the later 'forties were to prove no different. In the early days of motor bus operation, many companies rebodied chassis almost as a matter of routine, solid tyres and poor roads tending to make this the logical course, but as roads and vehicles improved it became less common in BET-managed companies. Although Crosville had been under BET influence in the 'thirties – its Chairman, W. S. Wreathall, was based at BET headquarters and was also Chairman of Ribble and East Yorkshire – its policy in regard to rebodying had much in common with such companies as Eastern Counties and Western/Southern National, under Tilling

management and also faced with the provision of services in large rural areas. There was also Tilling representation on the board at that time in the person of George Cardwell, who a little earlier had been General Manager of North Western, another company which continued to make rebodying of older chassis regular practice.

The switch to Tilling control in 1942 may have caused James Crosland Taylor misgivings in terms of enforced purchase of Bristol rather than Leyland chassis, but in regard to other aspects of vehicle policy it was more like a homecoming. The Tilling group, with more companies having predominantly rural areas, made a virtue of necessity in keeping buses for longer than favoured by BET, and accepting that rebodying or other means of major refurbishing would be needed. The BET companies also found themselves embarking on a similar course around 1947-50, but that was more of a reaction to shortage of new chassis.

Crosville was thus by no means alone among the Tilling companies in sending buses for rebodying in the post-war period, notably to ECW, where they emerged with much of the appearance of the all-new product. Inevitably they were largely Leyland – Lion, Tiger and Titan models, the latter extending back to the TD1 – but also included some AEC Regents. It was fortuitous that the rebodying was carried out soon after ECW had switched to its very durable aluminium-alloy structure from 1948. When it became evident that the ECW bodies built on new Bristol chassis in 1946/7 were fast deteriorating due to the poor timber available at that time, it was possible to transfer the bodies from old chassis to them, thus making the best use of chassis and bodywork with good life potential.

Use was also made of Burlingham, which rebodied the G-class Leyland Lion LT5A buses, and the Saunders concern. The latter was based at Beaumaris, Anglesey and hence doubtless regarding Crosville as the main 'local' operator, which may have been why a prototype of a new body design was based on a Crosville Tiger TS7, followed by thirteen more. In addition, the Company's own works built some new double-deck bodies, and if, except for one based on a Pearson frame, they were decidedly reminiscent of wartime utility designs in their angular outlines, they too played their part in enabling serviceable 1940 Titan TD7 chassis to outlive their Park Royal bodies which, like many buses of pre-war design for BET companies had been built on the assumption they would be replaced after a life of ten years or even less.

Facing page: Through the Gate Hole ! A view from Sealand into Crosville Central Works where so much of the fleet was reconstructed after the war. At least one E class Leyland can be seen. The works was to remain open until the division of the Company in 1986 eroded its raison d'être and paved the way for closure shortly afterwards. Volume Two will look at it in more detail.

Single-Deckers

Six dual purpose bodies were first to be constructed, which subsequently became the only bodies to be reused on post 1946 Bristol chassis.

Vehicle			New Body			Subsequent post 1946 recipient			
KA 189	FM 7468	Leyland TS4	ECW	DP31R	3443/2	1949	KB 10	FFM 478	1/58
KA 190	FM 7469	Leyland TS4	ECW	DP31R	3444/2	1949	KB 7	FFM 475	1/58
KA 191	FM 7470	Leyland TS4	ECW	DP31R	3445/2	1949	KB 6	FFM 474	1/58
KA 192	FM 7471	Leyland TS4	ECW	DP31R	3446/2	1949	KB 9	FFM 477	1/58
KA 193	FM 7472	Leyland TS4	ECW	DP31R	3447/2	1949	KB 13	FFM 481	2/58
KA 194	JC 1343	Leyland TS6	ECW	DP32R	3441/32	1949	KB 14	FFM 482	2/58

During 1949, 25 bodies were constructed by ECW to basic Bristol 'L' pattern and fitted to Leyland Lion chassis new in 1935. The chassis themselves had been updated with Leyland oil engines (JA) or Gardner 5LW oil engines (JG) classes. Although the bodies were not reused they did last for their full normal lifespan, the last being withdrawn in 1960. A further body was built in 1949 for the chassis of a 1933 Lion. It was fitted with an Albion engine as **FA2**.

JG 4	FM 8974	Leyland LT7	ECW	B35R	4246/2	JG 17	FM 8987	Leyland LT7	ECW	B35R	4250/2
JA 5	FM 8975	Leyland LT7	ECW	B35R	3116/2	JA 18	FM 8988	Leyland LT7	ECW	B35R	3109/2
JA 6	FM 8976	Leyland LT7	ECW	B35R	3117/2	JG 19	FM 8989	Leyland LT7	ECW	B35R	4252/2
JA 7	FM 8977	Leyland LT7	ECW	B35R	3111/2	JG 20	FM 8990	Leyland LT7	ECW	B35R	4251/2
JA 8	FM 8978	Leyland LT7	ECW	B35R	3121/2	JA 21	FM 8991	Leyland LT7	ECW	B35R	3120/2
JA 9	FM 8979	Leyland LT7	ECW	B35R	3108/2	JG 22	FM 8992	Leyland LT7	ECW	B35R	4254/2
JG 10	FM 8980	Leyland LT7	ECW	B35R	4247/2	JA 23	FM 8993	Leyland LT7	ECW	B35R	3110/2
JG 11	FM 8981	Leyland LT7	ECW	B35R	4248/2	JA 24	FM 8994	Leyland LT7	ECW	B35R	3115/2
JG 12	FM 8982	Leyland LT7	ECW	B35R	4249/2	JG 25	FM 8995	Leyland LT7	ECW	B35R	4253/2
JA 13	FM 8983	Leyland LT7	ECW	B35R	3113/2	JA 26	FM 8996	Leyland LT7	ECW	B35R	3112/2
JA 14	FM 8984	Leyland LT7	ECW	B35R	3107/2	JA 27	FM 8997	Leyland LT7	ECW	B35R	3119/2
JA 15	FM 8985	Leyland LT7	ECW	B35R	3118/2	JA 28	FM 8998	Leyland LT7	ECW	B35R	3114/2
JG 16	FM 8986	Leyland LT7	ECW	B35R	4245/2	FA 2	FM 7482	Leyland LT7	ECW	B35R	3122/2

In 1949 one B35R aluminium-framed body was built for the Company by Saunders Engineering of Anglesey on the chassis of **KA14**, *a 1936 Leyland Tiger TS7. This company enjoyed quite a large-scale involvement in bus bodybuilding around this time, notably for London Transport and subsequently the BET Group on early underfloor engined chassis. A further 13 bodies were built in 1950 on other chassis in the same batch. No body numbers are known for the new bodies which lasted until early 1960. One is illustrated on page 152*

KA 1 -10/12-15 FM 9965-74/5-79

A basically similar exercise was also carried out in 1949 on the G class of petrol Leyland Lion LT5A models, again being fitted with Leyland 8.6-litre oil engines, but in this case the new bvodies were by Burlingham, to that concern's standard front-entrance pattern of the time. All 21 of the class, dating from 1934 and originally fitted with bodies by Leyland, Eastern Counties or Tooth were so treated, being reclassified GA.

GA1-21 FM 8424, 8133-48, 8412-5

1949 ECW Bodies fitted to Older Double-Deck Chassis

ECW Body No. Series 2	Seats	First Chassis			Note	Second Chassis			Date	Note	Third Chassis			Date
		Fleet No.	Regn. No.	Chassis Type		Fleet No.	Regn. No.	Chassis Type			Fleet No.	Regn. No.	Chassis Type	
3074	L27/26R	M247	WX 2111	TD1		MB162	FXT 421	K6A	2/56					
3075	L27/26R	M39	FM 6415	TD1	1	M503	BWA 409	TD4	11/5					
3076	L27/26R	M572	CK 4418	TD1		M520	CTH 471	PD1A	7/55					
3077	L27/26R	M40	FM 6416	TD1		MB161	FXT 420	K6A	5/56					
3078	L27/26R	M248	UF 5644	TD1	2	MB163	FXT 422	K6A	2/56					
3079	L27/26R	M569	CK 4405	TD1	3	M510	CWB 985	TD4	12/50					
3080	L27/26R	M575	CK 4403	TD1		MB168	FXT 427	K6A	4/56					
3081	L27/26R	M578	EK 8106	TD1	4	M505	BWE 35	TD4	11/50		MW281	FFM 542	K6B	2/58
3082	L27/26R	M571	CK 4411	TD1	5	M509	CWB 479	TD4	1/51		MB 284	GFM 892	K6A	5/58
3083	L27/26R	M570	CK 4406	TD1		MB165	FXT 424	K6A	4/56					
3084	L27/26R	M515	HL 5339	TD2		MB273	FFM 454	K6A	1/57					
3085	L27/26R	M514	HL 5318	TD2		MB274	FFM 455	K6B	1/57					
3086	L27/26R	M580	KG 1148	TD2		M537	GFM 922	PD1A	7/56					
3087	L27/26R	M581	KG 1151	TD2		M548	HFM 70	PD1A	7/56					
3088	L27/26R	M35	FM 7467	TD2		MW286	GFM 894	K6B	1/57					
3089	L27/26R	M37	FM 7763	TD2	6	MW287	GFM 895	K6B	1/57					
3090	L27/26R	M27	FM 7234	TD2		MB271	FFM 452	K6A	11/56					
3091	L27/26R	M245	AG 8246	TD2		MB256	FFM 437	K6A	7/56					
3092	L27/26R	M24	FM 6918	TD2		M549	HFM 71	PD1A	10/56					
3093	L27/26R	M30	FM 7462	TD2		MB254	FFM 435	K6A	2/56					
3094	L27/26R	M246	AG 8258	TD2		MB264	FFM 445	K6A	10/56					
3095	L27/26R	M29	FM 7461	TD2	7	MB167	FXT 426	K6A	2/56					
3096	L27/26R	M25	FM 6919	TD2		MB283	GFM 891	K6A	1/57					
3097	L27/26R	M34	FM 7466	TD2		MB196	HGC 252	K6A	4/56					
3098	L27/26R	M31	FM 7463	TD2		MB259	FFM 440	K6A	7/56					
3099	L27/26R	M1	FM 6920	TD2		MB268	FFM 449	K6A	6/56					
3100	L27/26R	M10	FM 6276	TD3		M524	GFM 909	PD1A	3/56					
3101	L27/28R	MA601	GP 6231	AEC Reg		MB169	HGC 241	K6A	2/54					
3102	L27/28R	MA605	GP 6238	AEC Reg		MB193	HGC 237	K6A	11/54					
3103	L27/28R	MA602	GP 6242	AEC Reg		MB170	HGC 242	K6A	2/54					
3104	L27/28R	MA603	GN 6206	AEC Reg		MB160	FXT 419	K6A	11/54					
3105	L27/28R	MA606	GW 6255	AEC Reg		MB194	HGC 248	K6A	11/54					
3106	L27/28R	MA604	GW 6288	AEC Reg		MB166	FXT 425	K6A	11/54					
3325	L27/26R	M23	FM 6917	TD2		MW279	FFM 540	K6B	6/56					
3326	L27/26R	M32	FM 7464	TD2		MB195	HGC 249	K6A	1/56					

Notes:

The above new bodies, all lowbridge, were built at the same time as similar bodies on early Leyland Titan chassis for other members of the Tilling group, being delivered at various dates through 1949. The AEC Regents were rebuilt on new 16ft 3in wheelbase chassis frames, replacing the 15ft 6½in originals. In several cases the replaced bodies saw further use on other chassis, and in others the chassis rebodied in 1949 saw further use after their new bodies were moved to later chassis, the individual details being given below.

1. **M39** *rebodied Leyland L27/24R ex-L37 11-50 Body originally on L14.*
2. *Leyland L24/24R body to* **L131** *1949. Ran until 1952.*
3. **M569** *rebodied Leyland L27/24R body ex-***L120**. *Ran until 1956. (Body originally on Ribble 753, fitted by NNW 1944).*
4. **M578** *– original body to L123 1949. Rebodied NCME L27/24R ex-***L127** *11/50.*
   (Body originally Cardiff Corporation, fitted by BBW 1944-6).
5. **M571** *– rebodied NCME L27/24R ex-***L118** *1950. Ran until 1953.*
6. **M37** *– Leyland L24/24R body to* **L109** *1949. Ran until 1953.*
7. **M29** *– Leyland L24/24R body to* **L130** *1949. Ran until 1952.*

1949/50/1953 ECW Bodies fitted to Older Double-Deck Chassis

ECW Body No. Series 2	Seats	First Chassis				Second Chassis				Note
		Fleet No.	Regn. No.	Chassis Type	Note	Fleet	Regn. No.	Chassis No.	Date Type	
3870	L27/28R	M6	FM 8153	TD3		MB277	FFM 538	K6A	5/57	
3871	L27/28R	M3	FM 8150	TD3		MB258	FFM 439	K6A	4/57	
3872	L27/28R	M2	FM 8149	TD3		MB272	FFM 453	K6A	4/57	
3873	L27/28R	N8	FM 8155	TD3		MB272	FFM 453	K6A	4/57	
3874	L27/28R	M4	FM 8151	TD3		MB261	FFM 442	K6A	4/57	
3875	L27/28R	M5	FM 8152	TD3		MW280	FFM 451	K6B	6/57	
3876	L27/28R	M9	FM 8156	TD3		MB269	FFM 450	K6A	5/57	
3877	L27/28R	M20	FM 9056	TD4						
3878	L27/28R	M42	AFM 496	TD4		MW285	GFM 893	K6B	6/57	
3879	L27/28R	M21	FM 9057	TD4						
3880	L27/28R	M13	FM 9049	TD4		MB260	FFM 441	K6A	2/58	
3881	L27/28R	M15	FM 9051	TD4		MB266	FFM 447	K6A	5/58	
3882	L27/28R	M16	FM 9052	TD4		MB257	FFM 438	K6A	6/58	
3883	L27/28R	M46	AFM 501	TD4		MB270	FFM 451	K6A	5/58	
3884	L27/28R	M17	FM 9053	TD4		MB262	FFM 443	K6A	4/58	
3885	L27/28R	M18	FM 9054	TD4		MB265	FFM 446	K6A	3/58	
3886	L27/28R	M19	FM 9055	TD4						
3887	L27/28R	M41	AFM 495	TD4						
3888	L27/28R	M43	AFM 497	TD4		MB267	FFM 448	K6A	5/58	
3889	L27/28R	M45	AFM 499	TD4						
6302	L27/28R	MB171	FFM 310	K6A						
6303	L27/28R	MB172	FFM 311	K6A	1a					
6304	L27/28R	MB173	FFM 312	K6A						
6305	L27/28R	MB174	FFM 313	K6A	1b					
6306	L27/28R	MB175	FFM 314	K6A	1c					
6307	L27/28R	MB176	FFM 315	K6A	1d					
6308	L27/28R	MB177	FFM 316	K6A						
6309	L27/28R	MB178	FFM 334	K6A						
6310	L27/28R	MB179	FFM 335	K6A	1e					
6311	L27/28R	MB180	FFM 336	K6A						
6312	L27/28R	MB181	FFM 337	K6A						
6313	L27/28R	MB182	FFM 338	K6A						
6314	L27/28R	MB183	FFM 339	K6A						
6315	L27/28R	MB184	FFM 340	K6A						
6316	L27/28R	MB185	FFM 341	K6A						
6317	L27/28R	MB186	FFM 342	K6A						
6318	L27/28R	MB187	FFM 343	K6A	1f					
6319	L27/28R	MB188	FFM 344	K6A						
6320	L27/28R	MB189	FFM 379	K6A						
6321	L27/28R	MB190	FFM 380	K6A						
6322	L27/28R	MB191	FFM 381	K6A						
6323	L27/28R	MB192	FFM 382	K6A						

Notes:

1. Strachan body fitted to ex-LTE Bristol K6A chassis:
    1a **MB167** FXT 426 until 2/56
    1b **MB163** FXT 422 until 2/56
    1c **MB165** FXT 424 until 4/56
    1d **MB168** FXT 427 until 4/56
    1e **MB162** FXT 421 until 2/56
    1f **MB161** FXT 420 until 5/56

In the immediate post-war period, Crosville undertook some rebuilding work on its double-deck stock and many gained Tilling destination displays, grafted on with scant regard for the resulting appearance. The weariness of the years is still very evident in this 1936 ECW bodied Leyland Titan TD4, M44 (AFM 498), seen in Crewe in 1950, but it soldiered on until 1955 without benefit of new body. This particular batch of six bodies, delivered in ECW's first week of existence in July of 1936, were of a rare pattern, of which the only others seem to have been eight bodies, also on TD4 chassis, supplied from the same factory under Eastern Counties ownership the previous month to Ribble Motor Services Ltd.

Titans of all ages were given new bodies including early examples of the Leyland TD1 new with petrol engines in the L class, albeit fitted with oil engines and more modern Covrad radiator conversions. This gave rise to the need to adapt the ECW body frame as can clearly be seen on 1932 TD2 M29 (FM 7461). In this instance the cab is shorter as well as the bay immediately behind the engine. This view was taken in West Kirby in 1950 and already the side destination screen has fallen prey to the traditional Crosville routine of over painting. A Widd board bracket is thoughtfully in place in the nearside front window.

Number M45 (AFM 499), sister vehicle of the TD4 shown at the top of the page, did receive a new body – in this instance there being no need to foreshorten the bay behind the driver's cab. It is seen in Aberystwyth, in 1950. The TD3, TD4 and TD5 were dimensionally quite similar to the Bristol K, apart from bonnet height.

Number FA 2 (FM 7482) was based on the chassis of a 1933 Leyland Lion LT5 which had survived the Rhyl fire of 1945. It received an Albion four-cylinder oil engine and a new ECW 33-seat body in 1949. The latter was based on the standard design of the time, but had a foreshortened first bay, evident here by comparison with the 1946 Bristol L6A parked alongside in this scene in Wrexham in 1953. Somewhat surprisingly considering the work carried out, it survived only until 1955.

Five dual-purpose single-deck bodies were constructed on relatively early Leyland Tiger TS4s, new with petrol engines. Number KA 193 (FM 7472), seen here in Chester in May 1951, had been built as 745 in 1933, becoming K72 in 1935. They had begun life as coaches but the choice of such old-style chassis for new ECW bodies of the 'express' type in 1949 was unusual, even though the end result with Leyland 8.6-litre oil engine would have been a very competent vehicle, able to tackle coach duties.

A case of a broom which has gained a second head and a different stale – yet which broom? For some reason, possibly because it had been officially written off, another Lion LT5 casualty from the 1945 Rhyl fire was re-registered as HFM 232 on 3rd July 1947. It had begun life in 1933 as 765 (FM 7492), later running as F18. Here again, an Albion engine was fitted, accounting for the new fleet number FA1, but in this case the body was a second-hand ECW product, built in November 1937 on a 1928 Dennis E for Eastern Counties. Much of it can be identified as of the standard style built for United Automobile Services in the mid 'thirties, largely on Bristol chassis. Originally the front bulkhead was just in front of the emergency door. As the LT5 was longer, it had been necessary to build a short extra bay despite the set-back bulkhead of that generation of Leyland chassis – the cab seems to have been basically the original, but a post-war-style Tilling destination box had been added, rather more neatly than usual. It was withdrawn in 1955. Crosville's answer seems to have been to call it a new broom. The relief Driver to the front of the bus appears somewhat hot in heavy wool tunic and pullover !

The Leyland Lion LT5A, dating from 1934, despite its designation, was quite unlike the LT5 in terms of layout, belonging to the same design generation as the Tiger TS6 and Titan TD3. Crosville decided to update all 21 in the fleet in 1949, fitting Leyland 8.6-litre oil engines in place of the four-cylinder petrol units, a change which required an increase in bonnet length, but this was no problem since new Burlingham 35-seat bodywork was also fitted, the end result being redesignated GA instead of G. The body design was the bodybuilder's standard of the time, of front-entrance layout and not conforming to Tilling standards except in having the large destination display. Seen here in Caernarfon in 1950 is GA17 (FM 8148).

The 25 J-class Lion LT7 buses in the fleet, dating from 1935 and with chassis basically the same as the LT5A models apart from their vacuum-hydraulic brakes, were similarly rebuilt, also in 1949, save that the new bodywork was by ECW and hence generally to Tilling standard specification except for the different cab design. These were already oil-engined, but even so, it was decided to re-engine them; fifteen were fitted with Leyland 8.6-litre engines, creating type JA, and the remaining ten became JG, with Gardner 5LW engines. Seen here is JA7 (FM 8977).

When the Saunders concern developed a new metal-framed body design in 1949, Crosville provided a Leyland Tiger TS7 dating from 1936 as the basis for the prototype, and thirteen more received similar bodies the following year. As built, the new bodies carried the Clayton destination display in a manner unique in the fleet. One blind carried all the information; destinations, intermediate points and service number. A metal plate, operated by a drop handle, was used to mask the return destination point, being changed at each terminus. Later in their lives something of Crosville's old habits had returned with this single line display, as on KA1 (FM 9965) seen here. In fairness, very comprehensive information was given on the stands at Rhyl.

The best known rebuilds were those of the 1937 'BFM' Tigers. The following series of views, all from the Company's own collection shows the scope of the work involved.

The first stage was to completely strip the vehicles, the exterior panels being saved when possible.

Another feature of the post-1946 era was the complete rebuilds afforded to pre-war vehicles. As will be shown in Volume Two, the Company had one of the most comprehensively-equipped central workshops in the country. Thus with the final transfer of all residual activities from both Crane Wharf sites, reconstruction to the point of creating virtually new bodies could be pursued.

The 1937 batch of KA-class Leyland Tiger TS7 single-deckers are probably the best-known instance of its work at that time. In 1950, it was decided to rebuild 24 of these buses, and in the event, two more were later added to that, all selected from the 72 buses in the batch. At the time, mileages had reached around 700,000, but A. R. Goodhall, the Company's Chief Engineer at the time, said he contemplated getting five more years of trouble-free life out of the rebuilt buses when interviewed by 'Leyland Journal', which carried an article on the work in its September 1951 issue. In the event, some ran to 1960, fully justifying his confidence.

The procedure was to remove the seats, trim, windows and panels, and then specially-made wooden jacks were used to support the roof framing when the body side and rear-end framing were removed. Experience had shown that these latter sections would be extensively rotted after 13 years, so it was decided to use prefabricated sides and rear-end assemblies. Extruded aluminium alloy sections were considered but, at the time, there was a threatened shortage of this material and in addition, the facilities and staff, in the charge of Mr H. J. Halstead, Body Shop Superintendent, were well suited to working in wood. Ash would have been chosen, but was also scarce, and instead two African hardwoods, dabema and sapele, were used. Dabema, not unlike mahogany, was favoured for pillars, floorbearers etc, and sapele for waistrails, partly because Mr J. F. Burnley, Assistant Chief Engineer, had been able to buy logs of suitable length, which also proved useful in their untrimmed state by providing material for small parts.

What were described as standard ECW windows and fittings were used, though two quite distinct designs were used, with windows of markedly different size. In the larger of these, used for fourteen of the bodies, it seems as if the pillar spacing might have been that used on the contemporary standard ECW single-decker, there being five bays, seemingly of equal length, behind the entrance, with a shorter one at the rear. In this case, it seems that the waist level was lowered slightly as compared to the original design, and the pillar spacing changed, with one window more on each side than the 1937 original – the dimensions were

fairly close to the 1938-40 version, though the rearmost window was shorter. However the alternative version had shallower and shorter windows, with two extra pillars per side compared to the original, and the cantrail was also lowered.

The vehicles were then repanelled, it being claimed that old panels were re-used as far as possible, though clearly this was not possible on the sides, in view of the different pillar spacing. However the front and rear domes, which would have been hand-made and costly to reproduce, were retained. Rather surprisingly in view of the widespread use of the big Tilling destination box in less comprehensive rebuilds, it was not applied to these vehicles, possibly indicating that the enthusiasm for its use was waning. However, there was a clear affinity to post-war ECW practice in the new side windows, though the overall family resemblance was more marked in the large-window version.

Sides were prefabricated in the Sealand Road carpenter's shop and were ready for assembly on to the prepared chassis.

Here one of the vehicles was almost ready to accept the new framework. The rear part of the floor had yet to be renewed, but the main section was evidently to be kept, the wooden jack to support the roof framing in the correct position resting on it. At this point so little of the original body appeared to be left as to raise the question as to whether the finished job should be regarded as a rebuild or virtually a new Crosville body with elements of both original and post-war design. Two other KA buses, including KA41 to the right, are further advanced.

Here the framework was nearing completion on KA85 (BFM 202). The roof, with centre panels still in place, and parts of the front end are the original, but the new timber is clearly evident. The steel front and rear dash panels would have been supplied on the chassis when new and built into the body.

Here the panelling was complete. The altered spacing of the pillars – in this case, a small-window version – can be seen by the out-of-step positions of the roof panel joint beading in relation to the pillars. The side and rear panels were in shiny new aluminium sheet but the domes were the originals.

There were two principal variants, both with front entrances and either long or short windows. No reason has been established for this variety. The longer bay version was clearly the more attractive and KA 37 (BFM 154) represents these. This picture was taken shortly after completion as it awaited departure for Colwyn Bay. One vehicle of this type still survives, KA 27 (BFM 144) and has been fully rebuilt again by David Moores. It still holds a Class 6 PSV licence. It was a little unfortunate that the cab waist level no longer matched.

The short bay version also had shallower windows and its appearance suffered accordingly. KA46 is seen in Llandudno in 1956. Notice that the arch over the door, as well as the porch style entrance, were retained despite the thoroughness of the rebuilding. Another anomaly was the retention of the original destination screen at a time when Crosville was fitting standard Tilling equipment to many vehicles which only had a short lifespan ahead of them.

One curiosity was KA47 (BFM 164) which was further rebuilt in 1956 as a one man saloon, complete with full width canopy, yet still with small destination box. The vehicle remained unique and in the following year the first of a batch of Bristol L6As was converted instead. The row of holes in the bonnet give an odd appearance and are unusual, overheating not normally being a problem on this model.

Looking into the shell of the building. The heating radiator in the foreground has fallen from the club above and the remains of vehicles can clearly be seen. Many other vehicles were recovered from a side entrance and continued in service. Among the vehicles dimly visible in the back of the garage two of the Manchester TD1 buses can be recognised as among the damaged vehicles.

One of a series of photographs taken for the Company during the morning after shows the frontage on Crescent Road and the collapsed building. The crowds seem to have been permitted early access and clearly no particular thought was given to safety, but then damage of this kind had been a regular feature of life in many areas during the war.

CALAMITY AT RHYL !

During the night of the sixteenth July 1945, most of the populace would have been sleeping soundly – knowing that the war in Europe was over and hoping that in the South Pacific and Japan would not drag on too long. True, much was still rationed – and likely to remain so for some years, but that did not seem to matter for the moment. James Crosland Taylor would have been no exception – until about 1.00am. It was then that he was to be awoken by the Company's Traffic Manager, Captain Roberts, to be told that "Crescent Road Depot at Rhyl is ablaze from end to end. It started in the club....." Forty-nine buses were allocated to this important location in what was rising to the height of the season. The efforts of the fire brigade and others had saved some vehicles, whilst others were away from the seat of the conflagration, but nonetheless ten vehicles were lost.

The cause of the fire was almost certainly a cigarette smouldering in the club which was above the entrance, and the proximity of the fuel tanks with 2000 gallons of diesel stored overhead had served to intensify the blaze. Crosville had done more than most to promote Social Clubs for its staff yet here was one which dealt the most cruel blow, easily the worst disaster to befall the Company during the war years. Crosland Taylor records in *The Sowing and the Harvest* (originally published in 1948) that not one single mile was lost on the subsequent morning – buses being moved from around the Divisions through the night in a remarkable display of efficiency and team spirit. Crescent Road depot was eventually rebuilt on the same site and latterly was much used both as a Coach Station and to supplement the Albion Works site at Ffynongroew Road. It closed at the beginning of the 'eighties and was finally sold by NBC Estates late in that decade during the privatisation of the National Bus Company.

Vehicles destroyed:

L2/18/30/3/5/51/7/71/3   (FM 6392/6408/6270/3/5/5206/5885/91, TE9530,TF6358)

Vehicles Rebuilt:

F18 (FM 7492)   This vehicle was rebuilt with an Albion oil engine and a second-hand ECW bus body, being re-registered HFM 232, and renumbered FA1.

F8 (FM 7482)   This vehicle also received an Albion oil engine and an ECW body, in this case new, becoming FA2, but retained its original registration number.

In addition, two of the Leyland Titan TD1 buses with 1935/6 Metro-Cammell bodywork on loan from Manchester Corporation were written off after fire damage and scrapped by Crosville.,

ACKNOWLEDGMENTS & PHOTOCREDITS

Those interested in Crosville owe a great deal of gratitude to both Claude and later James Crosland Taylor, for throughout their stewardship of the company up to 1959 they sought to preserve many relics of the past including the magnificent Company Photographic Collection. Succeeding general managers perpetuated this and to David Meredith must go an appreciation for securing its future, in what has become the Crosville Archive Trust, at a time when his mind could reasonably have been expected to be on weightier matters, as he was forced to preside over the gradual dissolution of the English half of the company. So many company collections either 'vanished' or, worse, were thrust into skips by an incoming and unfeeling management bent on proving that this was the only way to start the 'new era'. The Crosville company and its sister Eastern Coach Works were always generous in granting use of their unique collections and over the years many photographs have found their ways into diverse collections. That has provided the Authors with the greatest difficulty, as they have been offered so many copies of the same views from a variety of different sources. It is against this background that the following listing has been made. I hope that those who have provided material for consideration will understand this dilemma and that all have been included.

Other sources whose assistance is gratefully acknowledged must particularly include Brian Horner who kindly afforded the Authors generous access to both his own personal collection and that of the late David Deacon. Deacon quietly pursued his interest in the company at a time when such activity might have jeopardised what was to become an illustrious career in the industry – indeed he was the first of the many Crosville trained Managers who rose to the very top of their profession.

This volume contains only a few of the many fine views available and more of these will appear throughout the Crosville series during the next two years. This selection will include more of the work of the late Peter Williams whose activities following the end of hostilities in 1945 provide a further lasting memorial to both him and the Crosville team.

The assistance of many other people is acknowledged, too many to mention by name unfortunately, but Jack Barlow, David Deacon, John Nickels, T B Maund and David Meredith were helpful in providing additional material whilst Alan Townsin spent many hours checking the fleet details. Permission to reproduce extracts from *Motor Coach Services from Merseyside* (Omnibus Society, 1980) and *Crosville on Merseyside* (TPC 1992) is acknowledged with thanks. My apologies to anyone I have inadvertently omitted.

Duncan Roberts
Sheffield
May 1995

All photographs from Crosville Company Archive except as below:-

G H F Atkins   96
G H F Atkins courtesy R Marshall   70
John Carroll Collection   13 (foot), 16, 85, 95 (foot), 103, 109 (top), 120 (top), 137
A B Cross   47 (lower), 48 (top), 101 (top), 116 (top)
Crosville Archive Trust   18 (top), 33 (both), 40 (both)
David Deacon courtesy Brian Horner   31, 37 (foot), 53 (foot), 86 (top), 109 (lower left), 157
A J Douglas   152 (foot)
D A Fletcher   106 (top left)
D Kerrison   34 (foot), 112, 115 (centre), 120 (foot left), rear cover
S Letts (J Carroll Collection)   127 (lower)
R F Mack   120 (centre), 131 (foot), 155 (centre)
R F Mack (J Carroll Collection)   133 (both)
Roy Marshall Collection   18 (foot), 23, 155 (foot)
T B Maund Collection   21, 71, 126
T B Maund courtesy Jack Barlow   11, 59 (foot)
John Nickels Collection   41, 43 (top right & foot), 44 (both), 45 (top), 47 (top), 46 (both), 60 (foot), 97 (foot), 99 (both),
John Nickels Collection courtesy W Noel Jackson   43 (top left), 97 (foot)
A E Old   127 (top)
David Randall   15
D F Roberts Collection   62 (top), 69
Senior Transport Archive   6, 7 (all), 9, 13 (top), 19, (both), 30, 37 (top), 48 (foot), 56, 73 (foot), 74, 77, 80, 82 (foot), 128 (centre & foot), 132, 134,
   ABC   35 (top), 89 (lower), 107 (top both)
   Brush   50, 59 (top), 104, 107 (lower)
   Duple   5, 68 (both), 118 (top)
   ECW   42 (foot), 45 (foot), 54 (top), 57 (both), 63, 92 (both), 95 (top), 119 (both), 123 (both), 124, 125 (all)
   R N Hannay   64 (both)
   Leyland   12, 22, 25, 27, 28, 52, 53 (top), 54 (foot), 60 (top), 61, 62 (foot), 65 (foot), 66 (both), 86 (bottom two), 89 (top), 90 (both), 91, 93 (both), 94 (top right), 97 (top), 105
   R F Mack   132
   Roy Marshall   81 (top)
   J A Senior   front cover, 129 (foot), 135
   J S Smith (J Carroll Collection)   151 (foot)
University of Wales (A J Moyes Collection)   36 (both)
J P Williams/D F Roberts Collection   26, 49, 58, 59 (centre), 79 (foot), 81 (lower), 82 (top), 84, 87, 100 (top), 102, 106 (top right), 109 (lower right), 111, 114, 115 (top & foot), 118 (lower), 120 (bottom right), 121, 128 (upper), 129 (centre), 130, 131 (top & centre), 150 (all), 151 (top & centre), 152 (top)

The task of assembling photographs has been made easier by the enthusiasm of both the company, in creating its archive, and certain individuals who took photographs when photography was an expensive hobby and the subject thought a great deal more odd than even in some quarters today. David Deacon was one of the earliest pioneers and is seen here at Aberystwyth in the 'thirties when he served as a trainee with the company. He is wearing a conductor's great coat and the Bell Punch ticket punch then in use – the plus-fours were almost certainly optional.

INDEX